THE ART OF TEACHING

THE ART

OF

TEACHING

Gilbert Highet

NEW YORK
VINTAGE BOOKS
A DIVISION OF RANDOM HOUSE

VINTAGE BOOKS

are published by Alfred A. Knopf, Inc.

and Random House, Inc.

Reprinted by arrangement with Alfred A. Knopf, Inc.

Manufactured in the United States of America

TO

CYRIL BAILEY

— χάλκεα χρυσείων

Preface

THIS is a book on the methods of teaching. It does not discuss the subjects which are taught (or should be taught) in schools, in colleges, and elsewhere. There are thousands of books on the subjects, but not nearly so many on the general principles of teaching. Yet it is necessary to distinguish subjects from methods. The development of propaganda shows us how lies and stupidities can be efficiently taught; and the history of schools shows us how good subjects and important truths can be badly taught. Our interest here, therefore, is not to distinguish the good subjects from the bad subjects, but to work out the principles by which a subject—once it has been chosen—can be well taught. This is not a book of educational theory, but a book of suggestions drawn from practice.

It is called *The Art of Teaching* because I believe that teaching is an art, not a science. It seems to me very dangerous to apply the aims and methods of science to human beings as individuals, although a statistical principle can often be used to explain their behavior in large groups and a scientific diagnosis of their physical structure is always valuable. But a "scientific" relationship between human beings is bound to be inadequate and perhaps distorted. Of course it is necessary for any teacher to be orderly in planning his work and precise in his dealing with facts. But that does not make his teaching "scientific." Teaching involves emotions, which cannot be systematically appraised and employed, and human values, which are quite outside the grasp of science. A "scientifically" brought-up child would be a pitiable monster. A "scientific" marriage would be only a thin and crippled version of a true marriage. A "scientific" friendship would be as cold as a chess problem. "Scientific" teaching, even of scientific subjects, will be inadequate as long as both teachers and pupils are human beings. Teaching is not like inducing a chemical reaction: it is much more like painting a picture or making a piece of music, or on a lower level like planting a garden or writing a friendly letter. You must throw your heart into it, you must realize that it cannot all be done by formulas, or you will spoil your work, and your pupils, and yourself.

* * *

The book begins by considering the character and abilities which make a good professional teacher, and then goes on to examine his methods. After that, it branches out further. One of the forces which have helped to make our own civilization is certainly the influence of famous teachers: therefore the most powerful teachers of the past are examined. First, the Greek intellectuals; then Socrates, Plato, Aristotle; then Jesus of Nazareth; then the teachers of the Renaissance; the Jesuits next; and the best nineteenth-century and twentieth-century teachers; and finally the fathers of great men, who taught their sons how to be great. Last of all, our survey turns to look at teaching in everyday life, as it is done by ordinary parents to their children, by husbands and wives to each other, by doctors, priests, psychiatrists, politicians, propagandists, and even by artists and authors who do not know that they are teaching the public. It ends with a declaration of the heavy but encouraging responsibility which rests on us all whenever we attempt to teach our fellow-men.

* * *

For discussing the book with me and for giving me valuable constructive criticism and factual information I am deeply indebted to a number of my friends and colleagues. First, to my own teacher, Dr. Cyril Bailey, Honorary Fellow of Balliol College, Oxford, to whom this work is dedicated as a very small expression of the gratitude I owe him for his guidance and friendship during twenty years. Then to Professor Mark Van Doren of Columbia University, who manifested his long experience of teaching and his characteristic humaneness by reading the entire manuscript and showing me how to remove some of its faults. And for advice on specific points, to Professor Ralph H. Blanchard of Columbia University; Mr. Abraham Flexner, New York; Dr. Albert D. Freiberg of the Psychological Corporation, New York; Professor Frederick C. Grant of the Union Theological Seminary; Professor Werner Jaeger of Harvard; Professor Arthur Jeffery of Columbia; Dr. Roger Lapham of New York, whose book *It's in Your Power* is a good practical demonstration of the doctor's ability to teach; Professor Gabriel Liegey of Fordham University; Mr. Denver Lindley, New York; Professor Clarence A. Manning of Columbia; Father Edwin A. Quain, S.J., of Fordham; Dr. W. H. Sheldon of the College of Physicians and Surgeons, Columbia University; Mr. L. O. Shuddle of the Social Security Administration; Mr. L. P. Wilkinson of King's College, Cambridge; and Professor Ben D. Wood of Columbia. I am also most grateful to the Reference staff of Columbia University Library, who with their wide bibliographical knowledge and their patient accuracy dug out a large quantity of references (particularly on the subjects discussed in Chapter IV) which would have cost me many months of searching; and for similar help to the Librarian and Library staff of Barnard College. Let me end with a tribute to my wife for her acute criticisms, which, like those of every good teacher, were always encouraging.

G. H.

March 1950
Columbia University
New York

Acknowledgments

Ishould like to express my thanks to the following persons and firms who have been kind enough to grant me permission to reprint illustrative passages from works in which they hold the copyright:

Mrs. George Bambridge, from Rudyard Kipling's *Something of Myself,* copyright 1937 by Caroline Kipling;

Jonathan Cape, Ltd., London, from A. E. Housman's *Last Poems* and James Joyce's *A Portrait of the Artist as a Young Man;*

Constable & Co., Ltd., London, from Logan Pearsall Smith's *Unforgotten Years;*

Doubleday & Co., Inc., New York, from Kipling's *Something of Myself;*

Henry Holt & Co., Inc., New York, from A. E. Housman's *Last Poems;*

Little, Brown & Co., Boston, from E. E. Slosson's *Six Major Prophets* and Logan Pearsall Smith's *Unforgotten Years;*

K. S. P. McDowall, Esq., from E. F. Benson's *As We Were,* published by Longmans, Green & Co.;

Macmillan & Co., London, from Kipling's *Something of Myself;*

The New Yorker, from R. Rice's "Penny-Arcade Philanthropist";

Ohio State University Press, Columbus, from J. D. Teller's *Louis Agassiz, Scientist and Teacher;*

Oxford University Press, from William Lyon Phelps's *Autobiography with Letters;*

Rutgers University Press, New Brunswick, from Houston Peterson's *Great Teachers;*

Charles Scribner's Sons, New York, from Nicholas Murray Butler's *Across the Busy Years* and Thomas Wolfe's *Of Time and the River;*

The estate of Logan Pearsall Smith, from Smith's *Unforgotten Years;*

The Society of Authors, London, as literary representative of the trustees of the estate of the late A. E. Housman, for a quotation from *Last Poems;*

The Viking Press, New York, from Irwin Edman's *Philosopher's Holiday* and James Joyce's *A Portrait of the Artist as a Young Man;*

The estate of Mrs. Gabriella Shaler Webb, from the *Autobiography of Nathaniel S. Shaler.*

Notes

In order to maintain the continuity of the argument, explanatory footnotes have not been added to this book. However, bibliographical notes, which give sources for quotations and for descriptions of certain methods of teaching, have been grouped together on pages 251-259. In these notes, references to the text are shown by page-number and by catch-phrase.

Contents

THE ART OF TEACHING

I

Introduction

It is difficult to write a book on the art of teaching, because the subject is constantly changing. There are different ways of teaching in different countries of the world, at any one time. Methods in any one country alter every generation or so, as the structure and ideals of society alter. One man will think of education as a privilege, work hard and save money to go to the university, and treasure all the knowledge he can get. Thirty years later his son may despise education, resist schooling, waste his time at college, and teach his children to hate books. Thirty years more, and the children will be eagerly educating themselves, perhaps in an unorthodox or wrongheaded way, perhaps late in life or without entering any educational institution, but still with a genuine hunger for learning. Each of these generations needs a different kind of teaching.

Then again, there are thousands of different things to learn and teach: so many that you might well ask whether they could all be brought under one system. Is there anything in common between a mother teaching a baby how to talk, a schoolmaster teaching a boy history, a trainer teaching a boxer how to feint, and a foreman teaching a crew of laborers how to lay a road? Even in one country, schools and universities teach a bewildering variety of things, from simple addition to higher physics, from dancing to brain-surgery. And over the whole world, with its thousands of schools and hundreds of universities, how many different subjects are being taught? Today, for instance, a boy is learning the Koran by heart. Another is working at calculus, and a third at double-

stopping on the violin. Another is practicing pole-vault-
ing, and another is reading a manual on demolition work
in underground warfare. A girl in Ecuador is being
taught lacemaking by Sister Teresa, a girl in India is
memorizing the teachings of Gandhi, and a girl in Japan
is learning the symbolic meanings of flower-arrangements.

All these subjects, and thousands more, are taught in
schools. But a great deal of teaching is done outside
school. Some things—and some of the most important
things—are taught by mothers and fathers to their children. This kind of teaching begins as soon as the baby
reaches for a knife and his mother takes it away. No, it
begins earlier than that. It really begins when the baby
gives his first cry and is first answered. In those days,
before he can even hear or see properly, he is finding out
something about the world and himself, he is communicating and being answered, he is exerting his will and
being victorious or controlled or frustrated, he is being
taught to suffer, to fear, to love, to be happy, or to be
violent. His mind is being made. Such teaching goes on
at a very obscure level, deep down among the foundations. We have all experienced it, and forgotten it. But it
is none the less crucially important because it is buried
so deep. You know how easy it is for a baby to slice his
hand open with a knife or scald his leg with a kettle. The
scar is still there, forty years later. Many of the twisted
minds and crippled characters in the world were made
by careless parents who kept their children away from
knives and fires, but put permanent scars on their souls.

All through school, and for years after school, parents
continue to teach their children. They do so whether
they want to or not. The father who never says
more than "Hello" to his son and goes out to the nearest
bar every evening is teaching the boy just as emphatically
as though he were standing over him with a strap. It is a
very tricky business, teaching. He may not be teaching
his son to drink and neglect responsibilities. The boy
may turn out to be a thin ascetic devoted to long plans
and hard work, like Shaw and Joyce. But, for good or ill,

the father is teaching him *something*. Many fathers either don't know this, or don't care. Yet it is impossible to have children without teaching them. Beat them, coddle them, ignore them, force-feed them, shun them or worry about them, love them or hate them, you are still teaching them something, all the time.

And teaching is not confined to parents and professional teachers. In every business and industry, there are learners and teachers. Wherever there are beginners and experts, old and young, there is some kind of learning going on, and some sort of teaching. We are all pupils and we are all teachers. Think of your own life as an individual. Much of it is routine. Some of it is amusement. The rest is made up of learning and of teaching: whether you are a doctor enlarging his knowledge of certain types of illness or a housewife planning her work more effectively, whether you are a trade-union official learning about economics or a typist learning about life on a minimum wage, whether you are a young husband cheering up his wife, a political speaker influencing an audience, a bus-driver covering a new route, or an author writing a book, you are learning for yourself and teaching others. Most people do not realize how much even of their private life is taken up with amateurish teaching and haphazard learning; and not many understand that most of us, as public beings, either learn or teach incessantly.

Dr. Johnson once boomed out the judgment that a woman's preaching was like a dog's walking on its hind legs. "It is not done well," he said, "but you are surprised to find it done at all." Now, most people are clumsy at learning and teaching, not because they are stupid, but because they have not thought about it. It is not done well, but we are thankful to find it done at all. Professional teachers vary. In some parts of the world, you can scarcely find enough of them to open a single school. In others, an efficient teacher appears in every village. There are some periods when good teachers start up everywhere. At other times, schools are dull and hateful, mas-

ters are lazy and ignorant, children are neglected and
vicious. But amateur teachers (if I may call them that)
vary still more. How often have we seen a charming husband and wife with a sullen and detestable daughter?
How many workshops are operating at half their poten-
tial efficiency because the foremen can neither plan the
jobs nor explain them to the workers? How many readers who are genuinely interested in art, or politics, or
religion, have gone halfway through a badly written
book on the subject, and thrown it down, and remained
baffled and discouraged because the author could not
manage to tell them what he knew? Bad teaching wastes
a great deal of effort, and spoils many lives which might
have been full of energy and happiness.

The subject, then, is an important one. But it is so
broad that no single book can hope to cover all of it. In
fact, I doubt that any single person knows enough to be
able to write a book on it. There are, of course, hundreds
of special treatises on separate types of teaching: how to
teach deaf children, how to teach dancing, how to teach
foreign languages. But such works are usually rather
limited, and seldom connect with one another. I have
been teaching for twenty years myself; I have several
times tried to find a book which would help me to learn
more about what I was doing. Having failed to find any,
I have decided to write this one, in the hope that it may
help other teachers, both professional and amateur, and
perhaps stimulate someone else to produce a better and
more complete work on the subject. For one of the chief
duties of a teacher is to stimulate.

One word of caution. This book does not deal with the
subjects which are taught. It does not try to discuss
whether science, or religion, or art, or foreign languages
should be taught, or what the relation between the various subjects ought to be. It is concerned only with
methods of teaching. There are many good books which
examine the subjects that ought to build the education of
children and of young men and women. The subjects
vary widely in different countries and different periods.

But the methods of teaching seem to remain, within broad limits, more or less the same. Therefore, in this book we shall try to find out, not *what* should be taught, but *how* the teaching can best be done.

II

The Teacher

THE best-known kind of teaching, and the most highly organized—although not the most important—is done in schools, in colleges, in universities, and in technical institutions. Everyone who is reading this book has had some of it, and knows what it is to be a pupil. Everyone owes something to professional teachers. Let us start, then, by looking at them. What kind of people are they, and how do they work?

*   *   *

The teacher has a very peculiar job. It is easy in some ways, and in others it is difficult. The easiest part about it is the spacious routine. There are not many teachers who, like business-men and professional people, are on duty forty-eight or fifty weeks a year every year, and there are still fewer who teach from nine to five every day, five or six days a week. Most schools and colleges run for only nine months in the year altogether, and there is seldom any necessity for a teacher to be on call every hour of the working day. Of course there is a great deal to be done outside teaching hours. Some of it is routine—preparing examinations, reading papers, interviewing pupils. Some of it is research and preparation. But much of this kind of work can be done in one's own time, at one's own home, or in the quiet of a book-room. The great advantage of this is that comparatively few teachers are tied to the desk, chained to the telephone which begins to ring at nine on Monday morning and is still chattering at noon on Saturday, or limited for vacations to a fortnight in July among the millions of exhausted factory-workers.

Leisure is one of the three greatest rewards of being a teacher. It is, unfortunately, the privilege which teachers most often misuse. But let us leave that point meanwhile: we can come back to it later, with some constructive suggestions. There is not too much leisure in the world.

The teacher's chief difficulty is poverty. He (or she) belongs to a badly paid profession. He cannot dress and live like a workman, but he is sometimes paid as little as an unskilled laborer. There are some big prizes at the top of the profession, and a few lucrative sidelines, but the average teacher in every land must be resigned to a life of genteel poverty. In some countries, where wealth is greatly admired as a symbol of success, this is a heavy sacrifice to make. In others, it is partly compensated by the rewards of prestige and respect. But it is always painful. Nevertheless, the job is secure, since there will always be young people who need teaching. A colleague of mine once told me that he lived better during the depression than ever before. In the roaring twenties, men who had been at Princeton with him pitied him for earning five thousand a year teaching when they were making fifty thousand a year selling bonds; but in 1932 he still had a job, and a salary which bought more at deflated prices, while they had neither. Still, even a safe poverty is galling, and many of the snarly bad-tempered teachers whom we remember with hatred were really nice people soured by years of anxiety and penny-pinching.

The teacher's second reward is that he is using his mind on valuable subjects. All over the world people are spending their lives either on doing jobs where the mind must be kept numb all day, or else on highly rewarded activities which are tedious or frivolous. One can get accustomed to operating an adding-machine for five and a half days a week, or to writing advertisements to persuade the public that one brand of cigarettes is better than another. Yet no one would do either of these things for its own sake. Only the money makes them tolerable. But if you really understand an important and interesting subject, like the structure of the human body or the history of the two World Wars, it is a genuine happiness to explain them to others, to feel your mind grappling with their difficulties, to welcome every new book on them, and to learn as you teach.

With this the third reward of teaching is very closely linked. That is the happiness of making something. When the pupils come to you, their minds are only half-formed, full of blank spaces and vague notions and over-simplifications. You do not merely insert a lot of facts, if you teach them properly. It is not like injecting 500 cc. of serum, or administering a year's dose of vitamins. You take the living mind, and mold it. It resists sometimes. It may lie passive and apparently refuse to accept any imprint. Sometimes it takes the mold too easily, and then seems to melt again and become featureless. But often it comes into firmer shape as you work, and gives you the incomparable happiness of helping to create a human being. To teach a boy the difference between truth and lies in print, to start him thinking about the meaning of poetry or patriotism, to hear him hammering back at you with the facts and arguments you have helped him to find, sharpened by himself and fitted to his own powers, gives the sort of satisfaction that an artist has when he makes a picture out of blank canvas and chemical color-ings, or a doctor when he hears a sick pulse pick up and carry the energies of new life under his hands.

Some teachers, however, seldom or never have this ex-perience. They are robbed of one of the rewards their job ought to bring them. Instead, they complain of an inflic-tion almost as severe as poverty. They say the boys and girls hate them; and often they hate the boys and girls. Over a period of years, their hatred becomes known and builds up a barrier which they can never break down. I remember when I was eight I went into a class domi-nated by a female Fury. We were all terrified of her be-fore she even entered the room. Whatever else we learnt that year, we certainly learnt to detest school, and grown-ups, and authority; and we got a fascinating insight into the power and horror of physical cruelty. On the other hand, no single teacher can ever be so devilish as a class of strong, badly disciplined children which has got out of hand. A few years later, in the same school, I recall helping to reduce an inoffensive master, with a good war record, almost to tears of rage and frustration; and I know a teacher in a city school who told me that her chief problem was to keep the boys in her class from attacking one another with furriers' knives.

Now, it is natural for a pupil to resist his teacher. It is healthy, and it can be invigorating for them both. The best works of art are created in difficult media: it is harder to shape marble than wax. Yet when the resistance is never broken down, but hardens into hostility, and when the teacher finds the same hostility—or at best a sniggering indifference—year after year, there is something very far wrong. Sometimes the pupils are wrong. Sometimes the teacher is wrong. Sometimes there is a deep-seated dislocation in the community to which they both belong, and their hostility reflects it. (We shall be discussing this a little later, when we come to discipline.) But whatever its cause may be, it is a sore trial to the teacher. It is one of the two worst drawbacks in the job. It is bitter to be poor; but it is torture to spend your life's energy, year after year, trying to awaken understanding and appreciation of genuinely important things in what seems to be a collection of spoiled, ill-mannered boobies, smirking or scowling, yawning or chattering, whose ideals are gangsters, footballers, and Hollywood divorcees. It is like giving a blood transfusion, and then seeing your precious blood spilt on the ground and trodden into mud.

This can happen, in certain conditions, even to a good teacher. But it is more likely to happen to bad teachers. How can it be avoided?

In other words, what are the qualities of a good teacher?

* * *

First, and most necessary of all, he must know the subject. He must know what he teaches. This sounds obvious; yet it is not always practiced. It means that, if his job is teaching chemistry, he must know chemistry. It is not enough for a chemistry teacher to know just that amount of chemistry which is taught in schools and required for the final examinations. He must really understand the science of chemistry. Its upper regions must be clear to him, at least in outline; and he should know what are the most important new discoveries made every year. If a boy shows a gift for chemistry, the master must be able to encourage him, by throwing open window after window into the future, showing him what he can learn at the university, what types of chemistry are most vital in peace and war, which big problems still remain to be solved, and (this is always important) how the great chemists of the past and present have lived and worked.

Therefore teaching is inseparable from learning. Every good teacher will learn more about his subject every year —every month, every week if possible. If a girl chooses the career of teaching French in school, she should not hope to commit the prescribed texts and grammars to memory and then turn her mind to other things. She should dedicate part of her life to the French language, to the superb literature of France, to French art and history and civilization. To become a good teacher of French, she will build up a growing library of her own French books, spending one year (for instance) reading Balzac, the next year reading Proust, the next with Molière, and the next with Giraudoux, Cocteau, Romains, and the other modern playwrights. She will visit France, if and when she can save up enough money to do so— which will be fearfully difficult with salaries at their present low level. She may take summer courses in French at a university. Certainly she will see every available French film, and learn to enjoy Raimu's rich Marseillais accent, to guffaw with Fernandel. For it will not all be serious work and planned self-improvement. It will be living, and therefore it will contain enjoyments, and even frivolities, like the latest records by Lucienne Boyer and Charles Trenet. But it will be learning at the same time, and it will make better teaching.

You may ask why this is necessary. Why can a teacher not simply learn the rudiments of the subject, master them thoroughly, and then stop? A postman does not learn every street in the city. He learns only his own area. A French teacher in a small town may never have a pupil who will be able to understand Proust. Why should she trouble to read Proust's novels? Why should a schoolmaster teaching elementary chemistry keep up to date with the latest discoveries? The elements of chemistry are limited in number, and do not change.

There are two answers to this. The first is that one cannot understand even the rudiments of an important subject without knowing its higher levels—at least, not well enough to teach it. Every day the grossest and most painful blunders are made not only by teachers but by journalists and radio commentators and others who have the public ear, because they confidently state a half-truth which they have read in an encyclopedia article, or because they lay down as gospel a conjecture once uttered by an authority they admired. And many teachers, trying to explain certain problems in their own subject, fall into explanations suggested to them by a colleague or thrown up by their own imagination, which are nevertheless totally wrong, and which an extending knowledge of the field would have corrected long ago.

The second answer is that the human mind is infinitely capacious. We know the minimum diet which will keep a child alive. We know the maximum quantity of food he can absorb. But no one knows, no one can even guess how much knowledge a child will want and, if it is presented to him in the right way, will digest. Therefore it is simply useless to teach a child even the elements of a subject, without being prepared to answer his questions about the upper ranges and the inner depths of the subject. And from the teacher's point of view it is far more difficult to do so. A limited field of material stirs very few imaginations. It can be learnt off by heart, but seldom creatively understood and never loved. A subject that carries the mind out in limitless journeys will, if it is well taught, make the learner eager to master all the preliminary essentials and press on.

Young people hate grown-ups for many reasons. One of the reasons is that they feel grown-ups' minds are fixed and limited. Whenever they meet a man or a woman who does not always say what they expect, who tells them novel stories about strange aspects of the world, who throws unexpected lights on what they sadly know as ordinary dull life, who seems as completely alive, sensitive, energetic, and zestful as they themselves, they usually admire him or her. It is true that we cannot all be fountains of energy and novelty throughout every day, but we ought, if we are teachers, to be so keen on our own subjects that we can talk interestingly about unusual aspects of them to young people who would otherwise have been dully neutral, or—worse—eager but disappointed. A teacher must believe in the value and interest of his subject as a doctor believes in health.

The neglect of this principle is one of the chief reasons for the bad teaching that makes pupils hate schools and universities and turn away from valuable fields of knowledge. The finest example of it I have ever encountered happened when a friend of mine was teaching at the summer session of a large university. A middle-aged man from one of the Southern states came to him and said: "I teach French at Woodside High School. I would like to take a refresher course." My friend said: "Good. Do you teach elementary French or one of the more advanced classes?" The teacher replied: "Elementary French, the first two years. I've never gone any further." My friend then said: "Right. We have an excellent man visiting us this summer from the Sorbonne. Suppose you take his class in La Fontaine and Molière."

Silence. Perplexity.

"You know, La Fontaine, who wrote those delightful fables, and Molière—you must have read *The Miser* or *The School for Wives?* Wonderful comedies, they get better every time you read them."

Still silence. Then the man said: "Well, no. I don't think I'll need any of that stuff. I just want a refresher course in elementary French."

"But you know that already!" said my colleague. "It's all in the book, a hundred pages of elementary grammer and vocabulary; you must know it off by heart. The only reason for learning it or teaching it is so that the boys can go on to read something worth while. They could certainly be given La Fontaine's fables on the side. If you take Sarrasat's course you will learn a lot about La Fontaine's humor, his satire, his subtle language, his psychological acuteness, valuable material which you can then use in your own teaching."

"Hm."

"And of course," said my friend, warming to his subject, "they would love Molière. Probably he's too hard for your beginners, but you could tell them about him, outline some of the best plots, read them a scene or two—try them with the monologue where Harpagon discovers he's been robbed and tries to arrest himself—you remember, '*Rends-moi mon argent, coquin! Ah! c'est moi!*'—it's a marvelous scene, and it's bound to make them want to read the whole play."

"No," said the visitor firmly, picking up his hat. "I'm paid to teach elementary French, and I don't see any use in getting all that extra stuff. Probably never be able to use it anyway."

"But even if you didn't use it in teaching," said my friend, "you would surely enjoy it yourself. Don't you like Molière?"

The tall man shook his head. "Nope," he said. "Never read him. Never will. I don't really like French at all. What I like is basketball. We've got a great little team at Woodside."

My colleague made a mistake at this point. He said: "In that case, why don't you give up French and teach basketball?"

"Guess I'd better do that," said the visitor at the door, "if you can't find me a refresher course in elementary French. That's what I came here for. Good-by."

We never saw him again. Yet it would not be safe to assume that he never read La Fontaine and Molière. The strangest and the best thing about teaching is that a seed dropped into what looks like rocky ground will often stick and take root gradually, and spring up years later, sometimes in a bizarre form and oddly hybridized, but still carrying the principle of life. Years afterwards the man from Woodside may have felt the principle working in him and, remembering my friend's words, may have taken a real interest in his subject. Probably he would go to some other university to learn about Molière and La Fontaine; and possibly he is now serving as producer and stage-manager of the Woodside Players in his own translation of *The Miser*.

However, he may not. If he did nothing about it, he is like millions of other people in the world, who hate the jobs on which they spend their lives, and will do nothing more than the bare minimum, sometimes scarcely that. I used to notice it in music shops in Britain. Whether you asked the girl behind the counter for a piece by Frédéric Chopin or a piece by Hoagy Carmichael, she had never heard of it, she didn't know where it would be, and would I rather wait till Mr. MacWhirter came in? *He* would know. If she had been selling silk stockings, you could be very sure she would have known the exact shades of difference between Gotham and Kayser, but she was only dealing in works of art, and who cares about them?

It reminds me of the story about Toscanini and the first violin. On a tour Toscanini once arrived in a new city and took over an orchestra he had never conducted before. He started them on something easy, like *Semira-mide*. After a minute or two he noticed that the first violin looked odd. He was playing well enough, but his face was all distorted, and when he turned a page to begin a new section, he really grimaced as though he were in great pain. Toscanini stopped the orchestra and said: "Concert-master! Are you ill?"

The first violin's face at once returned to normal. "No, thank you," he said, "I'm quite all right, maestro. Please go on."

"Very well, if you're sure you're fit. Begin at D, please, gentlemen." And off they went again. But the next time Toscanini glanced at the first violin, he saw him looking worse than ever. His face was all drawn up to one side, his teeth were showing between wolfish lips, his brow was furrowed with deep clefts, he was sweating painfully and breathing hard.

"One moment, please. Concert-master, you really look ill. Do you want to go home?"

"No, no, no, Mr. Toscanini, please go ahead."

"But I insist," said Toscanini. "What's wrong, are you having an attack, would you like to lie down for a while?"

"No, I'm not ill," said the first violin.

"Well, what on earth is the matter?" said Toscanini. "You look awful, you have been making the most agonizing faces, you're obviously suffering. . . ."

"To be quite frank," said the first violin, "I hate music."

Sounds ridiculous, doesn't it? But there are millions of people doing the same thing every day all over the world. They have a job they hate, they perform it grudgingly and inefficiently, they make it more difficult for themselves and for everybody associated with them. Sometimes it scarcely matters. If the girl in the music shop can't find the music, the customer can wait until Mr. MacWhirter comes in, or at worst he can order from the publishers. But it is terribly important when a teacher, whose job is to awaken young minds to a valuable subject, shows his pupils by every gesture, by every intonation of his voice (and remember, young people notice such things very quickly and sensitively), that he thinks the subject is not worth while learning; and that learning anything whatever is a waste of time.

* * *

The first essential of good teaching, then, is that the teacher must know the subject. That really means that he must continue to learn it.

The second essential is that he must like it. The two are connected, for it is almost impossible to go on learning anything year after year without feeling a spontaneous interest in it. I have a friend who is a stockbroker. He learns more about the market every year. He can recite the high and low quotations on forty leading stocks as far back as 1922; he knows the names of all their directors; he is an encyclopedia of knowledge on unlisted securities, including a lot of rather peculiar South American issues. It would kill me. I could do it—but only with a tremendous effort, for some other reason, clearly indicated. He honestly enjoys it. When he is in France he reads the Bourse page just as eagerly, although he never deals in European stocks. Whether this interest is acquired or natural scarcely matters. By now it is perfectly genuine. The result is that he is a good stockbroker. His interest gives him a steadily increasing knowledge, his knowledge strengthens his judgment, and he is not only successful but happy.

Suppose he met a young man entering business, with the intention of becoming a stockbroker, and saw clearly from his conversation and his manner that he neither knew nor cared whether General Electric was changing its price-policy: he would advise him to give up Wall Street and try some other job. In just the same way, if a girl sets out to make a living (or even a living until marriage) teaching history, and really cares nothing whatever for politics, for biography, for reconstructing the manners and mentalities of other ages, and for the different interpretations that can be put on such important events as the Crusades or the Versailles Treaty, it is useless for her to go on. She will teach it badly to begin with, and worse as she goes on, for she will come to hate it more and more. Eventually she will become like the horse harnessed to the millstone, plodding round and round the same circle, without hope, day after day.

Of course nearly every teacher dislikes some part of his subject. Many a good history teacher shies away from the early Middle Ages, or shuns economic manuals showing the relation of rent to prices and wages at various periods. But she (or he) acknowledges that defect, learns the essentials of that part of the subject, and then, with all the more energy because of a feeling of guilty neglect, throws herself into the part she really enjoys. But to dislike the entire subject, to be a history teacher and be bored by history, to teach French and never open a French book at home, that must be either a constant pain or a numbing narcosis. Think how astonished you would be if your doctor told you that personally he really cared nothing about the art of healing, that he never read the medical journals and paid no attention to new treatments for common complaints, that apart from making a living he thought it completely unimportant whether his patients were sick or sound, and that his real interest was mountain-climbing. You would change your doctor. But the young cannot change their teachers—at least, not until they reach university age, sometimes not even then. They have sometimes to submit to being treated by doctors of the mind, who seem to believe the treatment useless and the patient worthless. No wonder they often distrust education.

The young dislike their elders for having fixed minds. But they dislike them even more for being insincere. They themselves are simple, single-minded, straightforward, almost painfully naïve. A hypocritical boy or girl is rare, and is always a monster or a spiritual cripple. They know grown-ups are clever, they know grown-ups hold the power. What they cannot bear is that grown-ups should also be deceitful. Thousands of boys have admired and imitated bandits and gunmen because they felt these were at least brave and resolute characters, who had simply chosen to be spades instead of diamonds; but few boys have ever admired a forger or a poisoner. So they will tolerate a parent or a teacher who is energetic and violent, and sometimes even learn a good deal from him; but they loathe and despise a hypocrite.

And the teacher who dislikes his subject or is indifferent to it always runs the risk of becoming a hypocrite. Think of the alternatives. Suppose you are teaching chemistry without thinking it worth learning. Either you can tell your pupils to learn it because you will punish them if they don't; or you can tell them to learn it because it will help to get them good jobs in the future; or you can pretend that you think it is too, too fascinating, and just watch what happens when a little H_2 is exploded along with some SO_4. In the first case they will learn grudgingly and perhaps inadequately—it depends largely on the area where you live. (A class in Germany would learn well, a class in Australia would learn badly.) In the second case some of them may believe you and learn well. In the third case none of them will believe you, and you will throw disgust into someone who might have become a good chemist.

But if you do enjoy the subject, it will be easy to teach even when you are tired, and delightful when you are feeling fresh. You will never be at a loss for a new illlustration, for a topic of discussion, for an interesting point of view. Even if you do make a blunder, as every teacher does, if you forget a formula or mix up τύπτω with κρύπτω, you will not need to bluff your way out, you can admit that you have forgotten and even ask for the correct word (or, more wisely, promise to look it up), without sacrificing the respect and the attention of your class. For the young do not demand omniscience. They know it is unattainable. They do demand sincerity.

It follows from this that if you are going to be a teacher you must choose your subjects carefully. Of course, many schoolmasters have to take classes in anything and everything—at least to begin with. But even they can decide which are the really essential subjects, and guide their own interests in those directions; and they can mark out the type of subject they would like to teach later, when they get some seniority.

This kind of choice is surprisingly often neglected by young university teachers. They are apt to take a job teaching (say) "English," and to spend the first few years reading beginners' essays and giving simple general courses. Much of their attention at this time is taken up with getting married, having a family, and trying to meet the bills. Then they may slip into giving the series of lectures on the American novel formerly given by old Professor Crum, who has just retired; and another class on seventeenth-century prose to fit in with a newly announced course on seventeenth-century poetry. They spend three years working these up, and write a few articles on points of interest which they meet en route—a new source for Donne's 49th sermon, the first draft of *The Princess Casamassima*. They are still reading a large number of students' essays too. Meanwhile their administrative duties begin to pile up, they become members of the Hebdomadal Committee and Junior Deans, they take on outside work as adviser to the Periphrasis Press and examiner to the Joint Board and reviewer specializing in "avant-garde novels," the children are growing fast and food-bills are heavy, then one year there is the additional inducement of teaching in California during the summer session, they have to work up two new courses, and next summer these will be used again, perhaps they could be expanded for a winter series although neither of them really dovetails in with the American novel or seventeenth-century poetry, still it is a fine thing to be competent in a number of different fields, a reliable wheelhorse, you might say. And they go on like this, filling in here and fitting in there, half because of pressure, half through inertia, until they wake up at the age of forty and look around to discover that they have no really solid interests, no large book in the making, and so only a vaguely defined reputation. They can still be happy, for it is a delightful career to teach one of the world's great literatures. Yet they will have a sense of lost opportunity, and they have earned it.

They did not choose their field. They did not, in fact, plan their career. They allowed themselves to drift this way and be pushed that way—while the years passed. Some of the finest scholars in history have made this mistake. They were great men, and superb students; but they gave the world much less than they could and should have given it. Scholars less distinguished have often ruined their talents by neglecting to use them in the best possible way. How often have you heard it said that X might have written a fine book, but that he had put it off until it was too late!

You know how carefully the Germans plan things. When a young German scholar was beginning his career, he used to choose three or four large fields in which he felt a real interest, on which there was a good deal of work to be done, which—an important point—were all linked with one another, and which—most important of all—he felt to converge upon the very center of his subject. He would contrive as far as possible to make these the topics of his first classes and seminars. He would write groups of lectures on them, and nurse and nourish each group until it grew into a book. If he were energetic enough and percipient enough, he would thus become the author of three or four books, each of which would recommend and illuminate the others. He would then continue studying and lecturing on the area around each of these fields, enlarging it strategically from year to year until he had built up a really authoritative knowledge of almost the whole subject. Such a process gives cumulative dividends. Scholars who planned their learning and their teaching in that way usually found, by the time they were fifty or so, that they had enough interests and nearly enough knowledge to fill three careers.

Suppose, for instance, that such a man were setting out on a career as a teacher of philosophy. He might select, for his first course of lectures, the modern theories of

Truth. Another course could be a historical survey of man's ideas of God. He could also conduct a graduate discussion class on Perception (what happens in us when we see an external object? what kind of knowledge can we get through the senses?). And he could read and make notes for a future seminar on the problem of Soul and Body (how are they associated? does the body have a soul, or does the soul have a body? is one the matter and the other its form?). The lectures on Truth would keep him in close touch with such important fields as logic (including the new mathematical logic) and semantics, and would be extensible on the other side into moral problems. The course on the idea of God would help him to learn history—no one ever knows enough history—and would grow perhaps into a book on modern theology, perhaps into a study of the early church. The problem of Perception itself has occupied a number of philosophers all their lives, and would lead into other equally stirring subjects: how real is the external world? what are the final limitations of the individual's knowledge? what kind of knowledge does science give us? (And this, as you see, leads back into the problem of Truth from another direction.) Finally, his work on Soul and Body would take him into psychology, into the subject of immortality, into the very interesting and little studied field of animal intelligence and morality, and, by another glowing track over a field which is becoming more and more brightly lit, towards the theme of God and man's knowledge of God.

Not one of these subjects could be exhausted in any normal working career. But a man might learn more and more about each of them; and, as he learnt, become a better, more richly equipped, and more stimulating teacher. We should expect him to find new themes to investigate as he advanced further into each field, and not only to write several interesting books of his own, but to suggest, to pupils differently oriented, many other topics on which they might add to the knowledge of mankind. The only danger would be that he might always be so interested in moving on that he seldom stopped long enough to fix his ideas in a book. But if he planned his work at the beginning, he would probably have enough foresight and will-power to mark off its various stages by setting down the results he had achieved.

It is not enough, then, to choose your subject. A wise teacher will choose particular areas of his subject which he believes will be both interesting and illuminating, and will find that his increasing knowledge of them will give him a sense of mastery, will keep him from feeling he is merely plying a trade, and will somehow carry over to his pupils. When I learnt French at school, we had a plump, elderly, and charming teacher (Miss Groan we called her because her name was McCrone) who really loved Victor Hugo. Many teachers of French adore Racine's tragedies, and will tell you about notable performances they have heard; and some like Verlaine and Baudelaire. It is rare, even in France, to find one who loves Hugo, but Miss Groan did. When she read us the big firework displays from *The Chastisements,* like the description of Waterloo, she really sounded inspired; she knew the novels well too—it was she who guided me towards *The Toilers of the Sea,* and sent me to the submarine cave where, still panting from my long dive, I felt my wrist encircled by a cold tentacle (*La Pieuvre!*); when she read us the little poems about children, we were embarrassed but secretly charmed. Of course we sometimes steered her towards Hugo to keep her from asking awkward questions on a subject we hadn't prepared; but even then we admired the genuine enthusiasm which shone in her face and vibrated in her voice. None of us got out of that class without learning that Victor Hugo was the greatest of French poets. Even although we didn't all believe it, we at least learnt that poetry could be great, could be exciting and heart-warming, and we learnt what to look for in French poetry. Long afterwards, when I read Mallarmé's poem with the rarefied ending:

Je suis hanté. L'Azur! L'Azur! L'Azur! L'Azur!

I could still hear overtones of

>Waterloo! Waterloo! Waterloo! morne plaine!

in the rich and living voice of Miss Groan.

* * *

The third essential of good teaching is to like the pupils. If you do not actually like boys and girls, or young men and young women, give up teaching.

It is easy to like the young because they are young. They have no faults, except the very ones which they are asking you to eradicate: ignorance, shallowness, and inexperience. The really hateful faults are those which we grown men and women have. Some of these grow on us like diseases, others we build up and cherish as though they were virtues. Ingrained conceit, calculated cruelty, deep-rooted cowardice, slobbering greed, vulgar self-satisfaction, puffy laziness of mind and body—these and the other real sins result from years, decades of careful cultivation. They show on our faces, they ring harsh or hollow in our voices, they have become bone of our bone and flesh of our flesh. The young do not sin in those ways. Heaven knows they are infuriatingly lazy and unbelievably stupid and sometimes detestably cruel—but not for long, not all at once, and not (like grown-ups) as a matter of habit or policy. They are trying to be energetic and wise and kind. When you remember this, it is difficult not to like them.

A teacher must not only like the young because they are young. He must enjoy their company in groups. There is a famous American definition of a good education. It consists, says the epigram, of Mark Hopkins on one end of a bench and the student on the other. Mark Hopkins was a fine teacher, but he did better when he put ten students on the bench and stood in front of them. Later we shall discuss the advantages of man-to-man teaching and of classes of various kinds. Meanwhile it is enough to point out that there are many more pupils than teachers in the world, so that the average teacher must spend several hours a day with a collection of ten to thirty youngsters. Unless he likes groups of young people, he will not teach them well. It will be useless for him to wish that there were only two or three, or that they were all more mature. They will always be young, and there will always be lots of them.

In certain institutions, and given certain rather special conditions, someone who hates large groups and is nervous among young people can still be accepted and admired as a teacher. A scholar, for instance, who has spent a generation learning a difficult subject may not know how to teach it, and may be embarrassed or repelled by having a youthful audience. But if his reputation and his knowledge are distinguished enough, they will hold the attention of a class even when he himself is dull and inaudible. Many of his hearers will go away stimulated, not by his teaching, but by the excitement of contact, however remote, with a distinguished mind. Many of the world's great universities contain such scholars. Usually they are shocking bad teachers during the first twenty or thirty years, and continue to be bad teachers when they reach their peak; but by the time they have mastered genetics or iconography, most of the work of teaching is done for them, by the accumulated power of their knowledge. Their classes sit silent, attentive, eager. Their thin flat voices are magnified by the attention of their pupils. Incomplete ideas are filled in, obscure trains of thought are illuminated, by the keenness of the audience. I have never heard Dr. Einstein speak, I do not believe he would put much vital energy into teaching, and I do not understand astrophysics; but I should go to hear him lecture, and I know I should learn something from it.

But for most of us, who cannot reasonably count on being savants with a self-illuminating reputation, it is essential to enjoy the conditions of teaching, to feel at home in a room containing twenty or thirty healthy young people, and to make our enjoyment of this group-feeling give us energy for our teaching. Every profession has its atmosphere, its setting, and those who practice it must feel at home there. It is silly to become an actor if you want a settled home and time to think. Do not enter journalism unless you like the bustle of a large noisy office, welcome travel and the unexpected, and hope to like it all the rest of your life. If you do not enjoy the prospect of facing the young in large groups, if you would always prefer working in a laboratory or reading in a library, you will never be a good teacher.

Of course nobody can bear young people all the time. One of the pleasures and the necessities of the teacher's life is to escape—into a cool library or a little garden— away from their noise and their devilish energy. Among the most difficult jobs in the profession are those which give very little respite and condemn the dean to be always on call, the housemaster to spend every day of his working life among the boys. Still, these jobs are not thrust upon us, but taken by choice. Those who hold them usually relish them. Remember, you must not armor yourself against the energies of the young. You must not be the policeman watching the mob. You must be the leader of a group—something higher than the actor with his audience, something lower than the priest with his congregation, something kindlier than the officer with his unit. You must always feel what the orator feels when he addresses an audience partly friendly and partly docile, and senses after a little that they are with him. Such a man is borne upwards and swept onwards by energy which flows into him from outside, from the group of which he is the heart and the voice. The good teacher feels that same flow of energy, constantly supplied by the young. If he can canalize it, he will never be tired. At least, not while he is teaching.

* * *

At this point a serious objection can be raised. "There are some classes," you will say, "who cannot be liked. There are some teachers who have really loathsome pupils. There are some schools where the girls think of nothing but sex, and the boys think of nothing but sex and fighting, and all of them hate the teachers, and the school, and education. How is it possible to like them?"

This is perfectly true. Some schools are hell-holes. When Dickens described Dotheboys Hall, the horror of it was that the master and his family tyrannized over the pupils. When Keate was headmaster of Eton, the toughest bully quailed before him, and a mistake in Latin verse-writing was "expiated in tears and blood." But nowadays the pupils sometimes tyrannize over the teachers. There are schools in New York where the police have had to be called in to support the staff. In an interesting novel about a Negro schoolgirl living in Brooklyn, *Jadie Greenway,* Mr. I. S. Young (who has worked in New York schools for many years) describes some of the problems confronting city teachers. The heroine, aged sixteen, contracts venereal disease from a "boy-friend" in the navy. When one of the other girls mocks her for it, Jadie slashes her with a spring-knife, which she always carries to keep schoolboys from raping her on the way home. In such schools savage fights break out in classrooms, and a pupil who is punished may attack the teacher—or waylay him after school—or bring in a big brother to revenge the insult. I have met school-teachers who were literally terrified of their pupils, and sighed with relief when the bell rang and they were released from intimidation for another day.

And, what is just as bad, the boys and girls at these places do not want to learn. They think school is partly a waste of time and partly a prison. They would much rather be outside making money; or simply outside—at the movies, or standing on the street-corner. Being adolescents, they are terribly anxious to be grown-up. As one of them wrote in an essay, "the pleasures of childhood are nothing to the joys of adultery." They bitterly resent being kept in an institution with little boys and girls, when they would rather be men and women, earning wages and being independent. They can see no possible way in which it would do them any good whatever to learn the geography of the world, the history of their own continent, the literature of their own country.

Class distinctions and racial differences sometimes accentuate their resentment. In America a Negro boy is apt to dislike being taught by a white teacher, because the Negroes hate anything which reminds them that their ancestors were enslaved. ("She got no right tellin' me what to do.") Recently large numbers of migrants from Puerto Rico—who are American citizens but usually speak only Spanish—have moved into New York. The children are charming, with their big eyes and flashing smiles, but when they enter a class conducted in American English, they find learning difficult and become resentful. In many slum schools all over the world, from Glasgow to Valparaiso, the children hate the teacher because he sounds and looks middle-class, while they are working-class; and if their parents are Communists, they will also be told to hate the school because it is an instrument of capitalist oppression.

All that is true, and very serious. It is, however, true only for a minority of schools in any one country at any time. That does not make it any less a problem, but it keeps it from being the central problem of education.

It is a social problem, because it is caused not by a failure in education, but by the larger failure which is a maladjustment in society. It arose when the ideal of universal education was applied to highly populated industrial states, for that meant that education was no longer seen as a privilege, and not always as an aid to individual progress, but as a universal necessity, a tiresome discipline which some were bound to reject. Educators and social workers sometimes talk as though everyone in the past who was denied an education were secretly yearning for it. Of course many did, and if they were poor they sometimes made grave sacrifices to get it. But many of our ancestors cared no more about education than I do about bridge, and would no sooner have chosen to learn history than I would learn the two-no-trump convention. So today there are many children in the country who want to be farmers and want to learn nothing except farming; there are many children in the cities who want to be industrial workers and are unwilling to learn anything but what they can see in a pay-envelope. And beneath them there are thousands more who feel there is *no place* for them in society, and that a planned life and regular work will give them no rewards. They believe therefore (usually without reasoning it out) that a social institution such as school has nothing to give them, and that its discipline and routine are meant to trap them, maim them, torment them.

The worst problem is this last and lowest group. But it cannot be solved by the teacher alone. The best school in the world will scarcely save a boy who hates the school and the purpose it serves and the society that created it. No attempt to "make learning relevant" will permanently bridge the gap between the classroom and the juvenile gangster. This problem must be solved by the municipal authorities, the churches, the police, the local political organizations, by all the rest of the citizens, and by the parents themselves. The best work is already being done by the teachers and the policemen, and all the rest of the problem remains for others to solve. Education is doing as much as it can.

But meanwhile, what is the teacher to do? It is impossible for him to like a class if one of its members will show his contempt and hatred for learning by snatching a book from his hands and urinating on it in the classroom. How can he possibly teach such children? How should he think of them?

As far as possible, he should be sorry for them. Not pity them openly—that would infuriate them. But he should think of them as the doctor thinks of patients driven half-mad by pain. Even if a woman has brought on her own delirium by drinking herself ill and crazy, the doctor reserves his feelings of blame and contempt, and treats her as sympathetically as though she had had a street accident. These arrogant and brutal boys, these peevish and perverted girls, are really the victims of colliding forces more violent than those which make any car-smash. Like most sick people, they do not understand what fevers are burning them, what conflicts are tearing them apart. By the time they grow up, they will have been given some chance of making real moral choices and seeing the broader pattern of society. But when they are young, they do not act, they merely react. The best way to handle them is to make sure, as the doctor does, that they hurt neither themselves nor anyone else, and, like the doctor, to be sympathetic.

A woman teacher in such a situation has a far harder time than a man. The girls despise her because she is older, the boys despise her because she is weaker. It is worse than useless to post a woman to such tough schools. One of the essential reforms which should be made is to staff them all with men. Girls will respect a man, and boys will at any rate not despise him. If he has plenty of physical and psychical energy, he will be able to dominate them for a time. If he is a good sport, he may sometimes be able to bridge the gap and work with them. There was an early Russian film about the homeless boys who roamed the streets of the large cities after the revolution. It showed a bold but successful attempt at reclaiming a group of them. The first step was to capture them and send them off to a school in the country—and it was a police job, for they dodged like rats and fought like mustangs. (But note the implication of that. It is useless to attempt to teach tough youngsters as long as they are allowed to run free in bad surroundings.) As soon as they reached the country school they tore it to pieces. They burnt the furniture, started stills to make vodka in the cellars, wrecked the garden and the farm buildings, and fought one another to a standstill. There was a schoolmaster with them. He didn't attempt to resist. They would have torn him to pieces too. He joined in the orgies. Then, after the first excitements of freedom had died down, and after their protests against being sent away from the subways where they had been sleeping were growing hoarse, they began to be conscious of their own discomforts. The roof leaked. The windows were broken. The food was all over the floor. They had nothing to do. Partly from sheer boredom, partly to make the place less uncomfortable, a few of them began clearing up. This was the nucleus of a constructive group. The schoolmaster helped. They asked his advice. He showed them tricks of rebuilding. They made the place shipshape. They began to learn crafts. They constructed little comforts for themselves—there were plenty of tools. They began to enjoy what they had made, and to despise wasters and parasites. They accepted the schoolmaster, not as an external authority imposed upon them, but as a member of their own group whom they admired for his strength and dexterity and from whom they could always get impartial guidance. The film ended by showing a flourishing community run by youths who had only two years earlier been thieves and pimps and murderers in city streets.

In the United States Father Flanagan did a similar job of rehabilitation with his Boys' Town, and there have been many other successful educational projects of the same type in other countries. But they all depend on one preliminary step: taking the pupils away from the bad society which perverts them. The Russian teacher could never have saved the Bezprizorniki if they had been living in Moscow cellars. When sent out to the settlement, they could not escape, and so they had to find a new way of living. It was a little Siberia. Father Flanagan's Boys' Town is in a remote part of a thinly populated state. When the school is right in the center of the slum, what can the teacher do?

It is tempting to answer that he should make plans for the abolition of slums and propagandize for social improvement. But he is usually far too tired with his arduous and nerve-rending work. He has done his full share. Let others do theirs. I am reluctant to suggest anything to workers who serve society so gallantly as teachers in these difficult schools, and I certainly should not dream of recommending them to take on any more active social work in their rest hours. But I believe that much of the maladjustment in our societies is caused, not by malevolence and corruption, but simply by ignorance. In a large city, Fifth Avenue does not know how Tenth Avenue lives. It would therefore be very valuable if experienced teachers would report to groups of volunteer social workers—through churches, neighborly associations, welfare societies, and so on—telling them exactly what the problem is, as they see it, with suggestions for solving it. We do not ask the doctor to help in solving the problem of alcoholism. It is enough if he attends the delirious and the cirrhotics. But we need information from him on the causes of that social maladjustment, on its modes of expression, and on ways of eradicating it. Thereafter the responsibility is ours.

*   *   *

We have seen, then, that the third essential of teaching in ordinary schools and colleges is to like the pupils. Is it also essential to know the pupils?

It depends largely on the method of teaching that is being used—class instruction, lecturing, laboratory work, or tutoring. The distinction between these methods will be discussed later. Here it is enough to say that there is only one of them in which it is genuinely necessary to know every individual pupil well: the tutorial system.

In the other systems, how much must the teacher know of his pupils?

To begin with, he must know the young. They are quite unlike adults. They are so different that it would be easier to understand them if they looked like animals. You know how a baby, before it is born, passes through the main stages of evolution. It begins by looking like an amœba, goes on to look like a fish, resembles a big-headed monkey for some time, and ends up at birth still looking remarkably like a little red blind clutching grimacing ape. I have often thought that in its first fifteen years of life it passes through another series of animal existences. Boys of nine and ten, for instance, are very like dogs. Watch a pack of them hot on the scent, yapping, running and jumping, bouncing aimlessly around full of unexpendable energy, kicking one another or breaking down a door as carelessly as a dog nips at its neighbor's flanks or bursts through a hedge. When they are really enjoying the chase, all their teeth and eyes gleam and their breath and laughter go "huh, huh, huh, huh" like a leash of fox-terriers. Girls in their middle teens are like horses, strong, nervous, given to sudden illnesses and inexplicable terrors, able to work remarkably hard if they are kept firmly in hand, but really happiest when they are thinking of nothing in particular and prancing about with their manes flying. Both dogs and horses are amiable creatures and can be domesticated, but it is a mistake to treat them as though they were human. It is also a mistake to treat horses as though they were dogs, or dogs like horses.

So, if you are interested in teaching, do not even expect the young to be like yourself and the people you know. Learn the peculiar patterns of their thought and emotions just as you would learn to understand horses or dogs—or other animals (for there are all kinds of different animals implicit in children: the very small ones are often more like birds)—and then you will find that many of the inexplicable things they do are easy to understand, many of the unpardonable things easy to forget.

How can you learn this? Chiefly by experience. Watch them and talk to them. Mix with them sometimes off duty. Give them a party now and then, or play games with them. Listen to them, not to eavesdrop, but to understand, by learning the random careless rhythm of their chatter, how their emotions and minds really work. But as well as doing this, you can learn a great deal about them by remembering your own youth. The more intensely you can think yourself back into those parts of it which seem furthest away from your present adult life, the better you can understand the young. Some of the least successful teachers on general work are men and women who, even when they were boys and girls, had an air of premature solemnity and unchildlike primness, who studied hard and seldom played rough or silly games, and whose parents kept them in cotton-wool. Often they enjoyed themselves best, not as boys among boys, or girls among girls, but when assuming the teacher's authority and omniscience. Such youngsters often earn good marks, and then shrink from going out into the rude world to make a living by adventurous competition. Then they take up teaching as a career, and are surprised when they dislike so much of it. Sometimes, indeed, they are extremely good with bright hard-working boys and girls who remind them of themselves. They project all their ambitions onto such pupils, training them to get good scholarships and pass difficult examinations. But they are rarely much good with the ordinary youngsters who fill the average class, because they themselves have never been either ordinary or young.

The teacher, then, must know the young as such. Next, he must know the names and faces of his pupils. Some people find this easy, some very difficult, but it is a *must*. I do it so badly myself that I cannot advise anyone how to do it. Still, I know it must be done. One of the gravest mistakes made by A. E. Housman as a teacher at London University was to boast of his inability to recognize his pupils. The girls hated it, particularly because he would put what felt like really personal venom and vitality into correcting their blunders, and would pass them on the street next day. In his farewell address, before departing for Cambridge, he told them he was sorry, adding: "If I had remembered all your faces, I might have forgotten more important things"—meaning that if he had burdened his memory with the distinction between Miss Jones and Miss Smith, he might have forgotten the difference between the second and the fourth declension. You can imagine how this bogus humility and pedantic arrogance was welcomed by the young women he had snubbed. There was of course a certain amount of truth in it. He meant that it would have been an extra expenditure of time and energy for him to learn the names of his pupils; but he also implied that the effort was unnecessary, and not really part of his job. And there, since he was taking money for teaching, he was wrong. The young are trying desperately hard to become real people, to be individuals. If you wish to influence them in any way, you must convince them that you know them as individuals. The first step towards this is memorizing their faces and their names.

But the teacher will find that, beyond this, it is seldom feasible to treat all his pupils as individuals. Even if it were possible, it would be unwise. For it would mean that the problem presented by each young man or girl would have to be approached as though it were unique. This would make it very difficult to solve, would be exhausting for the teacher, and would waste the profits of experience. The art of teaching, like the art of healing, consists partly in recognizing, within each individual, a particular type or combination of types. If a doctor is asked to visit a sick man, he does not attempt to work out all the items of his individuality—the facts that he is a Freemason, has been twice married, enjoys chess and bird-watching do not interest him. He is the reverse of the modern novelists like Joyce and Proust who endeavor to bring out every infinitesimal wrinkle, every memory which shades a thought or alters a decision. What the doctor sees is not Leopold Bloom or Monsieur Bergotte, but a case of lobar pneumonia one day old, in a man of fifty with good heart and blood-pressure but poor metabolism and a history of respiratory infections. The combination of these factors is his problem. If the patient also has individual attributes which are really relevant— if, for instance, he is a Christian Scientist and believes lobar pneumonia is a mental delusion—the doctor will take them also into account. But the success of his treatment will depend on the penetration with which he can *generalize* about this particular individual.

Similarly, the best way to know one's pupils is to divide them into types. This is a skill which the teacher can learn only by experience. He will begin, early in his career, by thinking they are all different. Then he will observe that Clark is rather like Johansen, and that Verney and Lennox react in very much the same way to difficulties, and even write similar essays. Then, after four or five years' teaching, he will notice another Clark in his class—a youth who looks the same (except that he has red hair) and laughs at the same kind of jokes and writes the same big square hand . . . only this boy is called Macdonald and comes from a different part of the country. Next year another Verney will turn up. And so on, until the teacher, if he learns well, will in ten or fifteen years assemble a little gallery of types which, singly or combined, will account for eighty-five per cent of the average class.

It is a complicated business, typing one's pupils. It must not be oversimplified. It would be frankly impossible in a very broad sampling of humanity. For instance, it was extremely difficult in the army, where one had great strong farmers, quick little city boys, grave youths from the small towns, and dozens of unexpected blends of character and background and physique, all in the same unit. But schools and universities do not function in mid-air. They are each attached to one group of traditions and supplied chiefly by two or three localities; also, schools and local society and youth itself do a great deal of uniformizing, so that a teacher can usually count on a fairly even distribution and recurrence of types.

* * *

Is there any generally valid set of types which every young teacher might learn at the beginning of his career? Is it possible, for example, to begin classifying all one's pupils as introverts and extroverts, and to go on from there?

It does not appear so. The psychology of the normal has not gone far enough. The psychologists, who began by trying to cure the mentally ill, are still working on the maladjusted and the overstrained. They have not yet, as far as I know, worked out a useful set of basic psychological descriptions comparable to Best and Taylor's physiology of the normal healthy body. For American teachers of young men, however, there is a valuable approach to the question in W. H. Sheldon's *The Varieties of Temperament.*

This book is the result of some years of work at Chicago, where Mr. Sheldon took complete physical measurements of several thousand students, and then made careful psychological studies of the character and habits of two hundred of them. Starting with an entirely open mind (as far as anyone has an open mind) and searching for methods of classifying so many different individuals by working out sets of traits which repeatedly appeared together, he began to find that many youths were dominated by one out of three main elements in their physique. Some, tending to be fat and physically lazy, were governed by their stomach and bowels. These he called viscerotonic, because the tone of their life was set by their viscera. Others were muscular young men, with broad shoulders, lean hips, an almost inexhaustible supply of energy, loud voices and aggressive gestures. These he called somatotonic—perhaps not very appropriately, since *soma* is Greek for the entire body and is so used by Mr. Sheldon elsewhere. The third class, thin, clever, highly sensitive, were ruled by their brains and nervous systems. These he called cerebrotonic. Then he found that these physical types corresponded fairly closely to three main types of temperament: the easygoing man who *enjoys,* the energetic man who *acts* violently, the nervous man who *watches and thinks.*

But most of Mr. Sheldon's subjects did not belong to only one of these three types. Such a simple scheme would have misrepresented the complexity of human life. They were mostly mixtures. Some were plump and loved eating, but also had a good deal of somatotonic drive in them. (These were blends of the first two types.) Others looked like boldly muscled lifeguards, but had certain highly nervous reactions, a low pain-threshold, susceptibility to migraine, little hair on the body. (These were mixtures of the second and third groups.) To each of his three basic dispositions Mr. Sheldon allotted a scale of figures running from one to seven. Any youth who was classified as seven in one of the dispositions possessed the maximum number of its special qualities. The other end of the scale was one—for instance, an extremely thin and nervous boy would score 7 as a cerebrotonic and, probably, 1 as a viscerotonic.

Since everyone shares to some extent in each of these three dispositions, since everyone has some nerves and some muscle and some digestive and eliminative capacity, Mr. Sheldon's book suggests that everyone can be classified by a three-figure number, showing the proportion of each set of characteristics which makes up his temperament. A perfectly balanced man with a richly-endowed nature would be 4-4-4. A fat man with the minimum of muscular and nervous activity and the maximum of visceral activity, someone like the emperor Vitellius, would be 7-1-1. A professional boxer of the extremely violent and energetic type might be 1-7-1. The thinnest and most nervous man you know, the chain smoker with the bad cough and the gift for improvising at the piano, could be 1-1-7. The giant wrestlers who eat like elephants and yet fight like gorillas, and thus combine high proportions of muscular and digestive activity with the minimum of nerves, would be 7-7-1. The more rich and complicated figures of history, like Henry VIII, obviously run a high score in each class, and might turn out a surprising figure such as 6-7-6; but they are very rare.

Mr. Sheldon began by measuring his students and forming an index of their bodily shapes. He then tried to establish correlations between these physical dispositions and groups of psychological qualities. He found that the correlations did exist, and that they were clear and unmistakable for the extremes. He could soon tell that the fat greedy youth would be ceremonious in his behavior, and would enjoy family life and smoke big cigars or heavy pipes; that the somatotonic, or muscle-man, would be urgent and simple in his desires, liable also to suffer accidents and commit crimes of violence; that the cerebrotonic would be subject to anxiety, highly sensitive to music and art, a poor sleeper and a constant dreamer, a hater of plans and routine. Such was Sherlock Holmes. From the data supplied by Mr. Sheldon, admirers of Holmes will find it easy to deduce that, as a cerebrotonic, Holmes might have taken cocaine and played the violin, but could not possibly have smoked black shag in an old and oily clay pipe. The real owner of that pipe was Watson, the football-playing somatotonic, who was a projection of Conan Doyle, the energetic creator of his opposite, Mr. Sherlock Holmes.

The combinations of these dispositions are less easy to recognize than the extremes, but they exist, and they can be correlated with physical appearance. For the teacher, it is quite as valuable to know what a pupil cannot do, and should not be expected to do without a special reason, as to know what he is predisposed to do and will believe particularly important. Where Mr. Sheldon's system seems to me weakest, frankly, is in its rigidity. He tends to believe that each boy is born with his predispositions and never alters them. He says little or nothing of the effect of changes in environment, diet, and habits upon these groups of qualities. Yet many teachers know from their own experience that a boy who was thin, nervous, hypersensitive, and in most ways cerebrotonic while he was living at home often becomes tough, energetic, muscular, and somatotonic after two years' living among other youths. Everyone has seen a similar change from youth to middle age: the lean-flanked, square, bull-chested college athlete often puffs out and bags down into a curving pouch of well-filled intestines entirely surrounded by cozy fat. And Mr. Sheldon himself, although he does not discuss girls at length, has observed a similar change in some of them. He calls the type a PPJ—a "pyknic" (or thick-bodied) practical joke. When such a girl is eighteen, she is slender, blue-eyed, and blonde, vibrant with energy, full of fun, always organizing a new game or dashing off to play thirty-six holes of golf. She has many admirers, and one of them gets the prize. Five years after marriage she has three babies and three chins, and weighs two hundred pounds.

Despite its implied rigidity, Mr. Sheldon's system of classification is a valuable aid to the teacher. Certainly some kind of classification is necessary. The wise teacher will set to work, with his very first class, to observe the commonest traits that show character, to look for hidden resemblances of personality even between pupils who seem quite different to the eye, and to test his findings both by checking back with earlier records and by watching how his products turn out, years after they have left his class.

* * *

But after he has learnt the main types and subspecies, some unclassifiable individuals will always remain. These are the joys, the sorrows, and the horseflies of the teacher's life.

Rebels are not necessarily individuals. At certain times and in certain schools it is orthodox to be a rebel; and in general it is a very poor class that does not contain at least three pupils who can be counted on to oppose the teacher's authority and loudly and persistently to question everything he says. No, the individuals are those who go neither with the stream nor against it, but dart violently from side to side, spin slowly round in a backwater, bury themselves in the mud at the bottom, or, occasionally, take wings and soar in the air above. They may show up in any classroom, and come from any section of society. Their eccentricity may take any form; it may be so excessively complicated that it cannot be understood for years afterwards or so extreme that it is actively dangerous. They may be quiet, noisy, stupid, clever, sociable or solitary, handsome, hideous, or mousy, dim or dazzling: it is impossible to foresee them and unwise to overlook them. Often one eccentric will cause more trouble than all the rest of a class, and occasionally one will prove to be more rewarding than a thousand ordinary pupils. But the danger of all classifications is that they fail to prepare you for the eccentric. They may even make you mistreat him, by implying that if he does not fit into one of the accepted categories he does not really exist. On the contrary, he usually exists more intensely than his more typical classmates.

Since the eccentrics are all individuals, it is difficult to offer any general rules for treating them. But a few suggestions for the teacher himself are worth remembering.

First, always expect that one or two of your pupils will be eccentrics, even if they do not show at first. Never assume that you are addressing a group of types. That calm, fair-haired girl with the cheerful smile may turn out to be a cruel satirist with a bite like a rattlesnake. The plump short-sighted youth who seems to be bored and sleepy may be weighing and memorizing every word you say in the hope of proving you are an atheist, a Jesuit, a fascist, a Communist, or a vivisectionist. The earnest, pimpled hobbledehoy who writes down everything rather slowly may be three or four years ahead of the rest of the class. Watch them all. Human beings are infinitely complex.

Then, when you have discovered the eccentrics, treat them with extreme care. They are explosive mixtures. Some of them are as sensitive as those fulminates which can be detonated by a falling leaf. Others are fitted with a slow-burning, delayed-action fuse. You do not necessarily want to neutralize them. But you do want to employ all that force in a useful way—to economize and direct it instead of allowing it to blow itself to smithereens, perhaps taking your hand and arm with it.

These are the students whom you must learn to know as individuals. You must find out as many ingredients of the unstable compound as possible. The attempt to analyze may itself provoke an explosion. The risk, however, is worth taking, for the investigation is justifiable, and sometimes it relieves the dangerous tension.

In all your association with these eccentrics, weigh your acts and words with the utmost care. Make them clear. Make them unequivocal. Make them, as far as you can, verifiable. Eccentrics brood a great deal, and some are paranoiac. You may find that a chance word of yours sinks into the very soul of an eccentric pupil and alters his whole life in a way you had not intended. A colleague of mine, not very eccentric, has to overcome tortures of agony and doubt whenever he embarks on a new book or a new course of lectures, even in subjects on which he is an acknowledged and much-sought-after authority— because, when he was a young student, he ventured to ask an instructor for an estimate of his powers. The man replied: "You have sand in your foundations." My friend knows now that there is some sand, or clay, in the foundations of every mind, and that even his critic was conscious of far greater weaknesses in himself. Still, that early discouragement hampers him; for a time, it nearly ruined him. He still wonders if that was not the instructor's intention.

Sometimes you can make a rough division of your eccentric pupils into weaklings who need encouragement, and stronglings who need direction. Both of these groups want an unusually large quantity of spiritual food from you. But the weaklings must have it in small doses, mixed with honey and ice cream, smiles and sympathy, while the others are likely to complain if they do not get a bracing enough mixture. Every now and then, if you are both good and lively, you will get a pupil who can absorb all you can give him, and use it, grow on it, shout for more, and protest because you do not give him enough to feed and exercise the illimitable powers he feels growing in himself. It is then that you will curse yourself if you have not kept your mind open, if you have failed to think your way as far as possible into your subject, if you have stopped at the bare limits of the program imposed upon you. It is a crime to starve a growing talent, but many teachers, out of sheer idleness, commit it every year.

The most difficult eccentrics of all are the paranoiacs, silent youths with persecution mania, lip-twisted women whose minds are criss-crossed by hundreds of powerful conflicting currents, all searingly hot. These people can become dangerous. Nearly all priests and most doctors suffer from them. Many a clergyman is accustomed to have one or two fortyish women in the congregation who watch him with the ardent attention of a lover and distort his words and acts with the ingenuity of a spider. Many a doctor has had his practice damaged by a neurotic who decided that her complaints got too little attention and set out to prove the doctor was a homicidal quack. Here, as at other points, teaching touches the borders of psychiatry.

For dealing with these cases, there is one sovereign rule. *Keep the relationship impersonal.* Never step outside the bounds of your profession. If they want private interviews at which they can "really tell you all their problems," beware. Give them an interview in your study at a fixed hour, for a fixed time; take notes; and leave the door open as though you expected a colleague in ten minutes. If their personality swells up and becomes inflamed, make yourself into a cool, dry administrator who has a reasonable precedent for everything he does. Commit no dramatic personal gestures.

A colleague of mine once had a graduate student who came to his office and threatened to jump out of the window unless he revised her mark from C "to at least a B." I asked him what he did then. He said: "I opened the window for her. She didn't do it."

But he was taking a terrible risk. He was betting the woman's life against her sanity—not to mention his own career. I have often thought over this story, and the only way I can explain it is this. He himself was a quiet, hardheaded New Englander; and he knew that such a gesture, *from him,* would bring the woman to her senses. From nearly anyone else, it would have been a dangerous, a murderous provocation.

They are not uncommon, these people; and even quite normal pupils will, under a combination of strains, sometimes begin to behave strangely, whinnying, kicking, and shying at shadows. However, six such fits are amply compensated by the appearance of one really brilliant pupil.

He, or she, will be difficult to handle also, but infinitely rewarding. To train him or her properly is one of the chief functions for which the teacher should prepare; suggestions for this preparation will therefore emerge from the whole of this book, but a few general hints can be given here.

Most important of all is a negative. Do not try to make the brilliant pupil a replica of yourself. To begin with, that would be impossible, because individuals differ and brilliant individuals diverge widely. Even if it were possible, it would be stupid: because much of a man's creative energy flows from his knowledge of his own uniqueness and originality, whereas anyone who has been molded to fit the pattern of another personality usually spends the rest of his life *either* trying to conform and crushing out spontaneous and creative impulses, *or* rebelling in that dreary uncreative way which consists in saying "I don't care what I do, I just want to deny everything X stands for." (For X, read "my father," "my mother," or "my teacher.")

On the other hand, do not hesitate to train him in your skills and give him your experience. Many teachers tend to forget how valuable the wide reading and accumulated experience of a mature man or woman can be, to a pupil who is still groping around helplessly among untried experiments and unread books. If you can send him on into the world with frames of reference suggested by you and tricks of craftsmanship which he could get only from you, you will have made him your pupil, as much as he will ever be, and earned a right to his permanent gratitude.

Next, give him plenty of work, plenty to think about. Provided you are sure he is brilliant and his health is normally good, you should pile on as much as the traffic will bear. Even if he does not do all the work, he will know that it is there to be done some day. Unknown to you, after you have asked him if he has ever read Rousseau, he will buy a second-hand copy of *The Social Contract,* he will make notes saying *Mem. read Rousseau*

THIS WEEK, and he will, first in experimental dips and then in a splashing plunge of activity, read *The Social Contract,* and the *Confessions* too, and *The New Héloïse,* and *Émile.*

If he gets enough work to do and his health holds up, the chief danger for him will be wasting his energy. He will be apt to rush at everything he sees, jump every every fence, climb every hill, race down every valley, and then retain nothing but a feeling of exhaustion and disillusionment. In one of Thomas Wolfe's novels there is a weird picture of himself as he must have been when he went to Harvard. After being famished for years, he had a Gargantuan intellectual appetite. He used to go into the huge university library at night,

pulling books out of a thousand shelves and reading in them like a madman. The thought of these vast stacks of books would drive him mad: the more he read, the less he seemed to know—the greater the number of the books he read, the greater the immense uncountable number of those which he could never read would seem to be. Within a period of ten years he read at least 20,000 volumes—deliberately the number is set low—and opened the pages and looked through many times that number. This may seem unbelievable, but it happened. Dryden said this about Ben Jonson: "Other men read books but he read libraries"—and so now was it with this boy. Yet this terrific orgy of the books brought him no comfort, peace, or wisdom of the mind and heart. Instead, his fury and despair increased from what they fed upon, his hunger mounted with the food it ate.

He read insanely, by the hundreds, the thousands, the ten thousands, yet he had no desire to be bookish; no one could describe this mad assault upon print as scholarly: a ravening appetite in him demanded that he read everything that had ever been written about human experience. He read no more from pleasure: the thought that other books were waiting for him tore at his heart forever. He pictured himself as tearing the entrails from a book as from a fowl. At first, hovering over book stalls, or walking at night among the vast piled shelves of the library, he would read, watch in hand, muttering to himself in triumph or anger at the timing of each page: "Fifty seconds to do that one. Damn you, we'll see! You will, will you?"—and he would tear through the next page in twenty seconds,

evidently not really reading and digesting, but seizing a mouthful of every dish, anything to keep himself from feeling the old pangs of starvation. Pathetic and comic and true as it is, that is not how Wolfe learnt to be a good writer—and indeed, long afterwards, he would still have wasted his talents even more hopelessly if Maxwell Perkins of Scribner's publishing house, that admirable teacher, had not shown him how to direct their Vesuvian force.

The best way to avoid wasting the powers of a good pupil is to plan his work for him. You need not necessarily tell him that it is all laid out some distance ahead. Better not. Sometimes that discourages him. But you must arrange matters so that, at the end of a three-month or a six-month period, you will be able to make him look back over the journey he has made and be pleased and surprised at its extent. Make him keep records. Make him write. Extract from him groups of notes on the successive experiments he makes, or get him to put down a weekly summary of the period he has been studying, or set him a series of essays carefully designed to guide him through every sector of an important field. Then, at the end of three months, give him a rest and congratulate him, and while he is still elated, take him rapidly over his whole achievement. This gives him a sense of unexpected power; fixes the broad outlines of his work much more firmly in his mind; allows grand general ideas time to germinate in him; and often stimulates him to suggest further work in a direction that would not have occurred to you. It is also valuable insurance against those fits of depression that often afflict the brilliant. When he comes to you haggard and sullen after being baffled by a new set of problems, and says he is convinced all his effort has been wasted, then you will produce the solid collection of work he has already done, show him how far he pushed ahead during that period, persuade him that his profits there are inalienable, and, if you feel it wise, explain how the present period of work will dovetail into the earlier. Usually he will appear unconsoled. The young are easily changed, therefore they like to pose as being immutable. But after going away he will look back over the immediate past—his own, handmade, unique, indestructible past, the work that has become part of himself—and he will start again with new energy to hammer out his future.

Such pupils you must know. You must know the geniuses, the loonies, and the weaklings, all the eccentrics. You must know some of them for your own protection —in the same way as a wise physician with a new paranoiac patient telephones his previous doctor to get a complete history of his weaknesses and treatment. Others you must learn in order to draw the maximum out of them, and put the maximum in. The rest, the typical students, you need hardly know as separate persons.

But—one last word—never let them feel that they are only types: that would be quite wrong. If they ask for personal advice, it is your duty to give it freely and pleasantly. If they have special inclinations, they will be delighted to hear you discuss them. You should not, however, feel it your responsibility to know every single one of your pupils as well as you know the special individuals whom we have been discussing—since average youngsters, being easier to educate in a class and more friendly to the rest of their group, do not need such particular attention.

* * *

So far, we have said that a good teacher should know his subject, and, within limits, know his pupils. There is another necessary qualification. He or she should know much else. The good teacher is a man or woman of exceptionally wide and lively intellectual interests. It is useless to think of teaching as a business, like banking or insurance: to learn the necessary quota of rules and facts, to apply them day by day as the bank-manager applies his, to go home in the evening and sink into a routine of local gossip and middle-brow relaxation (radio, TV, the newspaper, and the detective-story), to pride oneself on being an average citizen, indistinguishable from the dentist and the superintendent of the gas-works—and then to hope to stimulate young and active minds. Teachers in schools and colleges must see more, think more, and understand more than the average man and woman of the society in which they live. This does not only mean that they must have a better command of language and know special subjects, such as Spanish literature and marine biology, which are closed to others. It means that they must know more about the world, have wider interests, keep a more active enthusiasm for the problems of the mind and the inexhaustible pleasures of art, have a keener taste even for some of the superficial enjoyments of life—yes, and spend the whole of their career widening the horizons of their spirit. Most people, as we see, stop growing between thirty and forty. They "settle down"—a phrase which implies stagnation—or at the utmost they "coast along," using their acquired momentum, applying no more energy, and gradually slowing down to a stop. No teacher should dream of doing this. His job is understanding a large and important area of the world's activity and achievement and making it viable for the young. He should expect to understand more and more of it as the years go by.

He has two special functions that make him different from other professional men and from the business-men and workers in his community.

The first of these is to make a bridge between school or college and the world. It is really very hard for the young to understand why they are shut up in classrooms and taught skills such as trigonometry, while the "real world" hums and clatters and shouts beyond the windows. They submit, poor creatures, but the pressure required to keep them there is intense. If they are allowed to think that school or college is an ingenious prison, a squirrel-cage in which they must whirl uselessly for a few years until they are let out, they will profit little or nothing from it. They may resent it bitterly. They cannot be told directly or convincingly how learning trigonometry will fit into their future existence: partly because no one really knows which of them will turn out to be a bridge-engineer or will make some now unimagined discovery in ballistics, partly because they themselves cannot realize the value of mathematical thinking during their adolescence and youth, and partly because they cannot foresee even the outlines of their adult lives. But they should be given to understand in as many ways as possible that the two worlds are closely and necessarily connected, and that light and energy from one flow into the other.

This is often done by "making subjects relevant." Little German boys used to be trained in mathematics by getting problems about the number of pounds of explosive required to demolish a (non-German) viaduct. Some teachers of English use current magazines like *Time* to demonstrate vivid and concise writing. Certainly every teacher of a modern foreign language ought to use the newspapers and films produced in that language. But this idea cannot be applied to all subjects, nor to some of the most valuable subjects, while in others it often leads to superficiality and lowers intellectual standards.

The best way to do it is for the teacher to make *himself* relevant. Nine thousand times more pupils have learnt a difficult subject well because they felt the teacher's vitality and energy proved its value than because they chose the subject for its own sake. If a youth, sizing up the professor of medieval history, decides that he is a tremendous expert in the history of the Middle Ages and a deadly bore in everything else, he is apt to conclude that medieval history makes a man a deadly bore. If on the other hand he finds that the man is filled with lively interest in the contemporary world, that he actually knows more about it because, through his training, he understands it better, that the practice of the intellectual life, so far from making him vague and remote, has made him wise and competent, the youth will conclude without further evidence that medieval history is a valuable interest.

The good teacher is an interesting man or woman. As such, he or she will make the work interesting for the students, in just the same way as he or she talks interestingly and writes an interesting letter. Most teaching is done by talking. If your mind is full of lively awareness of the world, you will never be at a loss for new points of view on your own subject. Novel illustrations will constantly suggest themselves to you. You will discard outworn types of argument and find fresh ones. Allusions and reminiscences will brighten your talk and keep your audience from suffering the awful torture of feeling that it knows exactly what you are going to say next. Much teaching consists in explaining. We explain the unknown by the known, the vague by the vivid. The students usually know so little that they are delighted to hear you explain what you know and tie it up with what they are trying to understand. A colleague of mine in Paris used to have great difficulty, when discussing *Don Quixote,* in convincing his intelligent youngsters that Quixote was not merely a farcical old lunatic who should have been locked up. Then he described a series of bull-fights he had seen on a holiday in Seville, with their cruelty, their pride, their useless courage, which is an art in itself, and the oddity of sixteenth-century costumes in a Roman arena for a twentieth-century entertainment, which struck none of the Spaniards as odd; and he reminded them of the same Spanish pride and idealism as expressed in tragedy by the French master Corneille. Then his pupils began to understand that their own standards had not been complex enough for judging all the world's great books, and that Don Quixote's insanity might be a kind of strange sense. From that point the discussions used to develop in a dozen equally interesting and instructive directions.

The second function of the teacher is to make a bridge

between youth and maturity. He has to interpret adult life to the young in such a way as to make them adults. To do this, he should belong to both worlds.

Many teachers find this extremely difficult. Some schoolmasters in Britain "live for the school." This means that their horizon is bounded at one edge by the preparatory institutions from which the youngsters come and on the other by the colleges to which they go. The great events of their lives are school cricket-matches and scholarship examinations. Like some officers of the regular army, they will talk for hours about the flap in Ingoldsby's unit, and "Whatever became of old Snoggins?" but they grow embarrassed when asked about new books or contemporary politics. At the other extreme are teachers who care less than nothing for the hopes and fears and gaieties of the young, who never open the college magazine or watch a school football game, who feel it is an infringement on their dignity to spend nearly every day with children and adolescents, and who would obviously be happier if all their pupils were fifty years old and graying at the temples.

Difficult though this bridge-building between two worlds may be, it is possible; it is necessary; it is done by the best teachers. After all, no one is entirely and exclusively thirty-three years old, or forty-eight, or whatever his legal age may be. Watch any group of people enjoying themselves, vividly interested, and you will see them growing decades younger. Within every one of us, not far from the surface, lie hidden many personalities, some of them as young as childhood, and only one as old as today. The good teacher will be able to draw vitality and variety from the younger layers of personality which are still alive within him, and to know what it is to be a youth again, or a boy, without ceasing to be a man.

For example, he will notice and remember not only the things that interest him as an adult, but those things which used to interest him as a youngster. If he does, and if he uses them to illustrate his teaching but discusses them from a mature level, his teaching will become easier and his explanations clearer. The young are not very deep and consistent thinkers, but they are highly sensitive to new impressions: so they notice things like fanciful advertising campaigns, eccentric new personalities, peculiar rather than essential pieces of news, far more than grown-ups do. They do not think much about such things, but—since they have not yet become blasé and have no very intense inner life—they do experience them. Allusions to such things therefore can clarify a difficult discussion. At the moment this is being written, for instance, it would be wise for anyone trying to explain the ancient Greek "tyrants," those ambitious independent despots, to begin by talking of Marshal Tito. Although the parallel is not really close, it is helpful.

* * *

One of the most important qualities of a good teacher is humor. Many are the purposes it serves. The most obvious one is that it keeps the pupils alive and attentive because they are never quite sure what is coming next. Another is that it does in fact help to give a true picture of many important subjects. Suppose you are discussing English literature of the early nineteenth century. If you confine yourself to talking about Wordsworth's lyrical simplicity, and Shelley pinnacled dim in the intense inane, you will be giving an incomplete picture of the group; whereas if you also d-d-describe Ch-Charles Lamb as both f-funny and ch-charming, and bring out the weird boyish comedy of some of Wordsworth's other poems, and read some of Byron's rougher letters, you will then establish the idea that these men were rich and varied and human personalities, not "classics" cast in a single mold of solid bronze, and you can proceed all the better to explain both the nobility of their achievement and the sadness of their failures.

Of course some subjects, notably the sciences, do not admit humorous treatment. There the wise teacher will continue to introduce flashes of humor extraneously, because he knows that fifty-five minutes of work plus five

minutes' laughter are worth twice as much as sixty minutes of unvaried work.

Some teachers speak of humor as a useful instrument
with which to control their classes. This is a dangerous
notion. Those who harbor it often make the mistake of
using humor as nineteenth-century schoolmasters used
the cane, to terrify the refractory and spur the slow. They
begin by mocking a particular set of mistakes. Then they
make fun of the boys who make these mistakes. Then
they develop a bitter wit which thrives on every kind of
personal defect, ruthlessly exposed. They will even feel
aggrieved if no boy in their class happens to be a fit subject for satire, and will single out a perfectly innocuous
youth simply because they cannot teach without having
a butt. They are like the Oriental monarchs who always
had a few malefactors impaled before their gates, to remind the citizenry that the master's word was law. Perhaps they would enjoy that comparison, for they are
usually so petty and insecure that they would like to be
maharajahs. I should compare them rather to the mag-
pies of the Western states which will find a sore patch on
a horse's back and perch on it, picking out raw flesh and
squawking with self-satisfaction, until the horse runs mad
down a cliff-side.

Kipling, who suffered a good deal of torture during his
childhood, got this treatment first from his guardians (see
Something of Myself, Chapter ii) and then from the master whom he immortalized as "King" (note the regal
pseudonym) in *Stalky & Co.* What "King" did to him certainly kept him mentally alert; and he says he enjoyed it
and profited from it; but it helped to increase that timidity and hypersensitivity which spoilt much of his adult
life, and it did something to produce his very odd belief
in the pulverizing force of ridicule as a political weapon
(see, for instance, "Little Foxes," "As Easy as A.B.C.,"
and "The Village that Voted the Earth was Flat"), his
absolute trust in authority, and his almost delighted contempt for lesser breeds without the Law. If he had only
had a teacher like Kim's Lama, he would have been wiser

and much happier. But part of his spirit was sacrificed to a schoolmaster who, perhaps, as some schoolmasters also do, detected and resented the superior intellectual brilliance of the grubby boy with the big glasses, and tried to make himself feel great by making young Rudyard Kipling feel small.

No, humor must not be used to tyrannize a class. It seldom is so used. Usually irony and sarcasm are used, because they imply intellectual domination; but not humor. The real purpose of humor in teaching is deeper and more worthy. It is to link the pupils and the teacher, and to link them through enjoyment. A very wise old teacher once said: "I consider a day's teaching is wasted if we do not all have one hearty laugh." He meant that when people laugh together, they cease to be young and old, master and pupils, workers and driver, jailer and prisoners, they become a single group of human beings enjoying its existence.

Jules Romains, the eminent French novelist and dramatist, began his career by working out a theory which he later put into several excellent plays and stories. This is the idea that collections of people remain individuals until a single event or purpose or emotion molds them into groups, and that then the group lives, feels, and thinks in a way of its own, superior in energy and intensity to the activity of any one of its members. Sometimes, no doubt, a collective emotion is silly or degrading, as in a riot or a panic. But sometimes, Romains believes, it can be a truly ennobling experience: it is our duty to understand such experiences fully when they come. To be a member of a meeting which is moved by an energetic speaker to take a generous resolution; to applaud with a crowd of friends when your own team, making a huge effort, wins; to share the emotion of actors and audience at the production of a good new play; to walk through a city and feel yourself part of its beating and driving life— these are worthy emotions, which help us out of our own pettiness.

Romains called this theory Unanimism. Obviously it

has its dangers. It leads very easily to the annulment of the individual, to the denial of intelligence, to "thinking with the blood" and believing that the majority is always right. Because it is easy to misapply, and because he knows that no eminent artist has ever been tied to one single theory, Romains has not concentrated on preaching and exploiting the doctrine. But it runs through most of his best work, and has inspired several younger writers. Now, Romains was for some time a teacher in French high schools. One of the most winning figures in his *Men of Good Will* is the schoolmaster Clanricard, while several others are in fact teachers though they are ostensibly priests, doctors, and authors. Although he got his first glimpse of Unanimism in a busy Paris street, I am sure that he confirmed it from his experiences as a pupil and as a teacher. For one of the greatest pleasures in teaching comes from those hours when you feel that every word you say is being heard, not by a collection of bored and dutiful individuals, but instead by a group which you create and which in turn creates you; that, instead of repeating facts learnt by rote, to be telephoned through the drowsy air to half-deaf ears and garbled down in notebooks, you are both stirring minds to ask questions and answering them; that you are being driven by the energy of the young on the search for truth, and drawing therefrom the power to lead the search; and, in fact, that you and your words and the class which listens and thinks are all part of the ceaseless activity of human Reason.

Your pupils will feel this too. If the feeling exists at all, it will be shared. To create it, or to help it to come into being, is one of the teacher's main tasks. It cannot exist unless there is a rapport, a give-and-take, something like a unanimist relationship between the pupils and the teacher. One of the means of establishing that rapport is humor. When a class and its teacher all laugh together, they cease for a time to be separated by individuality, authority, and age. They become a unit, feeling pleasure and enjoying the shared experience. If that community can be prolonged or re-established, and applied to the job of thinking, the teacher will have succeeded.

This can also be put in terms of traditional psychology. There are two powerful instincts which exist in all human beings, and which can be used in teaching. These are *gregariousness* and *the love of play*. Give fifty men four hours to cross a hill and walk down the valley beyond to the nearest town. If they try it separately, many will come in late, and nearly all will be tired. If they march in groups, they will be far less tired and come in sooner. If they do it in two teams competing with each other, or as a hiking party singing songs in rhythm, they will scarcely be tired at all, they will keep together, and they will enjoy the experience. In just the same way, if you can get a class of thirty youngsters to feel they are all pulling together, and if you can give them some reason to enjoy it, they will do nine times better work than thirty individuals working under compulsion. And one of the best appeals to both gregariousness and the play-instinct is a good joke.

We said that one function of the teacher was to make a bridge between youth and maturity. If he has a sense of humor, he can build the bridge. The young think their elders are dull. The elders think the young are silly. This is the basis of that mutual misunderstanding of the ages, on which scarcely anything can get done without compulsion. Yet a clever teacher, who can use his sense of humor in such a way as to show the young that not everyone over twenty-five is dead, will at the same time learn enough about his pupils to see that their silliness is only awkwardness, easy to penetrate and dissolve. Both sides will understand each other better, and work together. Togetherness is the essence of teaching.

* * *

Now we have listed the main things that a good teacher will know and like. But what kind of man or woman will the good teacher be? Are there any abilities which are absolutely essential?

Not many. But there are certainly three.

The first is memory. A teacher with a poor memory is ridiculous and dangerous. He is like a musician who announces an ambitious concert and plays innumerable wrong notes; or an actor who begins: "It is the cause, it is the cause, my soul," and then blows up; or a doctor who gives one gram of digitalis instead of one grain; or a policeman who directs three lines of traffic into one another; or a merchant who cannot find the goods his customers want ("I know they were in here somewhere; just a moment, it'll come to me where I left them, let me see now . . ."); or a painter who puts both eyes on the same side of the nose—no, no, hush, for Picasso is still alive and distinguished; but certainly those others. Of course he must remember all the essentials of his subject. So much we have already said; although if he now and then forgets a detail, the class will understand and sympathize. (Let him look it up freely and openly—preferably in his own notes, not in a book.) But his memory is also important in covering what is said in class. If a question is raised and discussed, let him remember it and bring it back a week or two later in another context. If a pupil volunteers a good illustration from his own reading, or from a hobby, let the teacher remember to ask him for another one later. If one little group find a problem unusually hard, let him give special attention to them when the next such problem appears. Memory is as important for the teacher as for other professional men. A creative memory is one of the qualities that differentiate the good lawyer, doctor, or teacher from the mediocre.

A display of good creative memory by a teacher helps the young in one of their most difficult jobs. Their attention is lively and their perception is keen, but they find it very hard to correlate. Many of the facts they learn merely drop into their minds like blocks of metal, and lie there. At examinations they take out the blocks, polish them, and show them to us. Then they put them back, or sometimes throw them away. If the facts simply remain on deposit, however neatly packed and highly polished, their possessors are not educated. The business of the teacher is to pass currents of interest and energy through the facts, while they are being learnt and afterwards, so that they melt, fuse, become interconnected, acquire life, and grow into vital parts of the minds which hold them. One excellent way to do this is to demonstrate *how* apparently remote facts are organically linked, and that can sometimes be done more happily as improvisation than as a prepared part of a lesson. When it comes off, the teacher's reward is there: he sees face after face light up as two blank areas of the brain, with the connections flashing between them, come alive.

* * *

Second to memory comes will-power. A good teacher is a determined person.

This was widely known in the nineteenth century. That was a time of strong-willed parents and tough teachers. Sometimes they were merely tyrants. But sometimes they were wise, firm, and efficient educators; and even if the children they produced did often rebel, they became well-educated rebels. This necessity is not so well known nowadays—at least in the schools of the Western democracies. It was recognized in Germany during the National Socialist regime, when will-power was classed as one of the essential qualifications of a schoolmaster and as one of the essential qualities he had to develop in his pupils. Teachers in America and Britain, France and Italy and elsewhere, often avoid the display of will, and prefer to be "nice"—which often means being cheery and indulgent and evasive on difficulties. On the whole, they do not teach so well as their resolute predecessors.

Yet it is obvious that a teacher needs will-power. Everyone who has ever faced a class and seen thirty pairs of eyes turned upon him knows that. Some nervous ladies stand behind their desks, as though they were hunting leopards from a hide, while there are men teachers who stride up and down among their pupils, catching every gaze and holding it, barking out short urgent phrases, lacking only the chair and whip to be lion-tamers. Still, it seems that some teachers do not know why they must have a strong will and exercise it: they are perhaps a little ashamed of the necessity, even afraid of it; they feel that in a perfect society no display of will-power would be needed in the schools. But it would.

Consider how many different kinds of resistance the teacher has to overcome. To begin with, the young do not like work. They would rather be playing football, or sitting in the movies eating popcorn. But they must learn to work, because they will assuredly have to work all the rest of their lives; and to teach them that work is unnecessary or avoidable is to deform their characters. (It is odd, by the way, that the word "school" means "leisure" or "pastime." When that name was coined, people felt that a boy was lucky to be in school, because if he weren't he would be sweeping out his father's shop or milking his father's cows: that was real work, and "school" was "play.")

Nor do the young like authority. They are natural anarchists. They would prefer a world of unpredictable disorder, without duties or responsibilities. Such a world is impracticable now. So the young must be taught to respect the principle of authority; and if they do not learn it in school they will find it very bitter to learn later. A subsequent duty of their teachers will be to teach them to distinguish between different types of authority, to choose the good and reject the bad. Only a determined teacher can teach them the first lesson. If he is both determined and wise, he can teach them both.

Also, the young hate concentration. It is an effort, an unfamiliar and painful effort. Watch a boy doing his home-work when he thinks he is not observed. He will read ten lines, then draw a funny face in the margin, then try to read ten lines more and give up, then stop to whistle two bars of "Blood on the Saddle," then rearrange all the books on his table and sharpen all his pencils, then make a dash at the book and read twenty-five lines, and then sit panting and vacant-eyed for at least three minutes before beginning the struggle once more. Even his moments of true attention are accompanied by all kinds of waste motion and diversion: he taps both heels rhythmically on the ground, bites his nails, shifts his position as though he were sitting in a red-hot torture-seat, and usually keeps the radio on full blast. All this side-effort means that he finds concentration to be so painful that he must mitigate the agony by every possible means. He is pretending to escape.

Yet he learns. By the time he gets to college he will be able to concentrate oftener and keep it up for longer periods. If he enters one of the professions, he will have to increase his ability until he can follow and reproduce nearly every stage of a complex operation, or summarize the essentials of six leading judicial decisions in one evening. If he goes to work on leaving school, life will teach him concentration—or else it will make him a nonentity, the sort of man who hops from job to job and has a constant struggle to keep alive in a world where the bees outnumber the butterflies.

Concentration must be learnt. It should be learnt in school. A good teacher can teach it to his pupils. It should not be imagined as nothing but an effort of the will. Concentration is also an intellectual process. It is choice. Take the same boy who reads his book slowly, grudgingly, five lines at a time, and increase the urgency of his study—somehow, anyhow—make the choice clearer to him, and the importance of his study paramount—put him to work on the prize essay—and then watch. "Turn that radio off!" he shouts. He clears the table, except for one photograph. He sits fixed in one position till he is cramped. Sometimes, when he is really intent, he will miss meals and forget about sleep. All this because he has chosen one aim and discarded others. And that, after all, is what we learn to do throughout life.

Many youngsters also resent the domination of one mind. They reject suggestions just in order to assert their own independence, as a horse will jerk its head and side-step when it is ridden on a tight rein. Indeed, one important and successful method of teaching (which we shall be discussing a little later) is based on the idea of provoking the student's resistance. This is the tutorial method used in Oxford and Cambridge and in special classes elsewhere. The student writes an essay on a complex and difficult subject—say the political influence of the nobility in modern Italy, or the relativity of color— and reads it to his tutor. One other student, who knows something of the subject, listens. The tutor may agree with nearly everything in the essay, but it is his duty to tear it to pieces. Ruthlessly he exposes the defects in its arguments. Relentlessly he searches out the passages copied from books and encyclopedias. Surgically he dissects every page, every paragraph: sometimes he will spend an hour on a single important sentence. But the student answers every criticism as far as he can, defends every assertion, and gradually, instead of allowing his essay to become a mass of quivering fragments, can, if he has thought out his subject, build it during the conversation into a fully documented and soundly reasoned paper. Should he do this, the tutor will be well satisfied. Should he make no reply to the tutor's criticisms, should he sit down under them without attempting to resist, he is a poor student, and, probably, the tutor is a poor teacher.

So then, the young naturally resist the domination of their elders' minds. It is good that they should do so. It is one of the aims of teaching to provoke their resistance, and then to direct it into the right channels. But when they are lively and energetic, or when their resistance is particularly strong, their teacher needs a great deal of solid will-power to control them and to retain his own independence.

Again, in some countries, although not in all, schoolboys and schoolgirls put up a strong resistance to the very idea of learning. They feel it as an attack on their own integrity. They think that their own natural endowments—good sense, courage, and vitality—will take them as far as they want to go. They believe, not only that it is useless to learn a lot of stuff out of books, but that it might be positively harmful—very much like the old army cook who declared: "All them vitamines only weakens the system." This is a point of view which is often found in the central and western United States, in Australia, in the English Midlands, and in certain other areas where toughness and energy are much prized. It is difficult for the educator to cope with, and will be discussed later. Meanwhile it can be marked as a common source of resistance to the teacher in his work.

To face all these resistances, then, the teacher needs a strong will. If he is to be a good teacher, he will master them and guide them, instead of merely meeting them head-on and wrestling with them; and for that he will need an even stronger and more mature will. Also, as well as definite currents of resistance, there is always perceptible in big schools and colleges a directionless, anarchist upsurge of revolt and idiocy. You know how, every now and then, three or four boys will break into an empty building and wreck the place as though a regiment of Cossacks had camped in it? And, when they are questioned, they always appear quite normal, in fact rather timid and subdued—as though they themselves were afraid of the forces that had possessed them? Well, in just the same way a whole class or a whole school can go *haywire*—the word comes from the wild whirling and tangling confusion of the wire in a broken hay-baling machine—and do unbelievable damage to themselves, to their teacher, to property, and to morale before they can be stopped. Wise teachers allow the young a large number of outlets through which this energy can escape. To draw it off into helpless, cheerful laughter is another of the functions of humor in teaching. But it takes a strong-minded teacher to resist its constant threat and to control it when it does reach the bursting-point.

* * *

Memory, then, and will-power are two of the qualities that make a good teacher. The third is kindness. It is very difficult to teach anything without kindness. It can be done, of course, by the exercise of strong compulsion—as lion-tamers teach their beastly pupils—but there are not many types of pupil on which such compulsion can be exercised. Lions are imprisoned, and partially cowed by hot irons and guns. Boys learning religious texts like the Koran and the Talmud are caged within generations of previous examples and prodded on by their own (and their families') ambition. Pupils at officers' schools, and certain other institutions where attendance is a guarded privilege, will drive themselves on within the tight disciplinary mechanism of the school even if the master hates them as much as they hate him. But in nearly all other kinds of learning the pupils should feel that the teacher wants to help them, wants them to improve, is interested in their growth, is sorry for their mistakes and pleased by their successes and sympathetic with their inadequacies. Learning anything worth while is difficult. Some people find it painful. Everyone finds it tiring. Few things will diminish the difficulty, the pain, and the fatigue like the kindness of a good teacher.

This kindness must be genuine. Pupils of all ages, from careless children up to hard-working graduates, easily and quickly detect the teacher who dislikes them, as easily as a dog detects someone who is afraid of him. It is useless to feign a liking for them if you do not really feel it.

On the other hand, it is not at all necessary to show it by pats on the shoulder, by nods and becks and wreathed smiles. A serious-faced lecturer, who seldom addresses a pupil by name and thinks only about the job of making the basic principles of economics or the powers of the Supreme Court absolutely clear and memorable, will often be recognized as a teacher genuinely interested in the job of teaching and anxious for the welfare of his classes. It is not enough for him to be interested in the subject. Many a man is interested in a subject without wanting to teach it to anyone else. But if he is really interested in making the subject better known and more correctly understood, and if he does not expect all his pupils to grasp its elements at the first attempt but will help the slow and correct the confused, then he will be counted kind, although his face remains immovably grave and his manner unemotional and impersonal.

Still, the kindness must be there. It may be the kindness of an elder brother or sister, even of a parent. It can well be the kindness of a fellow-student. Sometimes it is a sympathy based on local patriotism, where the teacher feels he is helping the younger generation of his own fellow-citizens to grow and prosper. (This is at the basis of the admirable plan for conquering illiteracy in Mexico, by getting every Mexican who can read to teach one other of his countrymen.) But if the teacher feels none of these emotions, nor anything like them, if he or she regards the students merely as a necessary evil, in the same way as he regards income-tax forms, then his or her job will be far more difficult to do, far more painful for the pupils, and far less effectively done. Every teacher dislikes *some* pupils—the cheeky lipsticked adolescent girls, the sullen hangdog youths, the cocky vulgar little comedians, how loathsome they can be, all the more so because they do it deliberately! But if any teacher finds himself disliking *all* his pupils, he should change his character, and if that fails, change his job.

III

The Teacher's Methods

W<small>E HAVE DISCUSSED</small> the character of a good teacher. Now we come to his methods.

Teaching has three stages. First, the teacher prepares the subject. Then he communicates it to his pupils, or those parts of it that he has selected. Then he makes sure that they have learnt it.

(a) PREPARATION

Preparation is usually done well on a small scale, but badly on a large scale. A teacher is apt to prepare his work for next day or next week, and to neglect the job of planning the whole of his work for the term or the year. He often knows exactly what ground he will cover as far ahead as Friday, but only vaguely understands how that part of his work will fit into the rest of his school year. It is only very strong-minded and far-sighted teachers who can draw up a scheme of work and then stick to it until the terminal point at which they have aimed. Most of us discover, a fortnight before the examinations, that we have spent too much time on the introductory material and have to rush the end. In this respect university teachers are generally worse, because they have more freedom to digress and less control in the shape of externally administered examinations.

Here is an example of this. It comes from the memoirs of Nicholas Murray Butler, who was President of Columbia University for many years, and who never allowed loyalty to his own college to alter his standards of good teaching. He attended Columbia College in the seventies of last century; he liked classical literature; but in his memoirs he wrote that Drisler, the professor of Greek, was

> so given to insistence upon the minutest details of grammar that our eyes were kept closely fixed on the ground and we hardly ever caught any glimpse of the beauty and larger significance of the great works upon which we were engaged. For example, I recall that during the first term of the sophomore year we were to read with Dr. Drisler the *Medea* of Euripides and that when the term came to an end we had completed but 246 lines. In other words, we never came to know what the *Medea* was all about or to see either the significance of the story or the quality of its literary art.

This is a serious indictment, especially from a man who was himself so devoted to the classics and to the whole cause of learning. It has its comic side too, for it reminds us of the story about the operatic baritone who never knew how a particular opera ended, because he was always killed in the second act and went home. The boys *could* have read the rest of *Medea* for themselves, at least in a translation. Doubtless, though, they were too disgusted.

But think for a moment of Drisler's planning. There are about fourteen hundred lines in *Medea*. There are fourteen weeks in the American academic term. It would seem obvious that he should have set out to read one hundred lines a week—or, allowing for introductory lectures and closing discussions, a little more. In fact he must have read an average of seventeen lines a week, which is pretty slow and careful if the class meets only once, and glacier-like if it meets three times. Now, why did he go at this hour-hand pace and leave over a thousand lines of the tragedy untouched? Was it because Butler's class was unusually slow? Scarcely, for Butler would have heard of that and made allowances; and Drisler himself would have noticed the fact and made other arrangements halfway through. Was it because he spent little time on translation and a great deal on explanatory lectures? No, because Butler implies he did not discuss the meanings of the myth, or Euripides' achievements as a tragic poet. It was because his real interests were grammar and syntax, and so long as he could teach them, he cared nothing about age-old myths and immortal tragedies, nothing about poetry and human character, nothing about that great gift of Greece, the sense of structure, which makes every work of art a perfect whole composed of perfectly harmonized parts, whether it is a temple or a philosophical dialogue, a vase or a play.

No doubt Drisler would have been surprised and shocked if you had accused him of obscuring several of the chief values to be found in the study of Greek. He would have explained that the class could not go much faster than 246 lines a term if he were to get in all he wanted to say. If you had then suggested that he might have treated the play as a whole, giving his pupils an outline of it, telling them he expected it to be finished by the end of term, reading and discussing the most important speeches and all the choruses (to the total number of 246 lines if necessary), and encouraging them to read the rest by themselves, he would probably have treated the idea as a scandalous perversion of academic standards. Or perhaps he really believed that he did read the whole play, and every year, when he stopped just before line 250, shook his head in astonishment because he had not got farther this time.

Teachers of literature are especially prone to this fault, because they often love part of their subject so much that they would rather dwell dotingly on it than push on to cover the whole area. This love is not a vice, but a virtue. A class nearly always enjoys a subject that draws out the enthusiasm of its teacher. Some of the best lessons I have ever heard have been unprepared talks, when the lecturer dropped his notes and stood looking at us earnestly and eagerly, talking about what lay nearest his heart, making us love the subject by showing us that he did, and why he did. When you have established an active sympathy with your class, you can tell when they are profiting from every word, enjoying every quotation, participating in the act of thought; and then it is your duty to go on improvising as far as the argument, your enthusiasm, and their understanding will carry you. But next day or next week you must re-establish the proportions. Point out and summarize what you have passed over. Explain what stage you have reached, and be sure the pupils are following you closely. You are a guide, not a fugitive.

One of the chief aids to learning is the sense of purpose. One of its chief rewards is the sense of achievement. One of its chief aims is to develop the structural faculty, which in intellectual matters shows itself as foresight and co-ordination, and in art gives the appreciation of harmony and the power to create it. The teacher should have all these in view as he prepares his work. By example and by practice, he can show the young that it is a weakness to live from day to day, and that accumulation and planning mean strength.

The best way to do this is to plan all the work which the class will do, to explain the plan to them, to make sure that they keep it in mind, and, after the work has been completed, to look back over it and sum it up. The young have very little ability to make long-term plans. They live from day to day, or at best from one Saturday to another. Teachers are sometimes infected by this malady, or take advantage of it, to save themselves the trouble of planning and the effort of sticking to the plan. They are sometimes apt to devote the term to reading one textbook, to studying one branch of their subject, and to let themselves drift week by week, carried on only by the flow of historical dates, the succession of chapters. Although this feels easier, it is vastly more tedious for their pupils, and even for themselves. Every teacher has overheard gloomy dialogues like this:

"What have you got for tomorrow?"

"Oh, thirty pages of Tremlett's *Nineteenth Century*. What have you got?"

"Oh, fifty lines of Goethe. So long."

"So long," with a sigh like that of the horse which, instead of being ridden through fields or even along a trail, is roused from its drooping rest to plod another thirty or three hundred or three thousand times around the same path, dragging the beam which turns the heavy millstone on its motionless axis.

Of course boys will talk like that no matter how clearly their work is planned, because they like to exaggerate their sufferings. But if they have a destination in their minds, they will work better and more quickly and more intelligently. If they know that those thirty pages will cover one of the greatest events that made the world they live in, and if they see, however dimly, how that passage in *Faust* is related to the episodes they have already read and those they are going on to study, they will approach their work with more liveliness than the horse turning the millstone.

Each class should therefore be given, before it starts work, a summary of the ground it will cover. Some teachers merely talk about the main outlines of their subject. Others dictate a neatly arranged program, paragraphed and subparagraphed. Others hand out a mimeographed leaflet, containing the main topics which will be discussed, arranged not week by week but in their logical order, so that the student can see their internal connections, prepare questions on subjects that interest him particularly, and, if he has been absent, find out what he missed. For the humanities—art, literature, languages, philosophy, history, politics—it is a little discouraging to have the work sliced up and packed into airtight compartments, each containing one week's ration. It is better in these subjects to allow the teacher and the class scope to develop their discussions without being kept to a timetable. It is the logical structure of the work that should be prepared and made known. In the sciences, and in law and medicine, it is probably better to maintain a suitably exact time-plan.

When the White Rabbit was presenting the evidence in the Knave's trial, he asked the King for directions. Gravely the King replied: "Begin at the beginning, and go on till you come to the end: then stop." This is excellent advice for storytellers, but it is bad counsel for teachers. Suppose you wanted to get to know a tract of country. The worst way to do it would be to jump into a car, drive straight from one end to the other, then turn your back on it and walk away. Yet that is what many teachers do with complex subjects, and that is why their pupils seem stupider than they really are. Actually, the students are bewildered. They don't know where they are going, what they should expect to see, where the difficult hills are and on which side the best views can be found, or what they will meet at the other end. All they know is that the car stops every Friday for forty-eight hours' rest. How much better would they learn the country if, before setting out, they were briefed and given maps to study; if they were rested and reoriented once or twice during the trip; and if they were shown photographs of the best spots and taken once more over the map when they reached the end of their journey?

Many textbooks make the King's mistake. They do not tell the reader clearly what he is going to learn. They do not, while he is learning it, show him the relation of each part to the whole. And they usually finish, not with a reasonable conclusion and a glance backwards, but abruptly and even rudely. Well do I remember the first book of Homer I ever read. It was an ugly brown book. The scholar who produced it had written explanatory notes on every line (mainly on that fascinating subject, Homeric grammar), but he had not thought to tell me

—who Homer was, if anybody
—where he lived, and when
—what the *Iliad* was
—what Book One of the *Iliad* was (I didn't see how a book could have Books inside it, and I didn't find out until I had learnt about individual papyrus rolls)
—what the general plan of the poem was, and how Book One fitted into it.

nor to answer a hundred other simple questions which occurred to me while I dutifully translated μέν "on the one hand" and δέ "on the other hand." He simply began talking at line 1, stopped at line 611, and disappeared—as though he were not a man, but a stream of words coming out of a dictaphone.

This was a common experience, and still is. Here is another description of bad teaching, written by someone who himself became a good teacher and loved literature. When William Lyon Phelps went to Yale in 1883, he found that "a curse hung over the Faculty, a blight on the art of teaching." He joined a class in Homer which ran three hours a week throughout the entire year. Now, with such an opportunity, you would expect that his teacher would really have given him and his fellows a mastery of those superb poems, bringing out the characterization and the plot-structure, the rich language and the infinitely melodious verse, describing the Homeric age and discussing the strange interpretations of Homer which other ages have held, showing Homer as the founder of tragedy, the educator of Greece, and through Greece one of the teachers of mankind. But no.

The instructor never changed the monotonous routine, never made a remark, but simply called on individuals to recite [i.e. to translate] or to scan [i.e. to read the verse metrically], said 'That will do,' put down a mark; so that in the last recitation in June, after a whole college year of this intolerable classroom drudgery, I was surprised to hear him say, and again without any emphasis, 'The poems of Homer are the greatest that have ever proceeded from the mind of man, class is dismissed,' and we went out into the sunshine.

That one sentence was evidently the only attempt made by the instructor to give a reason for all those hours and hours of work. It will be objected that no one requires a justification for the study of great literature. That may be true of adults. But the young need to have such things proved to them. They are not even sure that literature is worth studying, they cannot tell whether the Homeric poems are great literature until after reading them, and they have only a vague intuitive grasp of the meaning of greatness in literature. It is not necessary to glorify a good subject: but you must explain it, allow its merits to display themselves, fill in a suitable background. If you wanted to instill a taste for music into a group of young men or girls, would you order them to read the score of all the Beethoven symphonies, transposing two or three pages from them on the piano thrice a week for a year, and, without discussing the themes, the development of Beethoven's idea of the symphony, the changes in his orchestration, the strong reflections of his life and times in his work, his relation to earlier and later musicians, and the beauty and strength of separate movements and individual symphonies, leave it at that? If you did, a few would get to know music, most would remember snatches of Beethoven and acquire a certain facility in transposition, and many would hate and despise music for the rest of their lives.

How then should a long course like that be planned? Whether the subject is Homer or Milton, Beethoven or Dante, does not affect the plan very much, although the treatment would differ considerably according to the size of the class. The first essential would be to cut down the monotonous reading and scansion, and to increase the quantity of explanatory lectures and discussions; the next would be to vary the types of teaching, so that the class should not always expect exactly the same tasks (what Phelps calls "monotonous routine" and "intolerable drudgery"); and the third would be to conceive the subject-matter of the course not as a shapeless stream of foreign words to be read, translated, and scanned, but as an intellectual and artistic whole composed of various parts.

The course might begin with two or three lectures, punctuated by questions and discussions. In them, the teacher would give the class an outline of their entire year's work on the subject, telling them what books were necessary and which would be additionally useful, and advising them on methods of study. Then he would describe the two Homeric poems: first their history as far as it is known, then their nature and style, then their language, and then a brief summary of their plots. Next he might begin the actual study of the text with the *Odyssey*—since it is easier and moves faster, perhaps also because it is conventional to begin with the *Iliad*. After giving a fuller summary of its plot and characters and dividing it into easily surveyed sections, he would read it all through with the class—sometimes translating it himself, sometimes setting them to translate orally, sometimes giving them written "quizzes" to be carefully checked for accuracy, sometimes reading them passages from famous translations (Pope, Chapman, Newman—and Arnold on him, Butler, Lang and his colleagues, William Morris, Maurice Hewlett, T. E. Lawrence, and any newer versions) and asking them to criticize the translators' accuracy and grace. If he had not time for the whole poem, he should omit the duller and more repetitive passages, but summarize them with care and have them read in translation. After reaching the end of the *Odyssey,* he would pause to review the whole poem.

Next he might lecture on the *Odyssey* and the *Iliad* together, asking whether they were really produced by the same man or by the same school of poets, pointing out the many resemblances and the many differences, and quoting some of the fine remarks critics have made on the subject. ("Longinus" said that the *Odyssey,* like a setting sun, had grandeur without strength.) Then he would give a summary of the *Iliad* and go on to translate it in the same way. After reaching and dwelling on the end—those magnificent last four books, which are the highest sustained achievement of poetry in our Western world—he would review the entire epic, and call for questions on both poems.

Then to conclude he might sketch the history of the poems, their varying reputation in Greece and Rome, where they were the universal Greek schoolbook, where Plato and other philosophers attacked them as false and immoral, where they helped to create the craft of literary criticism, where they were parodied, emulated, disliked, and admired, but always used; the forgetfulness into which they sank in the Middle Ages, when Greek it-self was forgotten in western Europe save by a few ec-centrics; their rediscovery by men like Petrarch and Boc-caccio in the early Renaissance, with their effect on Renaissance literature (*Troilus and Cressida, Paradise Lost*); the misunderstandings of them which were cur-rent in the polite seventeenth and eighteenth centuries; their second rediscovery at the end of the eighteenth century, with its effects on Shelley and Chateaubriand, Goethe and Keats; and their continuing life in mod-ern literature. This, if properly arranged, would lead the class to a discussion of the epic as a form of literature, which the teacher would do well to dovetail into the work of his colleagues and into other branches of the hu-manities studied by that particular class. And then, hav-ing given them a broad survey of Homer, having answered a number of questions and having left others, like half-open doors, to attract the interest of his pu-pils, he should close the course by saying something a lit-tle more sympathetic than "class is dismissed."

The danger of teaching in this way is that one too easily becomes superficial and diffuse. But that is one of the dangers to which all teachers are liable. If they wish to be interesting, they are apt to be superficial. If they strive to be thorough, they can become boring. Thorough teaching and thorough learning, like all in-tense intellectual effort, are exhausting. That does not mean that they must be boring. It was not of exhaustion that Butler and Phelps and many others of their genera-tion complained: it was of the tedium of repetition, of the frustration of studying only one aspect of a subject. In fact, a course in Homer which is confined to transla-tion and scansion, without comment or discussion of any kind, is not less, but more superficial than a course con-taining lectures, summaries, and discussions as well as the indispensable groundwork of textual study. But if a good teacher is aware of the dangers of either policy, he can escape them both.

But was it only to avoid superficiality that Phelps's instructor became so crushingly, so mortally tedious? Was there no other reason? It is hard to say that he hated the subject—yet perhaps he did, and perhaps his real interests lay not in Homer but in Sanskrit roots. Certainly he did not like his pupils, and possibly he was suffering under the yoke of tyrannous or arrogant colleagues superior to him in rank. But many teachers who neglect to plan their work are, I believe, suffering from an occupational disease. Because their careers are not devoted to making quick profits and getting immediate results, they are apt to become ditherers. Sometimes they plan neither their work nor their lives. Nearly all other vocations demand something more closely resembling individual initiative and the balancing of expenditure and returns. The doctor must keep case-records, and if he has an acute surgical case he must arrange to see it every six hours. The lawyer is tied to court routine, and when his cases come up he must be ready with his strategy planned. Businessmen have monthly balances, annual inventories, stockholders' meetings, and directors' conferences, at which they must give an account of the past and prepare the future. But teachers and scholars, who receive regular though meager salaries and have long vacations, sometimes drift from month to month, from year to year, on the little breezes and ripples of class routine, without setting their course in any direction or pulling steadily at the oars.

Here is a sympathetic description of Walter Headlam, by his friend and colleague E. F. Benson. Headlam was a Cambridge don, who knew a great deal of Greek and Latin, far more than he ever communicated to his pupils and his readers. This account of his methods of working will show why:

One morning . . . his water for shaving was not hot, so after breakfast he put a small kettle to boil over his spirit lamp, and as he waited for that, he sat down in the armchair where he worked and casually looked at a note he had made the evening before. It was about a change of rhythm in a Greek chorus, or perhaps it was a word in his Herondas, which occurred in no dictionary, but which he knew he had seen before in some scholiast on Aristophanes. But where was the particular book he wanted? His room was lined with bookshelves, books that he was using paved the floor round his chair, and the table was piled high with them. There it was underneath a heap of others on the table, and he pulled it out: those on the top of it tumbled to the ground. He put down his pipe on the edge of the table, and as he turned the leaves, he found not just that which he was looking for, but something else he had wanted yesterday. He made a note of this on a slip of paper and picked up his pipe which had gone out. There were no matches, so he folded up the paper on which he had made his note, thrust it into the flame of the spirit-lamp and lit his pipe again. Then he found the passage he had originally started to hunt up. Awfully interesting: it was a slang word, not very polite, in use among the daughters of joy in Corinth during the fifth century B.C. These intelligent ladies seemed to have an argot of their own; there were several other words of the sort which he had come across. He became lost in this pursuit, his pipe had to be relit several times, and presently a smell of roasting metal brought him back for a brief moment to the surface of life. His shaving-water had all boiled away, and so he put out the spirit-lamp. Later in the morning his gyp [i.e. servant] came to see if he wanted any lunch ordered for him: bread and butter and cheese would do, with a tankard of beer. These were laid and left in the next room, and he wandered there after another hour or two deep in his investigation. The sight of food aroused no association of desire, but he had a drink out of the tankard and carrying it back with him, put it in a nest of books on his table. Presently more books got piled up round the tankard; he absently laid a folio notebook on the top of it, and so it completely vanished. Then he wanted more books from his shelves, in one of these excursions he stepped on his pipe and broke the stem. It did not matter for there were others about, but he forgot to look for them in the heat of this diverting chase. "I shall write a monograph on the slang current in Corinthian brothels," he said to himself.

It began to grow dark on this early close of the autumn afternoon. There was no electric light in those days, and he fetched a couple of candles and put them on the edge of his table. He was hungry now, and he gobbled up his bread and cheese, wondering what time it was, for his watch had stopped. Beer too: he felt sure he had ordered some beer, but where the devil was it? It should have been on his table with the bread and cheese. He looked everywhere for it, even in his bedroom, but it was nowhere to be seen. Then his razor lying ready on his dressing-table reminded him that he had not yet shaved. It was true there was no hot water, but cold water would do, and though it was rapidly getting dark, he had not yet found any matches to light his candles. But one ought to be able to shave in the dark, he thought, for an action, often repeated, became, as Aristotle said, an instinctive process, and it would be interesting to see if he could not make quite a good job of it. He made a fair job of it, there were a few negligible cuts, and finding that he had a box of matches in his pocket all the time, he lit his candles and went back to the ladies of Corinth. Then his gyp came in to see if he would go into Hall for dinner, or dine in his room: he settled to have some cold meat here, but where was the beer he had ordered for lunch? The gyp felt sure he had brought it, but evidently he was mistaken for there was no sign of it. So he brought the cold meat and another tankard and with this comfortless refreshment Walter Headlam pursued the ladies of Corinth till the small hours of the morning. The missing tankard came to light the next day.

(The details of my description are in no way composed but actually and collectively true.)

It is charming, isn't it? All Headlam's selflessness and breadth of interest, his devotion to knowledge for its own sake, his constant intellectual alertness, speak of a warm and generous heart, a subtle and energetic mind, a happy personality. Untidiness is human. But his inability to choose and group his interests, to plan even the work which enthralled him so deeply, much less his own daily life, is evidence of that weakness of will which sometimes characterizes scholars and spoils teachers. A number of the most brilliant savants suffer from this disability so gravely that they can never make up their minds to write, complete, and publish a large book on their own pet subject. A certain musical scholar has been admired for decades as the man who knows all about the origin and development of the fugue—but can his friends get him to publish a book on it? Never. He could. He lectures on it from time to time, although always refusing to make his lectures into a book in case he might repent of some of the suggestions and conjectures in them. On Bach's *Art of the Fugue* he has a fine seminar, which grows better year by year. When new books on counterpoint are published, he reviews them, sometimes acrimoniously, sometimes with an Olympian graciousness which is even more distressing for the author. And he has been engaged for the last thirty years in a bitter controversy with his rival in Milan about the relationship of Palestrina's canons to the earliest fugues. His friends often pray that his rival will issue a book on the fugue, so that he himself may be impelled to produce one of his own. But actually they will both die without finding—no, it is not *time* that they lack, nor adequate *knowledge* (they realize that knowledge can never be complete), but *will-power* enough to dedicate themselves to the completion of the books which are in them, and *courage* enough to face the inevitable criticism.

It takes will-power, then, to prepare a course for teaching and to stick to the plan once worked out. It also calls for a good deal of sympathy with the pupils. While he makes his plan, the teacher is forced to ask himself: "Is this useful to them? Will this be clear to them without illustrations? Can they be expected to know this?" and to shape his course accordingly. It is easier just to go out and start talking. But further, it demands a good deal of artistic sense, and those teachers who plan their teaching best are usually marked by strong aesthetic sensibilities. Gilbert Murray could not utter a sentence without shaping it beautifully. When he taught, there were none of those "Er's" and inconsequences and "But

I forgot to mention's." His sentences grew into paragraphs and his paragraphs without apparent compulsion into talks which were as wise as encyclopedia articles, as apparently informal as conversations, and as shapely as his published essays; while the whole course was so disposed as to encourage even the newest and instruct even the most learned of his hearers.

It is the structure of the whole course that matters most. The teacher who comes into a room without introduction and begins to talk about his subject without presenting it to the class as a whole composed of parts, each of which demands different treatment, is behaving like a newspaper editor who should print all the news just in the order in which it arrived, half a column of grain prices, one cartoon, an editorial, ten reports of fires, the closing quotations on the stock market, beauty hints, and then a two-column dispatch from Paris. Even there, there would be some differences in tone to guide the readers. But we have all heard teachers who sounded more like railway-station announcers reading off a long list of insignificant local stations, and who made their itinerary sound equally uninviting. To undertake to teach a complex subject without organizing one's treatment of it so as to bring out its structure, and to discuss an artistic subject without giving, in one's own teaching, a semblance of the order and harmony which are essential attributes of art, is to neglect an important opportunity of teaching something greater and more important than any set of facts, to discourage one's pupils, and to falsify one's own true appreciation of the subject.

* * *

After the initial preparation has been done—after the course has been planned and the notes written—what remains? Can the teacher then file his notes neatly away at the end of each year, take them out again for each new class, scan them over the night before, and deliver them year after year with minor variations for each class?

No. Obviously not. He can, and sometimes he does. But if he wants to be a good teacher, he will not do so.

Ask anyone outside of the profession what he thinks are the principal defects of teachers. He will give you two. One is impracticality, "being too academic," a mistake which we have discussed a little earlier. The other is repetition, "teaching the same old stuff year after year." The second fault is far worse than the first, and will be avoided at all costs by every good teacher.

Sometimes one can trace the same feeling in the casual remarks of former pupils. When they come back to school or college, a little paunchier, balder, and more complacent than they were when they were struggling with study, sex, and poverty all together, they are apt to say: "Well, hello! How are you? I *am* glad to see you! Are you *still* teaching ethics?"—or whatever it is one teaches. If one says: "Yes," they smile indulgently. If one says: "No, I've gone over to metaphysics," they look surprised and a little congratulatory. But if, after meeting them, one said: "Still selling insurance?" or "Still gazing at infected tonsils?" and looked indulgent, they would be a little irritated.

What they feel, subconsciously, is this: "I don't expect anything has changed here, and I rather like the idea, in a back-to-the-womb sort of way. So I bet everyone is teaching exactly the same course that he gave ten years ago. Dull, but reassuring. That's what teachers are like, monotonous but harmless." Yet they do not think of the monotony of other occupations in the same way. The monotony of selling insurance is its essence. Monotony in teaching is a fault.

It is a fault, because the world changes, and scholarship must change with it; and the teacher changes, and his teaching should change with him. Scarcely any subject is so static that it never alters from year to year. On nearly all the important subjects—history, law, languages and literatures, the organic sciences, geography, music and the arts, philosophy—there is a constant upsurge of discussions on new problems and points of view. It is every good teacher's duty to take account of all the important new discoveries and arguments that affect his own subject. He will often find, as he does so, that an essay on a topic he had thought settled or at least uninteresting throws a whole flood of new light into many aspects of his own thought, clearing up problems he believed insoluble, opening possibilities for speculation which had never occurred to him. Only in mathematics and the inorganic sciences, perhaps, do the foundations and the first three or four storeys of the subject stand firm and unaltered year by year. But the other subjects are in constant growth. That is a sign that they are alive. It would be as ill-judged for a teacher to discuss Shakespeare without having read the Shakespearean literature of the last ten years as for him to make the class read *Hamlet* in Bowdler's text—or for a doctor to operate using 1850 techniques and 1890 instruments.

How then can the important new literature be assimilated?

That is for the teacher himself to decide. Let him only resolve that it can and must be assimilated, and he will find time and energy. Some put aside a month every summer to read and excerpt the year's publications. Others go into the nearest large library each Saturday and read the periodicals that have been added that week. A colleague of mine has made an arrangement with the librarian to send him the next-to-current issue of each periodical as it leaves the shelves en route for the bindery. Such plans make the teacher's leisure really creative. Whenever the reading is done, it should be done with ample time to spare and in comfort, with plentiful facilities for taking notes.

For the books and periodicals should not merely be read over with the eyes, they should be taken in—as much of them as is nourishing. One of the master thinkers of the Renaissance says:

Some books are to be tasted, others to be swallowed, and some few to be chewed and digested. That is, some books are to be read only in parts; others to be read but not curiously [i.e., carefully], and some few to be read wholly, and with diligence and attention.

And although the chief part of this assimilation takes place in the mind, it should be accompanied and assisted, for the teacher's own subsequent benefit, by the taking of notes. These notes, on every new book and article that seems valuable, should be inserted into the manuscript of the teacher's own lectures or the outline of his discussions. Every teacher will keep notes to assist him in his teaching (their nature and use we shall consider later), and as soon as any new information or point of view on his subject presents itself to him, it should be entered in his notes. Then, when he reaches that part of his subject and prepares the relevant lesson, he will give some extra thought to working in the fresh material he has acquired. It may mean an alteration of his whole approach to that particular theme. It may be only an additional fact to be taken into account. Sometimes it will be enough for him to mention the new book with an illuminating comment, or to tell one of his class to read and report on it. Or he may decide to keep the information in reserve, as a confirmatory argument or a variation of his usual discussion. The effect, however, will be the same. Instead of teaching the same old stuff year after year, he will constantly enrich his knowledge, keep his teaching alive and dynamic, and prevent his mind from falling into the disease of authority and age, which is paralysis.

There is no other solution. Life is a process of constant change. No one can teach a subject in the same way two years running. Even if he uses the same books and teaches the same facts and conclusions, the second year he will have blurred a few outlines by repetition, cut a few corners because of age. The alternatives are only these: to allow your teaching to petrify by neglect, or constantly to refresh it by transfusions of new vitality and interest from your own reading. The choice is not too difficult, if it is clearly seen. One of the few consolations of age is that, while the body becomes weaker, the mind can grow stronger and richer.

* * *

One last word on preparation. Always read the original sources.

This is one of the commandments for scholars which old Lehrs laid down about a century ago. Some of them are now obsolete—they referred to contemporary fads like the philologists' passion for Sanskrit—and others are meant exclusively for university teachers; but two or three of them are excellent, and this is one. *Always read sources, everything flows from them naturally.*

It sounds easy enough, in fact inevitable: obvious, so obvious that it need not be brought to the attention of any teacher or scholar; insulting, almost. Yet the point should be made—partly for the benefit of young teachers who are just beginning their career and may not find it obvious, and partly as a necessary offset to the last part of this discussion. And for these reasons let me make it still more plain. Every teacher must know the original sources of his subject. He must also know the textbooks and the commentaries, and he should keep up with the new literature as it comes out. But the center of his thinking should be the original sources. If he teaches history, it is not enough for him to know what Robinson and Simpson's textbook says about the Treaty of Versailles. He must know the text of the Treaty itself, and that of the League Covenant too. If he teaches English literature, let him not rely on Bradley or Wilson Knight for his insight into Shakespeare's tragedies. Let him read one every month, and think about it. He will discover as much for himself as Bradley could have told him—at least, what he himself discovers will mean so much to him that it will be more valuable for his teaching than any second-hand learning.

True for school-teachers, this is even more true for university teachers. A friend of mine has lately finished a considerable book on a difficult subject, which has worried him for years. He spent several summers reading the voluminous periodical literature on it, and several winters analyzing, correcting, completing, and confuting the chief books which dealt with it. But when he started writing it, he got scholar's cramp—the malady of those who have read too much secondary material and think they can add nothing to it. For nearly three months he remained numb and helpless. He reread his notes. Useless. He reread his predecessors' books. Cold cabbage. Then, in desperation, he turned his back on his filing-cabinet and began to read, as though with a fresh eye, the original documents which formed the heart of his study. Scanty enough they seemed as he went through them, but new meanings, half-understood before, emerged clearly from every line, and the facts fell into a more strongly marked configuration than he had ever realized. In a single evening he had sketched the outline of his twelve chapters, in a week he wrote the first, and the back of his book was broken a month later. Halfway through, he had another attack of cramp, but it vanished at once when he turned back from his predecessors and competitors to the original documents: for then and only then he saw clearly what was the real purpose of his work.

This advice may seem to contradict the earlier suggestion that every teacher owes it to himself to keep in touch with all the new literature on his subject. But actually both prescriptions should be taken together. Suppose you teach Spanish. An important new book on Cervantes comes out. One of the chief purposes of learning Spanish is to read Cervantes: therefore you get the book, and go through it, and add to your own notes whatever assimilable ideas and facts you find in it. But after that you should give yourself the pleasure of rereading *Don Quixote*. Since you have changed, you will find something new in it. Your mind will be enriched and your teaching revitalized. And if you continue, you will work up a genuine rhythm of growth—now reading a new article on a group of authors you had thought of as interesting, and now turning with a fresh eye to read their writings and remake your opinions of them, until, with a constant interflow of new literature and familiar masterpieces, your whole mind becomes so intensely alive, so highly charged, that teaching is not an effort but a relief, a positive delight to you and your pupils.

Of course this is done by many teachers. It is one of the reasons for their success. That it is not done by all teachers is because some of them assume (often without thinking it through) that the mind stops growing with the body. Usually they themselves did most of their preparatory work in their late teens and early twenties. Since during that time they were developing physically, and then stopped, they tend to think that their brains follow the same pattern, growing quickly until twenty-five or so and then marking time until death. This assumption, usually unconscious, is based on a picture of the brain as an enclosed box into which no more than a limited amount of material can be inserted. But the picture is wrong, and the assumption is false and dangerous. The process of adult learning, as far as we know, does not involve increase in the size of the brain, but does mean that the paths and connections within it become at once clearer and more complex. The territory already held is explored and mapped; or, to use another image, the intricate machine grows capable of more and more skills as the operator finds his way about it. The mind which is exercised on books is not being strained and stretched. It is being used for its proper purpose. To smother it with newspaper pulp, shiny clay magazines, and gossip, so as to keep it from bursting, is like keeping the eyes shut all day to rest them.

* * *

(b) COMMUNICATION

After the teacher has prepared his subject, he has to communicate his knowledge of it to his pupils. If he fails in this, he has failed as a teacher. He may still be an inspiration for a few youngsters because of his selfless devotion to scholarship or the charm of his character; yet that will scarcely make up for his central failure. But let him be good at communication, and even if he is a mediocre scholar, he can be an excellent teacher. Communication, the transmission of thought from one mind to others, is one of the basic activities of the human race; it is a skill through which men make magnificent successes and startling failures, an art without which genius is dumb, power brutal and aimless, mankind a planetload of squabbling tribes. Communication is an essential function of civilization. Teaching is only one of the many occupations that depend upon it, and depend upon it absolutely.

There are three main methods of communicating knowledge from teacher to pupil. We shall discuss them separately, but first let us see all three clearly.

The first is lecturing. Here the teacher talks more or less continuously to the class. The class listens, takes notes of the facts and ideas worth remembering, and thinks over them later; but it does not converse with the teacher. At most, it may ask a few questions, but these are for the sake of clarification, not of discussion. The essence of this kind of teaching, and its purpose, are a steady flow of information going from the teacher to the pupils.

University lectures are mostly of this type, and so are many lessons in high schools. The surgeon demonstrating an operational technique, the physicist expounding a theory of the structure of the nebulæ, with working models and expository equations, the legal analyst examining the latest court decisions, the geologist distinguishing fire-made from water-made rocks—all these can best do their jobs if they can talk without interruption to pupils who are silent and receptive. Nearly all radio and TV commentators use the same technique. On a higher level it is that of the sermon. The best-known address in the Western world, the Sermon on the Mount, was delivered by Jesus (whom they called Rabbi, or Teacher) to his pupils and to a large crowd gathered around, attentive and still.

The second method was invented by Socrates, and can be called the tutorial system. Here the teacher does not talk. He asks questions, and the pupil talks. But the questions are so arranged as to make the pupil conscious of his own ignorance, and to guide him towards a deeper truth, which he will hold all the more firmly because it has not been presented to him ready-made but drawn out of his own mind by the joint efforts of his teacher and himself. It is important here that there should be some basis of discussion, so the pupil usually does some work in preparation, which his teacher then examines, criticizes, and by constructive questioning attempts to deepen.

In the third method, the pupils learn a prescribed lesson, as preliminary work. The lesson is then explained to them more fully and clearly by the teacher, who examines the pupils to make sure that they have assimilated it fully. Usually they have not. This is the standard way of teaching languages, literature, history and geography, and the descriptive sciences like botany. The gloomy routinist who took William Lyon Phelps through Homer (p. 72) was misusing this system. It is used in lower Hebrew schools, where the boys learn the text of the sacred writings off by heart and then prove their mastery of it by repeating every syllable; and then in higher Hebrew schools, where the teacher goes on to ask them for interpretations of the various meanings of the words. It differs from the other methods in that it assumes a written text, or a collection of documents, or a group of specimens, to be worth assimilating—almost to the point of memorizing—and proceeds to explain its implications and test the pupils' comprehension of it.

*   *   *

Of these three methods, you will naturally ask which is the best. The answer is: none. They are all equally good for different purposes, and a good education exposes the pupil to them all. Each of them has its difficulties and its defects; each of them contains unique advantages. A teacher who uses only one method is in danger of developing only one group of skills in his pupils and only part of his own powers as an educator. A pupil who knows only one way of learning will find it hard to conceive what rich possibilities lie unused in his own mind. All three are useful for some purposes, bad for others; all are valuable.

Let us examine them separately, from the teacher's point of view.

* * *

First, lecturing. A great orator was once asked what were the three essentials of public speaking. He replied: "First, delivery. Second, delivery. Third, delivery." For public speaking this is almost correct. For lecturing, it is overemphatic. But it is still true that for a lecture the single most important quality is delivery.

Delivery depends on the voice and on gestures. Of these, the voice is far more important. Obviously, it must be clear. Not many teachers make the mistake of speaking inaudibly. Yet some talk too fast to follow, while others chew their words, or gobble them, or hiss and splutter them, until the pupils tire of making the effort required to sort out the meaning from the noises, and take their revenge by mocking the noises. If you have a regional accent, or a curiously pitched voice, or a difficulty with any particular letter, watch your pupils' eyes. You will soon learn when they have ceased to understand and are merely listening for you to quack or hoot. If you are nervous or have a large class, don't hesitate to ask them to co-operate by telling you if you become inaudible. It gives them a certain interest in the success of your lecture, and thus helps to bridge the gap between teacher and pupil. A colleague of mine, who lectures to large groups in colleges where he is a stranger, sometimes begins by asking one little group in the back if they can hear him. At a suitable pause halfway through his lecture, he asks them if they can still hear him. By that time, of course, they always can; but he says that the question "keeps the fringes warm." In the Scottish universities there is a good deal of two-way communication between audience and lecturer. When they admire a phrase or an idea, the students applaud by stamping, none too gently; and when they miss something they shuffle their feet until the sentence is repeated. It may sound odd, but it is extremely helpful to the lecturer, and also ensures that the Scots get full value for their fees.

It is wise to remember also that, as you get older, your voice often gets weaker; or else the energy which you put into it tends to diminish without your noticing it. Speaking in public to any audience, large or small, always demands physical effort. A young teacher, if he is not inhibited by shyness or benumbed by vanity, will usually make that effort; but as he grows more familiar with his subject and realizes the ignorance and laziness of the average class, he will tend to save his strength and speak only to the intelligent, who will be listening. *He who has ears to hear,* said a great teacher, *let him hear;* but that was meant for grown-up pupils. The young all have ears, and we must speak clearly to them.

And some experienced teachers, like actors, learn the value of underplaying. It is really exhausting to listen to a speaker who shouts at you all the time. It diminishes attention. Good players like Alfred Lunt and James Mason sometimes throw lines away in an undertone, so that the contrast between an important thought and the offhand tone in which it is uttered will give it extra weight. Teachers of difficult and controversial subjects, who know it is essential for themselves and their pupils to keep calm and analyze the matter dispassionately, often adopt a tone of studied tranquillity which is very useful as long as they are audible, but is apt to sink into chattiness, triviality, and ultimate silence. Philosophers are prone to this because they spend their whole lives thinking about subjects of the highest importance and dignity, they know it is useless and dangerous to discuss them with emotional excitement, they have learnt that it is an insult to a good student to assume that he has not seen quite as far into the argument as his teacher, and sometimes they are discouraged by a lifetime of battling with problems which they know they will never solve. I have tried to discuss philosophy with a man like this, who was so tired and disillusioned about the whole business that he made half his remarks in a rapid whisper as though we were fellow-prisoners planning an escape, and filtered the other half down through the wet mouthpiece and bubbling bowl of a huge and greasy pipe.

The habit is more common among Englishmen than Americans, and is very rare among French and German teachers—who are usually clear to the point of being declamatory. In a romance dear to my childhood, Conan Doyle (who was Irish) introduced such a speaker as chairman at an important meeting:

Professor Murray will, I am sure, excuse me if I say that he has the common fault of most Englishmen of being inaudible. Why on earth people who have something to say which is worth hearing should not take the slight trouble to learn how to make it heard is one of the strange mysteries of modern life. Their methods are as reasonable as to try to pour some precious stuff from the spring to the reservoir through a non-conducting pipe, which could by the least effort be opened. Professor Murray made several profound remarks to his white tie and to the water-carafe upon the table, with a humorous, twinkling aside to the silver candlestick upon his right.

Of course this figure had no connection with Gilbert Murray, who has a beautifully clear and melodious utterance. Yet, although fictitious, he represented a common type which has helped to bring teachers into disrepute. The inaudible teacher is as useless as the statesman without a policy or the workman who breaks his tools.

It is not only the loudness of your voice that matters when you speak to a class. You must watch your speed. If you talk too quickly, they cannot follow your argument. If you talk too slowly, they will fall asleep. As far as my own observation goes, many teachers talk too slowly because they would rather be boring than unintelligible, and also because it saves effort. Some of them may be influenced by the practice of political speakers, who speak slowly both in order to be heard by large audiences and in order to avoid the very appearance of cleverness. The worst speaker I ever heard in my life was the late Stanley Baldwin. He spoke in a slow, weighty, pompous chant. He halted, not only at the logical pauses within each sentence, but after every three or four words, like this:

Mr. Chairman. Ladies. And Gentlemen. I have come here. Tonight. At the request. Of my good friend. The member for this constituency. My friend. Colonel Blp. Whom. I am glad to see. Among us. On this. Occasion.

Half an hour of this put everybody to sleep. Several years of it put Britain to sleep.

Yes, misplaced and multiplied pauses are a sure sign of a bad speaker. Sometimes they mean that he himself has not worked out the sentence he is uttering, and, like a driver on a skiddy road, is slowing down for every turn and checking the vehicle whenever it gains momentum. Sometimes they mean that he considers his audience to be halfwits. Who have. To be given. A few words. At a time. To avoid. Mental. Indigestion. Actually, if such a speaker realized it, it is *more* difficult to understand a speech when it is broken up into tiny fragments, as it is more difficult to read a page by intermittent light.

One fault still worse than making irrational pauses is punctuating every sentence by "Er." To Er is human, but it is unforgivable. Usually the speaker does not know how infuriating it sounds, and is shocked when he hears a recording of his own voice. It is a disastrous habit, for which every teacher should watch. Some of us acquire it in order to give the impression that we are "thinking on our feet," instead of repeating something

learnt by rote or reading off our notes. It sounds—Er—
kind of honest—and—Er—you know—Er—genuine. So
we think. In fact it sounds stupid and fuddy-duddy. Once
I heard the chairman of a large company, who apparently
wanted to convey the impression of transparent honesty,
mixing up "Er's" and clichés in equal proportions. This
had the same effect on his hearers as a cup of warm milk
and two tablets of phenobarbital. It is bad enough to talk
about leaving no stone unturned and exploring every avenue, but this performer hesitated so that we were never
sure whether he was going to improvise a brilliant variation on the current cliché or had simply forgotten the
words. He finished his survey of production during the
war years by saying:

> But since that time—Er
> a lot of water
> has flowed—Er
> under the—Er—Er—
> [is he going to say "dam"?]
> the bridge!

Of course every speaker must pause, to let his words
sink in and to let the echoes of his voice subside. But
when you pause, you should pause only after you have
uttered a fragment of thought big enough to be understood and examined by itself. It is silly to stop after every
three or four words. Pause as you punctuate in writing.
If you are a really good speaker, with a firm grasp of the
logical structure of your subject, an experienced reporter
could take down your whole speech, divide it up into
sentences, paragraphs, and sections, and subhead it, without help from you, because he understood it as you
spoke.

But remember this: no one, except an experienced reporter, can possibly take down all you say. Therefore it
is useless to speak slowly in order to let the pupils write
out your words. On the whole, this habit is responsible
for more bad lecturing than any other fault.

It has a long history. It goes back to the Middle Ages.

Books were scarce then, and annotated editions of great books were very rare indeed. (So low had Western civilization sunk since the elaborate culture of Greece and Rome, with its publishers, its multiple editions, and its multitudinous libraries.) In the newly built medieval universities, texts were so precious and the student's hope of obtaining an auxiliary handbook to explain them was so scanty that he treasured his own copy, and, as he listened to the teacher explaining it, wrote down every word. So at the end of his course he had a notebook in his own handwriting which closely resembled the ordinary annotated editions of today. He studied it with infinite care, meditating every word. If he himself became a professor, he introduced many of its explanations word for word into his own lectures, and then once more they were copied down word for word.

This method of teaching may possibly go back much beyond the largely illiterate Middle Ages. It may belong to the Hebrew tradition which flowed into Western culture through Christianity. The main part of the encyclopedia of Jewish learning is called the Mishnah, which means "teaching by repetition." The pupil in a Jewish school learnt his teacher's words off by heart until he could repeat them. It is not far from this to copying down the teacher's words and learning them off by heart.

Now, the fact that an educational system came to us from the Hebrews and was established in the Middle Ages is no reason for discarding it. But it is a good reason for examining it carefully to see what functions it fulfills today. How much of the average hour's lecture should a pupil write down? All of it? None of it? As much as he can?

Largely it depends on the lecturer and the subject. Distinguished scholars are so learned that, *if they have prepared their material well,* virtually every word is worth taking down: because it cannot be found in any book and it is so highly charged with wisdom that the student himself could not reproduce it in a hundred hours of research. Suppose Dr. Einstein were persuaded to lecture on the relationship of gravity to electricity, it would be worth having a recording machine and a cinema camera to make permanent every word, or, failing that, to transform oneself into such machines. Certain subjects also are so important, and, if they are to be taught at all, they have to be taught so intensely, that the facts and the arguments are difficult to follow and impossible to remember unless the student takes copious notes. For instance, a lecturer on metaphysics will discuss the three logical proofs of the existence of God. There are only three. They are all difficult to analyze, and are exceedingly important. A student who was introduced to this subject for the first time and had done no preliminary reading would be well advised to write down the three arguments word for word, and to copy as much as he could of the lecturer's discussion of each of them, so that he could think about the problems at his leisure.

But we have shifted our point of view from the lecturer to the student. We should rather ask: what is the duty of the lecturer? How much ought he to dictate, and how much should he merely talk?

The answer is made clear by common sense. No average teacher can expect his pupils to copy out every word of every lecture he gives them. On the other hand, he should expect them all to write down the salient facts and arguments, and, as individuals, to make notes on any other points that strike them as interesting. Therefore he should dictate to them clearly and unequivocally anything he judges important enough for them to transcribe. The rest of the time he should merely talk, commenting, discussing, arguing, explaining.

This means that he must put plenty of variety into his voice. He must be slow and emphatic when he is making statements he thinks worth copying. The rest of the time he should speak more easily and quickly almost at normal conversational speed. His pupils will soon learn to distinguish between the material meant for permanent record and the explanations from which they can pick out anything they choose. They will in fact be stimulated and interested by the changes of tempo, and they will be helped towards seeing the larger intellectual structure of argument which should underlie every course of lectures, binding separate hours together.

But this means much more careful preparation on the part of the lecturer. That is why good lecturing is so difficult, and why bad lecturers are so common. Recently I went to hear a lecture by an eminent scholar, whose books and essays I had often read and admired. He was speaking in a large college hall, before about a hundred guests and eight or nine hundred young men—who had been encouraged by his reputation (and perhaps by a few prods from their own teachers) to come to hear him. He was terrible. I knew something of the subject, I was anxious to hear what he had to say; but I gave up listening after twenty minutes. I was sitting among the students, and I could watch them without difficulty. They were polite. They listened dutifully. They learnt nothing. Those near me had started to take notes when the speaker began. They had the heading correct, and the subject-matter of the first few paragraphs, and a few names; but then their writing trailed off. They couldn't write everything down. Since the lecturer said everything in very much the same tone, conveying scarcely any emphasis by strength of utterance, by significant pauses, or by gestures, all they heard was a constant stream of words, with nothing to guide them in choosing which to select and transcribe. They resigned themselves to trying to remember the general outlines of the lecture, which few of those I met managed to do.

Afterwards I went up to the committee-room and met my friend the lecturer. I soon found out why he had so baffled and exhausted his audience. He wasn't talking to them. He merely took a chapter from a book he was writing, and read it out. Of course the result was a failure. Learned books are difficult to read, and often dull. Still, they have the advantage that you can go back over them again and again when you want to think over an argument or learn a series of facts. But even that advantage is lost if they are read aloud. So also is the sense of structure, which, in reading, is gained from the visual arrangement of the book in paragraphs, sections, and chapters. To compensate for these losses, nothing is gained by a lecture, except the trivial interest of seeing a man instead of a book. It is this practice that makes many critics of teaching say that lecturers are dull and prosy, and suggest that their lectures might just as well be mimeographed and distributed to the students to read at their leisure.

The good lecturer, therefore, will not read his lecture. And he will make a clear distinction between those parts of his lecture which he expects all his hearers to copy and remember, and those which are to be delivered more rapidly as explanation, illustration, or subsidiary argument. He will show this distinction in his voice, manner, and gesture. When he is preparing his lectures, and scanning them over before delivery, he will have this distinction clearly in mind.

* * *

Here we can discuss the use of notes in lecturing, and in speaking generally. We can begin with one general assertion. *It is impossible to make a speech without preparation.*

You will at once ask: "What about the distinguished wits who can be called on for an after-dinner speech without warning, and can keep the table in a roar for twenty minutes, not using a single note? What about the politicians who make extempore speeches at any hour of the day or night if someone turns on the tap?"

The answer is that all such speakers have already practiced what they are going to say. The after-dinner wit made many after-dinner speeches before his reputation became so reliable that he could be called upon without notice. In these he tried, tested, and learnt off by heart a dozen openings, twenty humorous references to the chairman, the food and wine, the guests, and himself, fifteen methods of introducing topical allusions, and three hundred anecdotes suitable to almost any occasion. As he sat at dinner, he ran over these and selected the best for the situation: ladies present, a bishop at the chairman's table, reporters excluded, but two editors among the guests, and so on—his selection was virtually made before he got the chairman's note. As for politicians, long before they start on a speaking tour, they have thrashed out every aspect of their official opinions on national and international affairs, in a hundred discussions with their advisers: so that they too know every sentence they are going to say about Russia or high prices long before they are called upon. Hitler is a special case of this. He seldom talked, even to his friends. He always made speeches, even to one or two intimates, sometimes to himself. His whole book, *Mein Kampf,* is a speech he made to Hess, taken down and reduced to order in the comfortable solitude of Landsberg Prison. Unable to converse with individuals, he was always, in silence or aloud, addressing an audience and trying to dominate it, hardening his thoughts and working out their connections by repetition. Never was there a better example of the oratorical power which an untrained man, with many disadvantages of manner and appearance, with a poor education and a repulsive accent, can gain by constant reflection and constant practice.

But Hitler was often incoherent and rambling, when he was overexcited or hurried. Other speakers, who think less intensely about their subjects, ramble and hesitate even worse when they have neglected their preparation. Speaking in public is as difficult as singing or acting, and it ought to have quite as careful rehearsals; even more careful, because one of the aims of the public speaker is to appear entirely spontaneous. The great speakers of Greece and Rome used to prepare an important speech as carefully as an opera star nowadays studies a new role. After writing it out a dozen times, they would deliver it before a few trusted friends, critics, and tutors, repeating it again and again until they knew every syllable and gesture, and yet the whole thing appeared, not a highly elaborate product of art, but a genuine outpouring of real and overwhelming emotion. When Cicero stood up to deliver his first attack on Catiline, he knew everything he was about to say and do—even the gestures of sudden horror and the hesitations—as an experienced actor, just before his cue, has his entry and his exit and all the intervening lines clear in his mind. That is why we still study the speeches of men like Cicero: a single page of them contains the results of more concentrated thought, active experience, intricate psychological knowledge, and training in language than most modern speakers can command in a whole lifetime. It is like the difference between a drawing by Dürer and a magazine full of advertisements; between a single movement from a Beethoven symphony and an evening's dance-music or a concert built up of *Humoresque, Narcissus,* and *In a Monastery Garden.*

It is therefore impossible to give a lecture without preparation. Before he opens his mouth, the lecturer must know exactly what points he wishes to tell his audience, in what order, and with what emphasis. He must have a scheme of the lecture clear in his mind—not simply as a set number of pages to be read over, but visualized as a well-articulated structure of thought, as the geologist sees the interlocking stresses of clay, sand, and water, igneous and aqueous rocks beneath a landscape, or as the architect looks through the chromium-and-plaster facings of a building to see its skeleton of steel.

If he is to know this, he must have written out notes for his lecture. He must have planned it, both as a separate utterance and in its place in the entire course he is delivering. Now, it is at this point that many lecturers make one of two important mistakes. Either they jot down a few notes on a single sheet of paper, and improvise; or else they work their material into book form, and read a section of it aloud. In the first case, the pupils are confused. In the second, they are bored.

In the hands of a very competent lecturer, both of these methods *can* be made to work. There is a story

about J. T. Sheppard, the eccentric, charming, and scholarly Provost of King's College, Cambridge, which illus-
trates this. He was lecturing on the artistic plan of the
Iliad. It is always difficult to detect and to describe the
structure of such a large book, especially when it is concealed with Greek subtlety. But Mr. Sheppard traced,
within the twenty-four books, through battle after battle,
debate after debate, under the rushing tides of emotion
and action, a strong pattern, which forms one of the chief
reasons why so many generations have felt the *Iliad* to
be a work of art without knowing why. After his third
lecture an earnest girl came up to him and said: "Oh, Dr.
Sheppard, I thought that was a marvellous lecture, I got
so much out of it even although I couldn't get it all down,
I took as many notes as I could, *would* you be so kind as
to lend me your own notes? I promise to return them as
soon as I've copied them out." "Certainly, my dear,"
said Mr. Sheppard, who had talked fluently and stimulat-
ingly for an hour, "certainly: here are my notes." And he
gave her an envelope on which were written the words:

ZEUS

AGAMEMNON

ZEUS.

Yet I have no doubt that the lecture was full of closely
packed reasoning and brilliant imagery, that it had a beginning, a middle, an end, and a complete, well-balanced
internal structure, and that it could have been tran-
scribed verbatim and printed without loss. Mr. Sheppard, with his long experience and his brilliantly critical
mind, can easily lecture from such notes as those. But
for most of us it is too dangerous.

The reverse is equally dangerous, although it has
rather more merit. If a lecturer has a complete text in
front of him, ready for the printer, he may be dull, but
at least he will not be incoherent. He won't "blow up."
But how dull can he be before mortification sets in?

When I was a student, I well remember hearing Professor X give the same lecture to the same class on two successive days. He had been reading out his own carefully typed material for so long that he had ceased to pay any attention to the audience, and this morning he started on page 140 instead of page 150. We stamped a little and shuffled a bit, but he merely beamed at us over his glasses, repeated the last sentence, and then read on. I took the opportunity to decorate my earlier batch of notes with striking designs in red and blue pencil, while on the bench behind me four fanatics played a complete rubber of bridge.

But it is not such a ludicrous accident that is the real danger of reading continuously from notes. The danger is losing touch with your audience. One of my first philosophy lecturers in Oxford was a thin, nervous young man who had a razor-sharp mind and was an excellent tutor, but had never considered the problem of conveying his ideas to a large group of undergraduates in a lecture-hall. He came in to lecture carrying a complete loose-leaf book filled with carefully typed and handwritten pages, which were evidently a series of articles he was preparing for the press. We were allowed to hear them before they were sent to the printer. Taking his place behind the baroque lectern, he glanced round the Tudor hall at the fifty undergraduates wearing thirteenth-century gowns, shuddered with obvious distaste, opened his typescript, and began to read in a low regular voice like the dripping of a distant tap. As he went on, and found himself interested by his own arguments about the possibility of perceiving color, he warmed into audibility. His glasses twinkled. He said things like "Kant was clearly too bold" and "We can assert as against Wittgenstein." His heated brains began to gutter: drops of wax melted out of his skull and moved slowly down his cheeks. Still he never looked at us, his audience—although some of us, who had never heard of Wittgenstein and knew Kant only as a ponderous bore, were watching him with fascinated anxiety. He glared angrily at the space between his eyeglasses and his notes, where he evidently saw, mopping and mowing, the faces of those morons and heretics, Bradley and Berkeley, Hegel and Schlegel.

Yet his lecture, although now audible, was no longer coherent. The typescript was like the magic book that Merlin described to his enchanting girl-friend:

> O aye, it is but twenty pages long,
> But every page having an ample marge,
> And every marge enclosing in the midst
> A square of text that looks a little blot,
> The text no larger than the limbs of fleas;
> And every square of text an awful charm . . .
> And every margin scribbled, crost, and cramm'd
> With comment, densest condensation, hard
> To mind and eye. . . .
> And none can read the text, not even I;
> And none can read the comment but myself.

And none could understand the speaker but himself. To us the problem of appearance and reality was obscure. We were prepared to admit that colors did not exist (except in so far as we existed) and that weight meant nothing really, but we needed to have all that explained to us, slowly, patiently, on our own level. Now this young lecturer, assuming that we had already fought our way through every question in the field of perception, made us second him in his intellectual duels with the other champions of metaphysics, although few of us knew their names, or what ideas they upheld. Meanwhile, day after day, he read on, first the typescript of his original essay, then a controversial paragraph from that fiend Cook Wilson, and then a long, difficult, word-for-word, concept-by-concept refutation by himself, ending in a triumphal march: "Thus I submit it has been proved, as against Cook Wilson, that perception of a colour *is itself sensed!*" Even the ranks of Tuscany could scarce forbear to cheer, but by that time none of us knew what on earth he was talking about.

* * *

It follows, then, that a lecture should be based on written notes, but should not be read out from them. After the lecturer has planned his entire course and reduced the separate sections of it to writing, he should go over each lecture and mark off

(a) THE SALIENT POINTS, which he should deliver slowly and emphatically, so that they can be copied verbatim by those who wish;

(b) *the connecting arguments,* which he should remember in outline, and deliver in a quicker, more conversational tone, leaving himself time and opportunity to expand them if the class finds them difficult or manifests unusual interest in any one of them.

It is the proper use of this contrast in tone that makes the difference between a bad lecturer and a good lecturer —or, you could say, between a teacher and a hack. The hack thinks his job is done if he writes out enough material on the Law of Torts to take up an hour's medium-speed reading, and then goes in and reads it. The teacher knows it is his duty to convey the material to the class. He therefore sets out the basic information clearly, and then, by explanation and illustration, by arguing points he sees are difficult and by passing quickly over generally accepted ideas (unless he wishes to examine and criticize them), by quoting an important passage or citing a new illustration, he makes sure, as sure as he can, that the class has not only accepted the information and swallowed it, but started to digest it.

The first lecturer we know to have done this systematically was one of the founders of modern education. It was Aristotle. Hardly any of the works which have come down to us under his name were published by Aristotle as books. They are nearly all notes of his lectures—made by his pupils or digested out of his own notebooks by his secretaries and successors. So again and again we find that he throws in a few words to summarize a difficult argument, puts in a single phrase to remind him of an illustration, jots down a word or two referring to something in the classroom which could be used for demonstrations, or by-passes a difficult word (e.g., catharsis) which was so central in his philosophy that he did not need notes to discuss it, which he would elaborate and exemplify differently for every class, every year. Whenever we open Aristotle, we should never read the paragraphs as continuous exposition in book-form. We should read them as lecture-notes, and try to hear through these echoes the voice of the teacher, and the questions from his class, and then the keen self-stimulating energy of the discussion.

But the main danger in lecturing on this plan is not that one's notes will be sketchy. It is that, if one establishes real rapport with the class, one will become so interested in talking to them that one fails to make them remember what one is talking about. For unless a lecture leaves in the minds of the class a lasting result—a new interpretation of facts, a technique of experiment, a chain of argument—it is only a display of learning or of acting. They must be interested. Yes; and also they must be taught.

The lecturer will therefore go over the salient points again and again in his own mind before he begins to speak. And, between the movements of exposition, he will use every method of making these points clear to the class. He himself knows very well what the steps of his argument are, what are its strongest and its weakest areas, what assertions are doubtful or controversial, what are the points most worth remembering. But as his lecture moves on, his audience hears only a stream of words, which he must help them to arrange into a system of ideas and statements corresponding to the one in his own mind. The best way to do this is to work over the material until its logical connections are so clear and strong that they are virtually impossible to miss. Numbering off the stages of each proof, the essentials of each operation described, and marking the numeration by gestures, are one of the oldest and safest devices of oratory, and although it is very easy to overdo, it is invaluable when carefully employed. With a class you know well or an audience which you feel to be really sympathetic, it is often possible to step out of character for a moment between paragraphs, and to run over what has been said (in a lighter and more conversational tone)—like a guide who stops during a climb, to rest his party and point out the difficult paths already overcome, or like those actors in the comedies of Shakespeare who confide in the audience to heighten its appeciation of the plot. And since the chief danger of teaching by lecturing is that the pupils will become merely passive and then unconscious, you can often ensure their alertness and co-operation by asking them: "Is that clear so far? You see these first two points, don't you? or should we run over them again?" (When you ask that, they always cry No!)

*　　*　　*

The next best way of making your lecture clear is to punctuate with the voice. Between sections of your argument, pause. Make it plain that you have finished a unit of thought. Silence can be more emphatic than a shout. And vary the speed and force and incision of your speech to suit the material. It is not often effective to roll out important periods in a rich episcopal boom, or to assume any manner of speaking that is artificially sweet or impressive, even for a short period; but your voice should change within a lecture at least as much as it does in private life, where it varies all the way from the energetic rapidity of an argument with your friends to the careful precision of a statement to your lawyer or doctor. No one would find it interesting to talk to a man who never raised or lowered his voice, never changed the speed of his words, and showed no change of feeling in his eyes and expression. No one finds it interesting to listen to a lecture delivered with the same monotony. Expressiveness in speech is natural. Repression and dullness in speech are artificial.

Still, a lecture is not a one-sided dialogue. It is partly a speech, and it should not be all in the tone of talk. The distinguished historian, Mr. A. J. Toynbee, writes with admirable vividness, variety, and articulation, but when he lectures he seems apt to communicate the boldest theories and the most poetic illustrations to a large and intent audience in the same light, chatty, sorry-for-talking-shop manner in which he would exchange politeness with a guest in the mahogany and silver of an Oxford Senior Common Room. Those who had the pleasure of hearing him speak at Columbia University in the winter of 1947 saw that he had much to tell them, and learned much from his lectures. But some of them also thought he was too clearly improvising upon his own themes—or, perhaps, translating the massive ideas and long perspectives of his *Study of History* into the flimsier and more fugitive phrases of conversation. He does this chiefly from politeness. He feels, probably, that a lecturer talks down to his audience, while a conversation can be carried on only between equals. He is reluctant to pose as an Authority explaining his own private doctrines, and would rather seem to be a student joining his hearers in the discovery and exploration of impersonal truth. Perhaps he is also thinking of the fact that large concepts cannot be swallowed at once, but must be slowly meditated and assimilated: so that it is better for their author to introduce them gently and allow the audience to ingest them gently. True as this is, it is nevertheless true also that every audience of non-specialists needs guidance, deserves to be shown the depths it cannot yet plumb, and, in Mr. Toynbee's own phrasing, must be given an adequate challenge by the lecturer if it is to give back the response of full attention and understanding.

Gesture and voice, then, will make the plan of your lecture clear. For school and college classes, the blackboard is valuable. Of course difficult names, formulas, and dates should be written on it so that they can be remembered and copied: that is obvious. But it is useful too to make the board, like the "smooth table" of the beginner's mind, receive the salient points of your lecture. One brief sentence or equation can be written down in a few seconds. It should stay on the blackboard then while you explain and qualify it, reasoning forward to the next. Then a pause while the next goes up. At the end of your lecture the blackboard will carry a summary of it, with the true movement of your ideas made clear by the spacing of the phrases and diagrams; and through the hour it will have offered something for the class to look at, as a relief from your perhaps-too-well-known features.

Television, as I write, is still in a very early and amateurish stage. But it is not hard to foresee the time when it will be one of the chief media for the dissemination of news, for political propaganda, and for some types of teaching. Many subjects in which adult learners are interested will be able to be taught in the evenings to mass audiences over TV. We already know from the films how hopeless it is to show nothing but a picture of an "expert" reading rapidly from his typescript and glancing up from time to time into the eye of the camera. The techniques for TV teaching will take years to work out; but it seems clear that one of the basic patterns will be a partial improvement on all existing methods of lecturing: a combination of the *personal interest* provided by the teacher's voice, face, and personality, with *illustrations* and *demonstrations* seen by a different camera and with *key phrases* displayed in such a way as to anchor the attention of the audience and remain in its memory. Through such a medium the possibilities of teaching in the future may be extended over the whole planet, to many different sections of our unhappily divided human race.

* * *

The second method of teaching, the tutorial system, was invented by Socrates. Really it sprang from the character of the Greek people, for they loved asking questions and arguing: as St. Luke observed, there was nothing they liked better than hearing and discussing new ideas. But Socrates was the first who thought that teaching might mean, not pouring new ideas into an entirely empty brain, but drawing out universal truths from the mind in which they already lay concealed. All his teaching was done by conversation. He merely asked questions. The other man was led on to answer. Of course, he could refuse to reply. Some did, or broke off the discussion in a rage. But the young were fascinated by Socrates' cheerful kindliness, the experts felt bound to defend their claims to special knowledge, and strangers were attracted, or sometimes deceived, by his pretense that he was absolutely ignorant and needed only a little instruction, answers to a few simple questions. . . .

Yet for Socrates, teaching was not merely asking a series of questions, with the aim of exposing the pupil's ignorance or piercing his pretensions. These are negative aims. He had a positive end in view, although that end was concealed from the pupil. He wanted to make every pupil realize that truth was in the pupil's own power to find, if he searched long enough and hard enough, refusing all "authoritative statements" and judging every solution by reason alone. And he himself had a very clear, though very broad, idea of where the truth lay. His questions always steered the pupil, slowly and imperceptibly, with frequent failures and digressions, and pauses to meet sudden objections, towards that region. In the combination of these two, the critical method and the positive purpose, lies the essence of the tutorial system.

This system is the most difficult, the least common, and the most thorough way to teach. It is most difficult because it demands constant alertness, invariable good humor, complete earnestness, and utter self-surrender to the cause of truth, on the part of both teacher and pupil. It is least common because it is expensive in time, money, and effort. Socrates was poor, and lived mainly on presents from his pupils; but there are not many professional teachers who could afford to live on the fees paid by the few pupils they could teach on this system, and there are not many pupils who would be willing to pay enough to make the life livable. (In another profession, that of medicine, Socrates has much more prosperous descendants—the psychoanalysts who, by relentless questioning, expose the weaknesses of their patients and lead them towards truths which they knew but did not know. Teachers, however, cannot charge twenty-five dollars an hour.) The expenditure in time and effort on this system is very great. It is far easier to give two one-hour lectures to classes of fifty or sixty than to tutor one or two pupils for two hours, questioning, objecting, remembering, following up, arguing, defending yourself and counterattacking, and always moving towards a definite end which must not be hurried or overemphasized. And after giving two such tutorials, you are exhausted. Virtue has gone out of you. You cannot teach any more. And, what is worse, you usually cannot work at anything else. It is very hard to finish an active session with a few vigorous and stimulating pupils and then to open your own books and continue with a job of research. It is sometimes possible, I believe, for teachers of mathematics, medicine, and laboratory subjects generally, whose tuition, although quite as intense, is shorter and less sustained; but for teachers of languages, literature, philosophy, history, and the humane subjects generally, it is very hard indeed. Consequently, those who teach these subjects in this way seldom have energy and time left to make another career in pure scholarship. Sometimes they can scarcely keep up with current work in their own field. When they are intimately occupied with developing the minds of a dozen or two pupils, all individuals, all growing, and all interesting, how can they turn to read the latest issue of *Metaphysics* and the *Hispano-Portuguese Review*? And the new book on the development of nationalism in the late Middle Ages: they mean to read it, but it must be postponed until—at least until the final examination is over, probably till the summer vacation; and sometimes it doesn't get read in the summer either.

But for the pupils, tutoring on this system is far the best kind of education. The tutor gets to know them very well—better than their parents know them, better sometimes than they know themselves. He cannot, in such a close relationship, be tyrannous or chilly. Often he becomes both an example and a friend. He learns the pupils' weaknesses and corrects them by gentle steady pressure. He knows the pupils' strengths, and develops them. The boys can always ask him for help in difficulties, and sometimes he can divine the need before he is asked. The only danger here is that the strong personality of the tutor may overpower the pupil and convert him into a carbon copy. (Socrates had at least one carbon copy, who followed him about everywhere and imitated his dress and mannerisms.) But it is the tutor's job to avoid this as far as possible, by playing down his own originality and refraining from turning on its full power. And usually the best tutors are flexible and changeable to suit the different characters of their pupils, rather than bold, strong, monolithic men of striking and determined personalities.

That self-forgetfulness which makes them good teachers very often causes us to forget them, sometimes even prevents their pupils from realizing how much they owe to the men who molded them. One of the best-educated men of modern times was Michel de Montaigne. He thought a good deal about education, and willingly wrote about it. From his essays on it we see that he always assumes that everyone who can afford it will be educated, at least as far as college age, by a private tutor—not to coddle him (sometimes indeed to punish him more resolutely than his parents), but to concentrate one hundred per cent on the business of making a weak and empty-headed child into a complete man. He himself had just such a tutor—a German who, following out an idea of Montaigne's father, took him over as a tiny child, taught him Latin as his first language, and thus set him five or six years ahead of nearly all his contemporaries as well as giving him the literary taste he enjoyed all his life. But he never mentions the tutor's name, and never seems to think he owed a special debt of gratitude to him, any more than to his fencing-master. It is the same in Rabelais. The bad tutor Holofernes (whose name implies "tyrant") and the good tutor Ponocrates (= "Power through work") play essential parts in the upbringing of the giant Prince Gargantua; but after the tuition has ended the young prince thinks little more of it and treats Ponocrates merely as another member of his retinue. Very few of its products will write, as Logan Pearsall Smith does in his autobiography, that it is "an intolerable waste of fine material" for first-class brains to be employed on tutoring half-baked youths when they might have been making their own mark in the world. But that is a proof of the success of the tutorial method. For, as I said, it is based on the principle that education is the art of drawing out what is already within the pupil's mind. It helps the pupil to become what, potentially, he already is. Therefore, when the work is over, the pupil feels that nothing has been given to him, merely that he himself has grown. We know, we who have taught him, but if we are wise we shall never tell the truth.

* * *

The methods of tutoring a single pupil or a small group vary as widely as subjects and individuals. But the principle is nearly always the same. The pupil prepares a body of work by himself. He takes it for criticism and correction to the tutor, who then goes over it with the greatest possible thoroughness, criticizing everything from the general conception to the tiniest detail. The pupil learns from three different activities: first, from doing his own work alone; second, from observing the mistakes he has missed, *and also* from defending himself on points where he believes he is right; third, from looking over the completed and corrected work and comparing it with the original assignment and his first draft. The first of these is the work of creation, the second is criticism, the third is appreciation of wholeness. It is the tutor's main task to see that the individual activities are not really separate: they must mesh together and work into a larger scheme, covering as much of the subject as the pupil needs.

In music, for example, a teacher may very well start his pupil with the elements—reading the notes, singing the simple scale, hitting the basic rhythms—and may carry her through progressively difficult exercises, week by week, planned to train her in breathing, tone-control, rapidity of utterance, and richness of overtones, while avoiding or eliminating the too numerous vices of young singers—blaring, trembling, hooting, and panting. Easy songs will be followed by longer and more complex ones, until at last, years later than the first lesson, he will be teaching her a group of Ravel songs and an entire part from *The Magic Flute*. (Yet he himself may not be a singer at all, far less a coloratura soprano.) If he manages this successfully, he will be a fine teacher. He will have solved the two most difficult of the teacher's problems, which are to plan the complete development of a single individual's learning, from beginnings to maturity, and to guide the pupil over the inevitable periods of discouragement by pointing back to the ground traversed and forward to the hopeful future.

The lessons assigned must not only be interconnected. They must be varied, to sustain the pupil's interest and encourage its multiple growth. There is a story that Caffarelli, the eunuch who became one of the finest sopranos of the baroque age, was tutored by a single faultless but relentless Italian master, who kept him at one single page of exercises for five years, and then dismissed him, saying: "You may go: you are the greatest singer in Europe." Certainly the unhappy creature became one of the finest singers in history. He could sing melodies more purely and sweetly, and execute difficult runs more flexibly and gracefully, than any modern opera star. But his teacher took a chance which was quite unwarrantable, and which might not have succeeded with anyone except a eunuch. Most pupils, all pupils but a very few, would have demanded proof of their progress, in the shape of new assignments, fresh challenges, a change of any kind. Disciplined monotony is good training, but it easily becomes mechanical repetition; and by mechanical repetition nothing higher than card-tricks and juggling can ever (with the rarest and most laborious exceptions) be learnt or taught.

The tutorial system is not very widespread. It flourishes at Oxford and Cambridge. It has been tried at Harvard, but because of the expense of time and effort it has not been entirely successful. At a number of universities it exists in an altered form in the graduate schools; for instance, in the small classes called seminars, where a student reads a carefully prepared report on a special problem he has chosen, defends his conclusions against the criticisms of the other members of the class, and, with further criticism as well as positive suggestions from the professor in charge, builds his paper up into part of a book-length piece of research. A professor who advises a graduate student on a thesis which takes a year or more to write, who sees every chapter in draft and talks over every problem as it emerges, is really tutoring him too, on a rather high level. But as far as I know, the intense and exhausting, but rewarding, relationship which was expressed by the American statesman in the phrase "a simple bench, Mark Hopkins on one end and I on the other" exists only in Oxford and Cambridge Universities.

I passed through it both as a pupil and as a tutor. From both ends, it was one of the best experiences of my life. It worked in this way when I was a student: I was paired off with one other youth, taking the same courses as myself. We were told to come to Mr. Harnish's room at five every Tuesday and Friday. For Tuesday I was invited to write an essay on a part of the field we were both studying. It was considerably ahead of the lectures we were attending meanwhile, and it took longer to do than I expected. However, I finished it about three on Tuesday morning, and read it to Mr. Harnish that evening. Dick listened. Mr. Harnish lay in his armchair smoking, with his eyes closed and an odd expression of mingled interest, pain, apprehension, and hope on his face. After I had finished, he looked into the fire for a minute or two without speaking. (Those were always uncomfortable moments, but one learned a good deal from them.) Then he began to ask me questions about my essay, page by page, paragraph by paragraph, word by word. What was my authority for the statement about the Allies on the first page? Yes, it was in all the books on the subject, but what was the original evidence? Didn't that deserve more careful analysis? What other interpretations of it were possible? Did I know who had proposed them? Shouldn't they have been given more attention in view of recent discoveries? And on page 5, what was the original text of the illustrative quotation? Was that the usual translation? How could the version I offered be justified? Let's look it up now and see. (Dick was brought in at this point, and we engaged in a three-sided argument.) The third page was a rehash of the Tuskar theory, wasn't it? What were the real weaknesses in that theory? And so on through the whole essay.

After that, Mr. Harnish took the essay as a whole and pointed out the omissions, calling on me to justify them or suggest how they could be filled in. He finished off by a few airy references to pieces of research just concluded, to arguments carried on last week at the Philobiblian Society, and to Caversham's new book on the subject, look at it some time, won't you? and for next week you might write about Mumble Mumble; and so shoved us off towards the Buttery and a well-earned glass of sherry.

That was Tuesday. On Friday Dick read an essay of his own, while I listened in silence and then heard Mr. Harnish dissecting it in the same way. Next week, the same. By the end of the term we had each written eight essays and heard eight more, all in the same field, about which we were also reading books and attending lectures. Eight weeks is a short term, but at the end of such an intensive stretch we knew that particular field fairly well.

At an earlier stage, while we were studying language and literature, our class did a piece of translation twice a week: German prose into English, English prose into Spanish, Russian verse into English verse, English lyrics into Latin lyrics, whatever we were studying, and usually made as difficult as the traffic would bear. Sometimes alone, sometimes with another man, we would take the composition to the tutor concerned, who went over it literally word by word, criticizing our choice of meter and vocabulary, making alternative suggestions for awkward phrases, checking the rhythm, occasionally wincing and writing: (!) in the margin for a real boner, and finally discussing the expressiveness and grace of the whole rendering. Then he usually gave us a version of the same piece done by himself, which we copied out or excerpted as we wished, and which for beauty and skill it was difficult not to admire. Once a week or so, at this stage, six or eight of us would gather in his room to read shorter essays on special subjects, which he would criticize handrunning, less intensively than Mr. Harnish was to do at a later stage, but in such a way as to throw out more numerous suggestions to stir up our diverse interests. After you have read one essay on Luther in the Peasants' War, and listened to five others on Erasmus and the Reformation, the tragic career of Ulrich von Hutten, Peter Canisius and the Jesuits in Germany, the Anabaptists of Münster, and the intrigues of emperor and pope, you have learned something about the German Reformation.

And while I am taking examples from my own experience (although they are a little altered), let me pay a debt of thanks to the schoolmaster who taught me Greek. He used the tutorial system because I was his only pupil; and what is more, he gave up half his lunch-hour to do it. We were both doing Greek as an extra: I because I liked the idea of learning the language written in the queer but charming letters; and he because—I don't know: he was a dour quiet Scotsman who seldom showed enthusiasm for anything but his garden. Perhaps he wanted a pupil who might go on to the university and do him credit; probably he liked teaching enough to give up spare time to it if he had a willing learner; certainly he liked Greek literature, for he introduced me to the best in it. Whatever his motives were, he tutored me kindly but relentlessly. I stood beside him at his desk (sometimes cocking an ear to the yells of my friends playing after-lunch football outside) and translated my daily stint of Homer, line by line. He missed nothing, not the smallest γε. He insisted on a straight literal translation, which was the best level for a beginner—like Charles Lamb's Mrs. Battle, he loved "a clear fire, a clean hearth, and the rigour of the game"—and if I finished ahead of time, I didn't pack up and go. No, I was made to push on into the unknown, and translate the next page or so unprepared and unseen. Buchanan helped now and then with the hard words. The rest of the time he stood there, stiff and silent, smelling of pipe-smoke and damp tweeds and garden mixtures, and, for one small boy who scarcely understood, representing the long and noble tradition of exact scholarship and sound teaching. Now I offer him this tribute, regretting only that it comes too late.

* * *

The third method of teaching is the commonest. This is classroom work. It is difficult to give it a single name. "Repetition" sounds too mechanical. "Discussion" is more of a free give-and-take than the average meeting of a class, at least in schools. The traditional American word is "recitation," which suffers from the same fault as "repetition." Classroom study of this kind ought to be much more than memory-work, although it is based on memorizing.

Whatever it is called, the basis of this method is, as I have said, the study of a single book, or one set of documents, or one well-marked area of knowledge. The class sets out to read *Macbeth,* or to study Stubbs's *Charters,* or to learn the anatomy of the thorax. The teacher divides the subject into sections, each of which is to be studied privately in preparation for one session of the class. When the class meets, he has two duties. One is to explain what the pupils have been trying to learn: this he does by filling in the gaps in their understanding, pointing out things they have missed, sometimes helping them by practice and repetition and public reading to deepen their confidence. The other is to ensure that they have actually done the preparation. The second of these is less important than the first, but unfortunately it has come, in many schools, to seem much more important. The real job for which teachers are trained and paid is to *help* the young to learn. It should not be necessary also to *make* them learn.

I am not sure when this second necessity grew up to overshadow the first. I think it must have come with the establishment of universal education in the Western countries. Of course there has always been resistance to school discipline and reluctance to learn hard and boring things. Scarcely anybody learns the multiplication-table for fun. Certainly as early as Shakespeare we recognize the schoolboy with shining morning face, creeping like snail unwillingly to school. But it seems to me that resistance was not shown by *entire classes* of youths and girls, year after year, until education ceased to be a privilege sought after by the few and became a compulsion inflicted on everybody. In countries where education is imposed on every boy and girl under the age of sixteen, it is very hard for them to see it as the most valuable gift of the state, next to national security and public health and the rule of law. If it is surrounded and sanctioned by disciplines, they come to hate it. If it is made easy and delightful, they don't take it seriously—as in some schools where pupils are "automatically promoted" every year. This means that even if they have been too lazy or stupid to master first-year geography they are pushed on to second-year geography to get them off the teacher's hands, and to avoid the danger of giving them a feeling of inferiority to their intelligent and hard-working classmates. For this problem I see no solution except the radical one of declaring such numskulls to be unfit for education in book-work, and devising trade-schools, outdoor schools like the CCC camps, and domestic schools, to occupy their strong hands until they grow up. (Montaigne, who was a mild enough man and devoted to kindness as an educational ideal, had no solution either. He said that if a boy refused to learn or proved quite incapable of it, "his tutor should strangle him, if there are no witnesses, or else he should be apprenticed to a pastry-cook in some good town.")

Meanwhile, however, how is the teacher to make his class learn?

Much of it depends on his own brains and character. There are some men who strike us as boring even if we meet them only for half an hour in a ship's smoking-room. There are some women who stand out as dull and silly even if we only overhear them making a telephone call. Such people cannot teach except by bitter compulsion. But this has been touched on in our discussion of the teacher's personality. What can we add about methods?

The obvious method of discovering whether the class has studied its work, and of prodding them on to study in the future, is to ask them questions. Written questions with written answers are "tests," "quizzes," or "examinations." Horrible words. My soul sickens at their very sound. I sat so many scores of them, and I have marked so many hundreds of them. . . . Yet I have never been able to think of a substitute, and have yet to meet anyone else who has. Thinking back over the history of education, it strikes me as interesting that, in other times when people were well educated, the higher examinations were all oral. The Greeks and Romans had excellent schools, but when their children were being tested, they had to recite poetry or make speeches. There is a little exam in Shakespeare (*The Merry Wives of Windsor*, IV, i), but it is by word of mouth. In the great medieval universities, the graduating Masters and Doctors announced a thesis and defended it by debating against critics and rivals—a custom which still survives in the oral part of our own doctoral examinations. But the written examination, with all the heads bent over the same paper and brows wrinkled and nails bitten over the same problems, does not seem to be heard of until the nine-

teenth century. Perhaps it goes with the enormous increase in population (both inside and outside the schools)
and with the elaboration of modern industrial techniques.
A room full of candidates for a state examination, timed
exactly by electric clocks and supervised by watchful foremen, resembles nothing so much as an assembly-line at
the Ford works.

This is proved by the fact that specialists in educational technique are getting closer and closer to the production of an examination-system which can be run like
a machine. Their aim is to produce a series of wholly
objective tests of learning and intelligence comparable to
the laboratory tests of blood and lymph and tissue which
are made by the big hospitals for hundreds of different
patients who never see the examiner but merely receive
his verdict. The papers are made up by an expert, but
marked on the assembly-line technique. The expert
merely devises the questions, and puts down the right
answer and three wrong ones for each question. The
right answer is there, on the paper. The examinees have
only to recognize it. They look over the four possible
answers. They write down a number, 1, 2, 3, or 4, corresponding to the answer they choose. Then a staff of girls,
trained like lamp-testers in a factory, runs through each
paper, matching the numbers with a master-list which
gives the right number for the correct answer to each
question. The wrong answers are subtracted from the
right ones. A percentage is deducted for successful guess-
ing. The result is the candidate's mark.

From the teacher's point of view, this is delightfully
easy. For testing memory-work it is very useful. Why
should anyone trouble to go round his pupils one by one,
asking for the dates of the European revolutions or the
valences of the elements, when he can have their knowledge checked more rapidly and less personally?

But at the level above memorization, these tests are de-
ceptive. Suppose the examination is on the New Testament. The first question runs:

Peter was a (1) soldier
          (2) rich Pharisee
          (3) poor fisherman
          (4) well-to-do farmer.

These answers are set out as though they were equal. Whoever answers (3) is right. Whoever answers (1) or (4) has something to be said for him. But anyone who says (2) ought to be not merely marked wrong, but penalized several points. How many? As we ask that, the "subjective" factor rears its ugly head. The teacher must estimate the intelligence and the application the pupil has been showing, his grasp of the *whole subject*. More and more he must do that as the work he teaches rises higher above memorizing of individual elements and becomes creative understanding of a large and complex pattern of thought.

A test entirely composed of such questions must fatally alter the student's attitude to the work he is doing: because he must, for the purposes of the test, see it as a congeries of unrelated little facts: "Napoleon made Fouché . . . ," "Napoleon compelled Austria . . . ," "Napoleon divorced Josephine . . ." And yet the sense which teachers must strive hardest to develop in their students is the sense of structure: the power of grasping a broad historical process, a large geographical nexus, the plot and purpose of a great book. As students become more inured to this type of examination, their attention is shifted away from these broader questions to the atomic facts which can be learnt almost entirely without real knowledge and real education.

However, these tests were devised to ensure greater fairness for the pupils. The earliest ones were built by researchers who had found that sometimes there were shockingly unfair differences in the standards used by different examiners in marking the same examination, so that a boy would pass comfortably if his paper were read by examiner X, while he would be failed on the same paper by examiner Y. Not only that, but the investigators found that sometimes X would pass a paper if he read it in the morning when he was fresh, and fail it in the evening when he was tired. Hence these papers, in which the answers are fixed beforehand, and the standards are immutable. No matter who reads them or when, the answer to question 1 is always (3).

Yet this has only shifted the problem back one stage. Formerly the trouble was that X and Y and X-tired marked on different standards. Now, when composing the papers, X and Y and X-next-year work on different standards. It is next to impossible to select fifty questions which, when answered together, will be an equable test of the student's knowledge of any large and important subject, like world trade between the World Wars, or the role of the genes in heredity. It is quite impossible for X and Y to select questions which will be both equally important and equally difficult to answer, and still more so over a large area.

We are also told that mechanization will bring in the millennium, as we are told in every other sphere of life. Here is a quotation from the 28th bulletin of the Carnegie Foundation for the Advancement of Teaching, in its own phrasing: "the items in a new type test . . . can . . . eliminate from instruction the attempts to guess at or to emphasize or gamble on 'examinable topics.'" How wonderful it would be if this were true! Once students were given lists of dates and formulas to learn: if you memorized the fact that Justinian reigned from 527 to 565, or that all words in -ment were masculine except jument, you were sure to be asked to reproduce these facts. So an intelligent teacher soon discovered the "examinable" topics and questions. Has this changed? No. After half a dozen "new type" tests have been set and marked, every intelligent teacher will discover and most intelligent students will learn the fifty "examinable" facts in each area of each subject—with the absolute certainty of seeing at least thirty-five of them turning up. And they will turn up, again and again; or else the examination will be badly set. In this type of test you must ask, at least once every three years, whether St. Peter was a farmer or a fisherman: you have no choice, unless to imitate the emperor Tiberius, who asked "what song the Syrens sang, or what name Achilles assumed when he hid himself among women."

In more complex subjects, or in the same subjects treated with greater depth of penetration, it is virtually impossible to devise such examinations. There are dozens of possible answers to questions like *What were the weaknesses of Napoleon's continental policy?* and *Estimate the importance of Bellini's operas,* and a fixed set of answers would simplify them to the point of imbecility. What is the solution, then? How can we possibly manage to mark the papers without intruding our own personal weaknesses and blindnesses?

The surest method is to have them read by a committee. If two experts read a paper separately—each knowing that the other is going to read it and therefore a little more alert and less arbitrary—and then give it separate marks, and then discuss it before setting a final mark, the result is likely to be fairly reliable. They should have a third colleague in reserve, to call in if they differ. The most serious examination I have ever taken part in was run by a board of five. No paper was read by fewer than two men. Every doubtful paper and every paper of every doubtful candidate were read by three or four examiners several times over. After it was finished, we felt that our results were as fair as human effort could make them.

But when a teacher has to read his own papers, can he ever be sure his marking is impersonal?

Really, it is very difficult. A has a good memory, but he writes such a filthy hand that his papers are repulsive to read. B is intelligent and interesting, but he writes *beleive, imagnation, hopeless, rymth:* away with him. C's pen ran dry and he did four questions in blunt pencil, which gives you a headache. D is the tall thin youth who sat slumped on his shoulder-blades throughout every class meeting, seldom raising his eyes and often appearing to sleep—how *can* his paper be worth reading carefully? But our duty is to forget all their defects and our dislikes, to read their papers with the calm passionless memory-free reason alone.

It is hard to do this at a first reading. Therefore all exam papers should be read at least twice, with a day's interval between readings. It is hard to forget personalities. Therefore the candidate's name should be folded over and hidden, if possible, and the papers should be arranged in an arbitrary order—not one where you can expect D after C. It is hard not to overestimate the cumulative effect of a whole paper, which forces the writer's personality upon you. Therefore the best way—although the most tedious and exhausting—to mark a group of papers is to dissect them, and to read separate questions, to give each its mark, and then to total the whole. Thus, instead of reading all A's examination paper, putting down a mark, and going on to B, you should read question 1 in A's paper, give it a tentative mark, then read B's question 1 and give it its tentative mark, and so on through the list. Reading all the different answers to the same question is quite painful. But it compels one to be objective. If D makes more points and explains more ably than C, he must be graded higher. If you read their answers together, comparison makes the marks obvious.

Suppose, then, that the examination contains five questions. Before starting work, you will study it and jot down the essential and the secondary points which you think could properly be made in response to each question. No candidate, probably, can make them all. Some candidates can probably make others—all the more credit to them, and another reason for reading the papers twice. Some points you may find have been entirely omitted by everyone. If so, your teaching has been deficient there: note it for next year.

Then give each question a maximum numerical mark, so that the total maximum will add up to an easily manageable figure, 100 or 500 or 1,000. You may have to alter your marks after one reading, when you see how fully the various questions have been answered, but they will usually stay put. Then prepare a mark-sheet with five columns, another for the total, a space for notes on individuals, and sometimes another column for marks expressed in grade-letters. (It is often possible to estimate an answer as clearly second-rate or outstandingly first-rate while you read it; then you put down II or I, B or A, as a guide to estimating the whole paper later.) Then fill up each of the five columns separately as you read the questions, total the figures against each candidate's name, and you will have a fairly objective set of results, which will sometimes surprise you by its clarity and emphasis. Do the same a day or two later, on a new sheet. Compare the figures. Reread any papers which you have graded very unevenly, and compare them with others until you reach a solid decision. Then add up, sprinkle with pepper, and serve.

Seriously, though, this method is fairly rapid and yet very fair. It will enable you to justify any grade, whether to a dissatisfied candidate or to yourself. And it can be used to convert the examination into an instrument for learning. A post-mortem is sometimes quite valuable if you can explain what the *full* answer to the question on Napoleon's continental policy would be, and can quote one or two good remarks from the best papers. It is even permissible to quote some of the most outrageous boners, provided you give no hint of their authors. The others will relish them because they feel superior and sophisticated. The perpetrators will learn, from the shout of laughter which greets each atrocity, and they will be grateful to you for not exposing them. And apart from the comic relief, the whole class will know that you have done your best to give justice, and they will also have been brought back to think of the subject not merely as an examination hurdle, but as a topic for sensible discussion.

* * *

It is impossible, and it would be unwise, to have a written test every day. Every week is often enough. But every day you should find out whether your pupils have improved or not. A class, like a teacher, never stands still. It progresses, or it deteriorates. If it does not learn, it forgets. If it does not change, it ossifies. Therefore you must keep pressing it on by encouragement and elaboration, all the time. Teaching is constant expansion and development.

The usual way of verifying this development is to question the class on the new work it has done since the last meeting. There is probably as much bad teaching done through bad questioning as in all the other fields put together. We have all heard men asking railway officials for train-times in a tone of voice that made us want to kick them. We have all met women who stabbed out inquisitive personal questions as though they were killing flies with a hatpin. That manner is too often adopted by the discouraged, harassed, or peevish teacher, and it automatically provokes hostility and stupidity in the pupils.

There are really two different reasons for asking questions of a class: to find out if each individual has done his work in preparation, and to expose the difficulties they have found collectively in preparing the work. The former is a method of making them learn, the latter helps them to learn. The latter is much more important, but it is sometimes quite forgotten. Why should it be forgotten? Because teachers try to believe that the subject they teach is perfectly easy, that anyone can learn it fully without positive help, that any failure to master it must be due to laziness, and also, perhaps, that no amount of explanation from them can add much to the preparation already done by a really industrious pupil.

All these assumptions are wrong. It is more important to explain a new field of study to a class than to check their home-work on it. It is also more creative, because a class soon learns if you are interested merely in catching them out, proving them wrong, showing them up, making them squirm; and if you are, it thinks of methods to evade and to irritate you. But if it realizes that you care more about the subject than about their personal deficiencies, and that you are not merely a taskmaster who expects them to do all the work so that you can take the credit, they will begin to see their learning and your teaching as a co-operative endeavor, and some of them will do more than before, while few will do less.

Therefore questions asked of a class on a piece of newly prepared work should always be positive and creative, aimed at strengthening their understanding of it, sharpening their alertness to its implications, and exposing problems which they can help to solve. Suppose they have been told to prepare the geography and resources of the Middle East, pages 299–309 in the geography manual. The easy and the bad way of passing the "recitation" hour is to open the manual, divide its ten pages mentally into ten five-minute cross-examinations, and start round the class asking each boy and girl to echo some sentence from each page. *Where is Baku? What are its resources? What are the chief harbors in the Red Sea? Name the products of Bahrein.* An industrious pupil will be able, on this system, to list the chief harbors in the Red Sea twenty years after leaving school, and a careless one may be able to list them until the next examination, but neither will have a real understanding of that peculiar and important territory, or the faintest wish to go on and learn more about it.

The better way to teach such a lesson would be to assume that the class had done its best to ingest all the scattered facts given by the manual, and then to make them (a) more completely integrated, and (b) more vivid. It is an effort, painful for the young, to remember isolated fragments of information which they cannot relate to their own lives or fit into a larger scheme. But it is no effort, almost a pleasure, to remember a bright picture, rich but clear. This can be done by choosing for discussion a single topic which will bring in a good many of the facts as prepared, but set them in a new and vital light. The topic depends on the age of the class.

With young pupils of twelve or so, you might draw a map (making an occasional mistake and omission), and then ask them to help you fill it in. Make sure that the helpers are not all the six or seven top pupils. Ask them all, in turn, for contributions—but without browbeating them if they are dumb. Challenge them to fill in not only towns and harbors but difficult things like oil-pipe-lines and deserts and ruined cities, the Negeb Desert and Nazareth, the Kurds and the Armenians. With help, they will do it, and some will go away and bring you back more maps or pictures next day.

With a higher school class you could do a more elaborate map and discuss it. For example, above the physical lines of coast and mountain you could superimpose colored areas to show (1) religious groupings—white for the Moslems, yellow for the Jews, blue for the Christians, and red for the Parsees, as in the old *Arabian Nights* tale? (2) language areas—who, of all these diverse peoples, can really understand each other? what kind of speech do they use? (3) wealth—which are the sections that produce the great prizes like oil and pearls? where is there abject poverty? how many regions are there like Lebanon where the living standard is reasonably high? And so forth, always choosing ideas that will mesh in with the work already done on the geography manual, and yet will keep the minds of your pupils moving on outwards.

A class of undergraduates at college could be challenged to discuss more difficult problems. For example, you could invite them to work out a fifty-year plan of economic development for the whole region, to be sponsored by the United Nations and to depend as largely as possible on *local* contributions in manpower, finance, and administration. What would be its chief purposes? What difficulties would it have to solve? What oppositions would it provoke and how could they be overcome or circumvented? To offset such an idealistic discussion, you could give another hour to the strategy of a Middle Eastern war between two or three world powers. What would be their principal targets for capture and for destruction? What would be the function of Israel, Egypt, and Iran? Two hours of keen discussion on these lines, with constant reference to maps drawn by and for the class, would very soon bring all the prepared material together in their minds, lighten up many half-forgotten facts, and integrate the whole subject with their own present and future lives.

Even when the discussion is not carried on with a map, the blackboard should nearly always be used. The chief difficulty about arguing out a problem in the classroom is to control and guide the argument—to make sure that it reaches some kind of conclusion, or at least that the issues become clearer, and to keep the minds of the pupils from hopping like sparrows in a dozen different directions at once. This is best solved by using the device of Marshal Foch. At staff-meetings, when the various branches of the services and the representatives of different Allied forces and the gold-epauleted prima donnas had all wrangled with one another for an appreciable time without reaching any conclusion or even approaching one, Foch used to take a large sheet of paper and write at the top, in bold capitals:

WHAT IS THE PROBLEM?

In a matter of minutes, the debate took shape. It was not a supply matter; intelligence would be consulted, but only at a later stage; infantry had nothing to do with it; transport was urgently concerned, transport and the engineers, now the issues became clear, and the gunners too were interested, estimates could be submitted and priorities allotted on that basis—and the problem, once so hazy and difficult, grew easy as soon as its boundaries were fixed and its relevance cleared.

So then, almost every discussion ought to have its subject put clearly and inescapably in front of the eyes of the class. Write down the problem. Write down the partial solutions as they are suggested by various members of the class: modify and rephrase them as you feel necessary. Be particularly careful to arrange the problem and its solution in a clear and forcible logical scheme, as in this simplified instance:

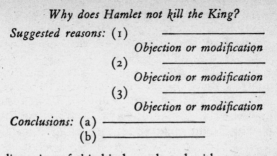

Why does Hamlet not kill the King?

Suggested reasons: (1) —————————————
                            Objection or modification
                      (2) —————————————
                            Objection or modification
                      (3) —————————————
                            Objection or modification
Conclusions: (a) ————————————
             (b) ————————————

A discussion of this kind, conducted with constant reference to the material the pupils have been studying, and so organized as to bring in the maximum number of suggestions and answers from the class, will not only deepen their understanding of that particular field, but teach them the invaluable lesson of organizing their thoughts. They soon learn by example. They will half-unconsciously start to arrange their own essays and plan their own work on similar logical models. They will jump the gap between memorizing and creative thinking.

* * *

It is difficult to conduct a class like this without bringing out the spirit of competition. Even if the teacher does not stress it, the pupils feel it. Lazy pupils are abashed when they fail at easy questions which others solve. Slow but industrious pupils work harder, when encouraged, and challenge the brilliant but superficial ones. Competition keeps a class from being merely a group of faceless nonentities, and gives it something of the diversity of life.

How far should the instinct of competition be used in teaching? Should it be emphasized, so that every week rewards and punishments, praise and disgrace, are distributed? Should it be ignored? Or should the teacher try to diminish it and as far as possible abolish it?

It is used very differently in different countries. In some, competition in school-work is a long-standing and deeply rooted tradition. Others, among them the United States, play it down and would prefer to eliminate it. Its value varies from one region to another and at different ages. But a few general remarks may still be made about it.

In the first place, competition is a natural instinct in the young. Listen to them outshouting and outboasting one another when they are having fun. Watch the innumerable games and stunts which they enjoy, all blended between co-operation and competition, team-spirit and rivalry. Think of the more serious competition practiced by adults not only in business and politics, but in personal display (houses, furniture, clothes, cars, and other gadgets), in the craving for publicity, and in the innumerable spectator sports on which we spend so many hours and so much money. (It is interesting to note that the Bolsheviks, who often denounce the free democracies for depending on the "ruthless spirit of competition," have themselves admitted the persistence and value of the instinct. They give special rewards to workers such as Stakhanov in Russia and Hennecke in Germany who produce far more than the average; and they habitually pit one factory or workshop against another in "Socialist competition" to increase the output of both.) Evidently an instinct so strong cannot be eradicated. Therefore in education it should be used constructively.

It is not only natural but apparently valuable. Being young, and growing up, is like making something out of nothing. You cannot quite tell what you are. You do not know what you want to be. You have scarcely a notion of what you can be or do. And so you make yourself, by differentiating yourself from others. Later the differences will be qualitative; but at first they are only differences of degree. You can run faster than A, jump higher than B; you beat C at diving, although he swims faster. X can draw caricatures better than all the others, Y tells the best ghost-stories, Z writes funny poems about the masters. Outside school, competition develops many good qualities as well as some bad ones: courage, determination, industry; conceit, selfishness, envy. Inside school, therefore, it should be used—and controlled. It should be used with moderation and a very careful sense of fitness, so that it brings out good qualities and encourages keen learning—and is braked, if possible, before it becomes bitter. It would really be alarming if one's fourteen-year-old pupils burned with as desperate a passion to win the Western Region school award in mathematics as to beat Forgan School at football. Or are we merely phlegmatic Anglo-Saxons? I remember a visitor to Oxford from a French college asking me what was our average number of suicides after the examinations, and I cannot think which of us was more astonished, I by the question or he by the answer.

The Jesuits, who worked out in the sixteenth and seventeenth centuries one of the most successful educational techniques the Western world has seen, used the spirit of competition very strongly and variously. They treated it not as a method of making the boys learn, but as a way of helping them to learn by bringing out their own hidden energies. As well as pitting the best individual pupils against each other, they used the technique familiar to modern leaders of mass meetings, and balanced groups against groups, half the class against the other half, teams of six against each other, and finally the whole class against another class slightly more or less advanced. They got the best boys to challenge each other to feats of brainwork which would astonish us nowadays. A top-notch pupil would volunteer to repeat a page of poetry after reading it only once; another would offer to repeat two pages. (The Jesuit teachers paid the greatest attention to the development of memory. Even their punishments were often designed to strengthen the memorizing powers, making a late or lazy pupil learn a hundred lines of poetry by heart, and the like.) A group of specially gifted boys would challenge another—always under the smiling, flexible, encouraging, but canny Jesuit supervision—to meet them in debate on a series of important problems, and would spend weeks preparing the logic, the phrases, and the delivery of their speeches. Perhaps the fathers overdid it, although we do not seem to hear of nervous breakdowns among their pupils. Certainly they made more of the spirit of competition than we could possibly do nowadays. Yet that was part of the technique which produced Corneille and Molière, Descartes and Voltaire, Bourdaloue and Tasso. No bad educational system ever produced geniuses.

It is, then, the teacher's duty to use the competitive spirit as variously as possible to bring out the energies of his pupils. The simple carrot-and-stick principle does not work, except for donkeys. Really interesting challenges are required to elicit the hidden strengths of really complex minds. They are sometimes difficult to devise. But when established, they are invaluable. It is sad, sometimes, to see a potentially brilliant pupil slouching through his work, sulky and willful, wasting his time and thought on trifles, because he has no real equals in his own class; and it is heartening to see how quickly, when a rival is transferred from another section or enters from another school, the first boy will find a fierce joy in learning and a real purpose in life. In this situation—and in all situations involving keen emulation—the teacher must watch carefully for the time when competition becomes obsessive and the legitimate wish to excel turns into self-torture and hatred. Long before that, the competition must be resolved into a kindlier co-operation.

*   *   *

This is the place to mention another valuable stimulus which a few teachers can use. Most, unfortunately, cannot. In its own way, it is inimitable and irreplaceable. It is not indispensable, though some of its defenders think it is. Often it is not even calculable. Results unexpected and bizarre may issue from its workings. Its products may hate it and, with an eloquence of speech and brilliance of reasoning created by its action, call for it to be utterly destroyed. Yet it is increasing in distribution, if not in intensity, in various places over the world.

Educational theorists who work on scientific methods rarely mention it, because it is a surd. It cannot be co-ordinated with plans drawn up in a central office, or controlled by a ministry. It can be studied by analysts, although it may be injured in the process and will certainly not be fully explained. It is best when talked about very little. Some of those who feel its power most vitally never mention it, may not know that it affects them, or may even spend their lives denying it. He who proclaims its value most loudly is often one of its mediocre products. Those who stand outside it entirely sometimes belittle it, sometimes hate and loathe it, but sometimes respect it. A teacher who is connected with it can usually make no direct and overt use of it, but must be content with allowing it to be felt by his pupils and now and then emphasizing one or another aspect of it. Even then he can seldom be sure how it will work.

This force is the tradition of a school or college. An old school, where many great men have once been boys, where their names are remembered and relics of them are preserved—a tree beneath which one used to read, a name cut in a panel; or a college of several centuries' growth, its library filled with the books used by famous students and enriched by bequests from them at the close of their careers, its rooms known by the names of once poor, or unhappy, or eagerly ambitious, or startlingly brilliant youths who passed a year or two in them at a creative crisis of their lives before going out to change the world, its walls alive with the faces of its elder sons, looking out at the later generation with eyes that invite and challenge and yet reassure the newcomers—such a college and such a school have a spiritual life of their own, which is much more than the buildings, the teachers, and the pupils of any particular epoch, and which acts as a most powerful developing force upon the character and mind of everyone who joins it. Those who have attended an average school with no distinguishing traditions (as most of us have done), and those of us who, if we went to college, entered an institution which was relatively new and was not invigorated by creative memories, but was a sort of factory for producing graduates (as most of us did)—we can scarcely understand the immense strength of the current that passes through a young mind when it feels itself part of a tradition of learning, living, and becoming which has lasted two hundred, four hundred, six hundred years. It would be strong enough to paralyze most people if it were only a restrictive tradition like belonging to an archducal family. But it is a tradition of learning, a creative current which sweeps them along towards richness and maturity, which, instead of numbing, exercises the muscles of their minds.

Essentially this current began to flow in the later Middle Ages, and has been growing stronger ever since. It was then that the great universities established themselves—Oxford, Cambridge, Paris, Salamanca, Bologna, Cracow, Prague, and others—and then the first great schools were founded, like Eton and Winchester. Of course the source of the current was in Rome and Greece, but it had been buried under the ruins and jungles of the Dark Ages until about the eleventh century. Then later, with the Renaissance, the flow became stronger. More colleges were founded. More universities grew up and the old ones enlarged their scope. School after school arose all over western Europe. In the seventeenth and eighteenth centuries the current swelled still more, and in the nineteenth it grew to a flood, as universal education changed from a dream into a nearly realized potentiality, as every town got its school and every province its college, as universities multiplied themselves and turned from collaboration towards competition. There are many schools now and many universities whose history is far younger than that of Harvard (1636) or Halle (1693), Charterhouse (1611) or Boston Public Latin School (1635), not to mention the grand medieval foundations—

but which have produced so many eminent men and developed such a habit of excellence that their tradition is now quite as potent, if not yet as varied. In France the École Normale Supérieure (1795) has taught hundreds of playwrights, philosophers, scientists, and statesmen. New universities like Johns Hopkins, London, and Berlin have released many untapped spiritual energies. To the general foundations, schools, colleges, and universities, we must add the special institutions—the military establishments such as St. Cyr, West Point, and Sandhurst; the research centers like the Institute for Advanced Study and the Schools of Rome and Athens; religious and sectarian schools, Jesuit and Quaker and Islamic; many more. No doubt some of the most ancient have the weakest reputations, and like an old, old dowager are sustained chiefly by their bankbooks and their corsets. Some of the newest and most ambitious are little more than façades, lacking foundations. But if we were to make a list of the hundred thousand men who have done most to uphold and advance civilization in the last century or so, we should, I believe, find that while some of them (for instance, Lincoln and Tolstoy and Picasso) had a broken and unsatisfactory education, and some were excellently well taught by tutors or parents (to these we shall return later), the majority (for instance, Pasteur and Roosevelt, Nietzsche and Byron) came from a relatively small group of schools and universities whose tradition helped to make them what they became.

* * *

But how does this tradition work? How does it create outstanding men out of ordinary boys?

It is difficult to answer this, except in the broadest terms; and it is unwise to analyze the force from within its field, so that the closest participants in such a tradition seldom explain it; but we can trace four or five ways in which it develops minds. Their relative importance will vary for each individual, and will sometimes change at different periods of his career.

Encouragement is the first. Many promising young men are nervous and self-distrustful. More closely than their brash extroverted friends, they see the vastness of life's problems and the inadequacy of their own talents. If they stay in their own homes or work in a little local school, they are apt to give way to despair and do nothing with their brains—or at most to limit themselves strictly to a small field in which they feel they can do something and still be safe. But when they join a school or college that has already given birth to famous men, they realize that they also, if they expand their minds and use all their energies, can achieve careers of the same distinction. The conditions have not changed. Usually they have bettered—it is easier to study in the new library with improved lighting, the rooms are enlarged. The great men of the past were no richer, came from no better homes, had no more friends. They even *looked* just as odd, in youth, as the oddest and most self-conscious freshman of today. Yet they built strong characters, they laid vast plans and carried them out, they discovered new drugs, became ministers of state, wrote the finest dramas of their time, worked out the laws of climate, won wars and made peace. *What man has done, man can do* is a good saying. Yet the young sometimes do not believe it until they enter the very place where great things were done and see its evidence around them.

Tradition also offers *a range of possibilities*. There is a good deal of wasted talent in the world, and some of the waste comes from sheer ignorance. People simply do not know how to apply their energies. Young men are nearly always very vague. They do not know the world. They do not know themselves. They confuse what they would like to be with what they can be. They will accept or reject a career simply because their father or their brother has chosen it. They have hardly any idea of the careful forward-looking process of building a life-work. In default of a good model, they will choose a faulty or an inadequate one—someone from the movies, a historical figure, a character in a book.

But the student who enters a school or college of long standing learns, almost unconsciously, who are the leaders of men. He hears names which are respected, and sees portraits of the famous. Gradually he builds up a hierarchy (not necessarily in the order accepted by tradition) of the different ways of achieving eminence. He comes to realize that the fields of human endeavor have been mapped from the air, although not fully explored. He learns which of them are easy and which difficult; which bring quick rewards, and which may (like Africa swallowing up an explorer) accept a new adventurer and obliterate him from human sight. He sees which of them can be combined, and which are mutually exclusive. By brooding on the careers of former students, sometimes by hearing stories of them or seeing them in the flesh, he decides more accurately whether he wants to resemble them or to reject their ideals. The techniques of attaining political success or artistic fulfillment, of making money or serving mankind, or making social acquaintances without surrendering his integrity, or doing prolonged research without growing eccentrically lonely— all these and many more patterns of living he learns, and can test by examples.

Membership in a great educational tradition also instills *a sense of order*. This is a difficult thing to explain, and is easily misunderstood. It is not that students who have attended a distinguished school or college always become Blimps and uphold the established system, defending its defects as stoutly as its merits. Often they do; but so do most people all over the world. From China to Arabia, from Sweden to Chile, the average man is conservative. He changes less than he preserves. What I mean rather is that students in such places acquire a clear sense of the fact that human living is a matter of organization. The state, the family, the arts, religion, trade, finance, education, law, medicine, farming and all kinds of production, science, architecture, navigation, war and peace and diplomacy—all these aspects of our life and work are highly organized. They must be planned. They must be

kept going by people who understand long-range planning. Without system of some kind they collapse into arbitrary individualisms and wasted efforts. Now, a long-
established school is itself a triumph of organization,
and it has usually produced a number of distinguished
contributors to the order which lies beneath human affairs. Therefore its graduates may be conservatives, or
revolutionaries, or reformers, or eccentrics; but they almost always know that their own life is (whether they
will it or not) going to be part of the human organization. They determine, then, to alter that organization, to
shatter it and then remold it, to improve it slowly or simply to utilize it, but they rarely behave as though it did
not exist. They seldom wish to destroy it and replace it
by *nothing*. Take Shelley as an example. He was odd and
persecuted at Eton (always a sign of talent) and got himself expelled from Oxford. Yet he retained the learning
and the love of learning which both institutions gave
him. He was a thorough revolutionary, preaching athe-
ism, sexual liberty, and something very close to an anarchist revolution. But the ideal that lit up his mind was
the creation of a new heaven and a new earth.

In ordinary schools, however, this sense of order is
much harder to attain. Each generation seems to live for
itself alone. Time, which is one of the essential frames of
human life, scarcely exists. The organization of the
school itself, and of the educational and political system
to which it belongs, does not mean very much to the pupils. It looks, not like a way to help them to live better,
but like a clumsy device to keep them from living as they
want to. At best, going to school is only a channel to
"getting a job." At worst, it is a trap.

At a much lower stage, far beneath ordinary schools,
the feeling that schools are prisons and that society is a
torture-machine is widespread. This is the other extreme
from the established schools and colleges we have been
discussing. This is the level on which the Russian educators found the young street gangsters (pp. 31-2), the level
from which habitual criminals are often drawn, the most

recalcitrant and ignorant group of people in any country, and at the same time the most pathetic and the most desperately in need of help.

The real anarchists in our world are the people who have never been to any school long enough to realize the inevitability of order, or who have been so badly taught that they think order—any order—is only a machine to spoil their own lives. These are the men with no fixed homes and no jobs they can do well, the women who make love without thinking it means children, who have children without thinking of bringing them up, who marry men without being able to run a two-room house; these are the people who drift about the big cities and lie stagnant in squalid villages, usually halfway between the bar and the pawnshop, miserably unhappy, their faces (after thirty) swollen with illness and seamed with conflicts, kept alive by the incredible vital force which endures so much abuse, yet alive to no good, even their own; wasted material; dead souls. In dark ages, in collapsed societies, in slums and backward country areas (like vermin in ruined houses), these people multiply. One of the chief purposes of education is to keep their numbers down, to help their children towards an orderly and reasonable life. Any school can do something towards abolishing their spiritual anarchy. The better the school, the more powerful its influence. An old school or university with a notable tradition often produces reformers and revolutionaries, but they are not anarchists. They are trying to make a better order in the world.

Another way of describing the sense of order which an old and eminent school or university inculcates is to say that it teaches *responsibility*. Life cannot really go on if everyone looks out for himself alone. Even if we do nothing more than refrain from getting in each other's way, if we do not "break the other man's rice-bowl," human society will roll along slowly and painfully, but more or less continuously. But we need men and women who will actually find their own career in helping their fellow human beings, in shaping and directing the organizations through whose help we all live better—running the hospitals and the Red Cross subscription lists, serving voluntarily as social advisers and pioneers of slum-clearance, working for the best political party they know and the betterment of the state—and it is hard to find such people. It is hard even to become such a man, such a woman. The three forces that produce most of them seem to be religion, the tradition of a community, and the tradition of a school or university. And the steadiest flow of men and women who make public service their lifework seems to come from schools and colleges whose tradition inspires them with that ideal.

The boy who lives at home with his family, who goes to a relatively new school which was designed like a factory instead of growing like a garden, and who spends only a few hours daily there, to return to a different community for part of his work and all his amusement and friendships, will naturally tend to grow up into a strong and wary individualist. Any association larger than the family and a loose group of friends he will tend to distrust, and will scarcely wish to serve. (It is to correct this very tendency that Scout troops are necessary, particularly in cities, and that the schools try to inculcate group loyalties in their sports teams and so forth. In small towns, where the school is an organ of the entire community, the situation does not arise.) Membership in a school of that type is no more likely to form a sense of responsibility than traveling on the same bus every day. The newer colleges and universities suffer from the same handicap —unless they have been able to attract a group of distinguished and magnetic teachers early in their existence, and to line up a number of students whom newcomers are proud to follow, whose examples create a sense of solidarity, they are apt to be institutions as mechanically conceived and run as a new, clean, busy hotel. Technical institutions can sometimes be run like that, but education demands more. It involves the entire personality—whether the pupil knows and wills it to do so or not. A school or college, then, which will give mind and character the

greatest amount of nourishment and exercise is a better
school or college than those which merely communicate
techniques or give injections of information every hour
on the hour. And since part of every complete character
is the will and ability to serve society, the school which
can inculcate them easily and unconsciously through its
tradition will deserve better of the nation than the school
that neglects to teach social responsibility or does so only
in neatly packaged courses.

*   *   *

After saying all this, I must admit that some of the most
complete wasters and scoundrels I ever met came from
schools and universities with traditions as old as oaks. I
can see them now, wearing the inimitable, the sacrosanct
tie, standing in an attitude of baroque grace, speaking in
a voice resonant of many exquisitely modulated generations, smiling with not even a hint of hauteur, as genial
as any cardiac nobleman out of the charmed Thirkell,
and telling a long and eloquent series of thundering lies.
They are not freaks, but a subspecies regularly produced
from the same ancestry. They express tradition almost
as truly as the solemn public servant. Sometimes they are
more delightful to watch, provided you don't endorse
checks for them. But how can they emerge from the same
tradition that creates the others, the reformers, the or-
ganizers of charity, the benefactors? How is it possible?
We shall look into this problem a little later.

*   *   *

The fifth of the powers exercised by a school or college
through its tradition is the obvious one, which brings us
back to the beginning of this discussion. It is *challenge*.
If there has never been a good scientist at your school,
you may want to be a physicist yourself, but you will
not be apt to work so hard, and you will have more
doubts and divagations. If five or six Fellows of the Royal
Society or members of the Institute for Advanced Study
have been trained in the same laboratories, perhaps by

the same masters, you will have clear targets to aim at. Even a failure will spur you on instead of discouraging you. They failed too. You must not fail again. Work. It is not necessary to model yourself on any individual. You can be yourself, unlike them all. You must equal them first, then excel them. Work. What they did, you can do, and more.

At this point tradition appeals to the same instinct as the master who sets four or five clever boys to the same job, knowing they will do far better in competition than working separately. Progress is successful rivalry with the past. As soon as reverence for tradition shrinks to nothing more than dutiful imitation, it becomes a deadening weight. As long as tradition provides an urge to strong, constant, and varied creative activity, it is a healthy stimulus and a wise guide.

* * *

Tradition and competition are two powerful stimuli to help teachers in teaching and pupils in learning. There is one other, much better known and more often used. This is *punishment*. Is it really useful? When, if ever, is it useful? What safeguards are there against its misuse?

The simplest kind of punishment is a reproof given to a pupil immediately after his fault. Like the scolding given to a child after it has thrown down its cup, this is quick and almost painless. It forms good habits by checking the bad ones in formation, as a boy learns not to kick sharp stones by wincing when he kicks them.

The most useful kind of punishment is repetition of the work done badly. If Tina gets her seam crooked, she has to pick it out and sew it again. If Joe gets the wrong answer in his arithmetic, he goes over the problem again until he gets it right. (But they should both be given a little help, a few words of advice and encouragement.) This punishment is valuable because it is a perfect preparation for life. They will both have similar jobs to do a thousand times, and they must learn to do them correctly. He will have his income-tax forms to fill up, his mileage records to keep straight, his bank-account to balance; she will have quantities to remember in cooking, and household expenditures to calculate, and who knows what else? If they do not learn now, they will have to learn later, and then far more painfully. Some adults who have been spared this kind of discipline in childhood spend their lives in a dream world, and are constantly tortured by its unlikeness to reality. As Housman says,

> To think that two and two are four
> And neither five nor three
> The heart of man has long been sore
> And long 'tis like to be.

For misbehavior, it is often useful to take away privileges. A friend of mine who is nearly fifty still remembers how, when he was eleven years old, he was exceptionally talkative and cheeky. It is hard to imagine it now, for he is a cool, smiling lawyer, economical of words. When did his character change, then? He says it changed one afternoon when his whole class was being taken to visit a big observatory, by their favorite master, a keen amateur astronomer. They were going to see something very special, a shower of meteors, or a comet revisiting the glimpses of the sun. He was so excited that he gabbled and giggled and interrupted and shouted all day. Although he got two warnings, he says he scarcely noticed them. The third time he was forbidden to go with the class to see the observatory, because he had spoilt his own work and some of the others' work for the day. "It was," he says now, "an epoch in my life."

All these types of punishment can be used in school without bringing in the parents. But when the school complains to the parents, asks for their help in enforcing discipline, or expels the pupil for an irremediable offense, it is using the most serious punishment that it can command. Here we see most clearly how schools are not a separate world, but a projection of society and the family. Bad homes, where there is little sense of order and responsibility, refuse to take any action and even encourage the children to defy their teachers. Some schoolmasters, doing their best on a poor salary to teach working-class children the skills that will fit them for life, are visited by truculent fathers who threaten to bash them in the jaw if they don't stop picking on little Danny. In other households a boy whose master writes to his father about him is likely to get a worse beating than he would ever receive in any school. Both extremes are bad. This type of discipline, like others, depends on a fairly close link of understanding between parents and teachers.

A failure in learning should *never* be punished by blows. Learning is difficult enough. To add fear to it simply makes it more difficult. Fear does not encourage, it drives on blindly. It blocks the movement of the mind. It produces the opposite effect to that of true education, because it makes frightened pupils dull and imitative, instead of making them original and eager. And it is useless to object: "Boys don't fear physical punishment, they laugh at it and forget it": for it can always be made tough enough, by a brutal master, to make most of them secretly afraid and some of them paralyzed with terror.

It has another counter-effect even more damaging: it causes hate. When Homer is mentioned, an officer in *Tom Jones* shouts out: "Damn Homo with all my heart, I have the marks of him on my backside yet"; and he is only one of many thousands who have burnt the books that meant nothing to them except tears and bruises. You could easily gather a heart-rending anthology of protests against such punishment, from the autobiographical memories of decent men who suffered under it. Here is little David Copperfield, trying to do arithmetic under the eye of Mr. Murdstone, who has just been "binding something round the bottom of a cane—a lithe and limber cane, which he left off binding when I came in, and poised and switched in the air."

"Now, David," he said—and I saw that cast [in his eye] again, as he said it—"you must be far more careful to-day than usual." He gave the cane another poise, and another switch; and having finished his preparation of it, laid it down beside him, with an expressive look, and took up his book. This was a good freshener to my presence of mind, as a beginning. I felt the words of my lessons slipping off, not one by one, or line by line, but by the entire page. I tried to lay hold of them; but they seemed, if I may so express it, to have put skates on, and to skim away from me with a smoothness there was no checking. . . .

He walked me up to my room slowly and gravely—I am certain he had a delight in that formal parade of executing justice—and when we got there, suddenly twisted my head under his arm. "Mr. Murdstone! Sir!" I cried to him. "Don't! Pray don't beat me! I have tried to learn, sir, but I can't learn while you and Miss Murdstone are by. I can't indeed!"

"Can't you, indeed, David?" he said. "We'll try that." He had my head as in a vice. . . .

Or here is Stephen Dedalus, half-blind after his glasses had been broken, facing Father Dolan, the "prefect of studies" or official beater.

"Lazy idle little loafer! Broke my glasses! An old schoolboy trick! Out with your hand this moment!"

Stephen closed his eyes and held out in the air his trembling hand with the palm upwards. He felt the prefect of studies touch it for a moment at the fingers to straighten it and then the swish of the sleeve of the soutane as the pandybat was lifted to strike. A hot burning stinging tingling blow like the loud crack of a broken stick made his trembling hand crumple together like a leaf in the fire. . . .

There are many more such memories. None of their authors ever praised the idea of physical punishment by saying that, although it was painful, it had taught them to study. Many of them said that it almost discouraged them for life, by associating the worst of things, cruelty and pain and fear and hate, with the best of things, art and learning and beauty.

The other types of discipline are the only acceptable bases of control in a school. The boy who cannot learn needs help. The boy who learns only half what he can learn should be shown that it will be uncomfortable for him if he does not do his duty. The boy who refuses to learn altogether is really a problem for his parents, and, beyond them, for the whole of society; I doubt if any treatment in a school, short of a complete psychological overhaul, could do him much good. Sometimes, though, he is only passing through a phase of disorder, an upset or a bad companionship, in which "the bread of affliction and the water of affliction," together with a little serious encouragement, will help him to rearrange his mind. If you are patient, and show that you really want to help them, even the most difficult and stubborn boys will often be moved, and change.

* * *

(c) FIXING THE IMPRESSION

The teacher has not finished his work when he has communicated the required knowledge to his pupils. Their minds are not stone, to be engraved. They are wax, to be molded and then hardened. Often they do not take the first impression; or, if they do, they lose it again. Often and often they take wrong impressions and distort right ones. Illness and football, love and carelessness and many other things help to make the impressions incomplete. If the teacher leaves the minds of his pupils inadequately informed, he has done a poor job. He resembles a doctor who sees a patient past the crisis, makes sure that his temperature is down to normal, and then stops calling, instead of giving advice about convalescence, prescribing a tonic, and watching carefully for dangerous sequelæ and a possible relapse.

The last three or four days of teaching can make a good course or spoil it. Usually they are given up to a mad rush through the last ten experiments, a sketchy outline of the century still to be covered, an earnest but hollow adjuration to "look over this for yourselves, with special attention to" or something else of that kind. During eight years of university attendance, I had only five courses which covered all the ground described in the announcement, and only two of these had any time over at the end for reviewing and fixing the impression. This is the same fault we have already discussed in dealing with preparation (pp. 66 f.): the fault of bad planning. But in this case its origin is different. A teacher who maps out his course badly, and neither sees where he is going nor tells his class what to expect, usually fails because he does not quite command his material. A teacher who huddles the last quarter of his course into a rapid-fire survey and says good-by after the last paragraph does not quite understand his pupils. He does not realize how new it all is to them, and how vague. He does not see that points which seem perfectly clear to him and names he has known for years are nothing but gaps and question-marks in his pupils' notebooks. He cannot understand how fast the boldest outlines are fading from their minds.

This is one distinction between good and bad teaching which the general public grasps firmly. Talk to them about their school days. Ask what teachers they remember; and what subjects. They always recall the ill-tempered and eccentric teachers—Miss Crab, who hit them with the pointer, and Mr. Fizz, who blew bubbles. But next to those, and more pleasantly, they remember the teachers who made them remember. They say: "There was Miss Mapp, she taught geography: I've forgotten most of the things I learned at school now, but I still know the capitals and boundaries of all the forty-eight states, and the principal rivers of the world." They speak of Miss Mapp with respect. She made their education last. She gave them their time's worth.

The Jesuit teachers also knew that fixing the impression was extremely important. This fits in with their stress on memory-work—and it was not automatic memorizing, it had to be thorough understanding. Their manuals of teaching never tire of saying: *Repeat, repeat and repeat*. They nearly always add that the master must watch carefully and vary his questions to ensure that there is nothing mechanical about this repetition, but then they urge once more *Repeat* and once more *Repeat*.

There are three chief methods of fixing the impression on the minds of pupils whom you have just finished teaching. The first is probably the most important. It is to *review* the ground you have covered.

The advantages of this have been hinted at in our discussion of the planning which should be done before the start of a course (pp. 66 f.). The two things—initial planning and final review—go together and complement each other. If the class was told, before the journey started, where it was going and what it was to see, it will welcome an opportunity to pause at the end and gaze back over the ground crossed. The view will be quite different. You will of course take advantage of this. In the two or three hours you devote to retrospect, you will be careful to deviate from the emphasis given in your original program, so as to show new aspects of the field which might possibly seem too familiar otherwise. Winston Churchill says, in his history of the first World War, that one of the finest strategic advisers of the War Cabinet was Sir Henry Wilson. Instead of summing up the factors of strength from the Allied point of view, or even from the angle of the impartial observer above the battlefield, he began one day: "Prime Minister, today I am Boche," and delivered a brilliant report on the state of the war as seen by the German General Staff.

One of the sharpest worries of the conscientious teacher is his own inadequacy. He has not made this vital point clear. Did they really understand his sketch of that theory, and his refutation of it? Should he have given more time to the first half of the program? These worries can be removed, or at least mitigated, by three or four hours saved at the end of the term for reviewing the ground, filling in the gaps, and reemphasizing the important points. It is tempting sometimes to end a lecture-course with a rousing peroration on the final topic, but its impression soon fades, whereas a steady, cool, clear review of the entire ground will, in a comparatively short time and with comparatively little effort, make a far deeper and more lasting mark on these flexible minds.

As the class retraces its journey, it will have a fine opportunity to ask *questions,* and you to prompt them and answer them. Never underestimate the power of a well-put question to illuminate the darkness. Students who have been passively absorbing information and allowing it to trickle out almost as fast as it was poured in will often come to life and take an active interest in their work when questions start flying. But the real value of the question-period at the end is for the conscientious students. It is worth while to read through a lecture-notebook kept by a student of good intelligence and industry. The gaps and misunderstandings in it will astound you. Often these youngsters are afraid to ask you to fill in the gaps, because they do not want to give themselves away. They think you will snub them, or brush them off. If you do, you are committing a crime. Instead, you should make it easy for them to ask for corrections, full names, the exact figures, the complete references. Don't simply wait for them to demand help. Offer it. You have not always spoken clearly. Foreign names and complex formulas are difficult to write down quickly. A cough will cover up half a vital sentence; and, in most cities nowadays, at least five minutes of every hour's teaching is made inaudible by the roar of transport aircraft apparently flying just above the roofs. The last few meetings of the class are your opportunity to wash away all that mud, and reveal your own lost pearls.

I still have a number of the notebooks I kept while I was an undergraduate. Before beginning this book, I looked through them. They were full of queries, one or two on every page. In some courses I had made a hard effort to solve the queries for myself, looking up references and trying to verify names. In others I had left them with large question-marks in the margin, apparently hoping for divine intervention to solve them. I had never ventured to go and ask the lecturers what on earth they meant. It was strange too to notice that, in some of the courses which covered the subjects I now teach myself, I could solve all the queries today without much trouble; but in others outside my field the gaps remained and will remain for ever—or at least until I get to heaven and once again meet the kindly Joachim, the suave and mannered Phillimore, and that master of analysis, H. W. B. Joseph.

Medieval methods of education are so often abused that it is a pleasure now and then to point out their virtues. In particular it is worth noting here that some medieval universities knew the value of this questioning process. At the University of Paris in the thirteenth and fourteenth centuries the chief teachers made themselves available on special occasions to answer *quodlibets*. The word means "whatever you like," and in theory their students could question them on any subject. In practice the questions ranged very widely but concentrated on philosophy; sometimes when we read them we have the impression that the students are trying to puzzle the master, to show up problems which he has skipped over, to convict him of inconsistency or even of heresy. But it was very good for both the students and the professors. Minutes of the meetings were kept, and are still available. As we read them, we have the pleasure of hearing, behind the formal apparatus, the perpetual duel of the young and bold against the mature and experienced, which has sharpened so many minds, and which is an essential part of the process of education.

After retracing the ground covered, so as to make all the students feel at home in it, and after calling for their questions, to be answered as clearly as possible, the good teacher will take one more step to round off his work. He has not taught them all he knows, and he has not taught them all they can learn about this particular subject. Whether he acknowledges this or not, they will realize it. If he attempts to conceal the fact, they will see through it and call him a fraud. He should therefore expose and explain it, and use it to awake their interest still further. This he can do by describing *outstanding problems* which are still to be solved.

This often acts as a challenge to good pupils, and sometimes to a certain number of intelligent but lazy students who have failed to find in class-work the scope they need for their restless energies and high spirits. One of the worst depressants in school learning is the feeling that everything is already known and filed away, that knowledge is all dead wood which every generation has to saw up and grind down all over again. Youngsters do not always admire their elders enough to work hard at school-books just in order to become replicas of Father and Mother or of Mr. Brown the schoolmaster and Miss White the schoolmistress. Often it does them good to feel that, by hard work, they will go further; and one way to inculcate this feeling is to show them problems which the best brains have so far failed to solve. They may never solve them. They may not even try—they may become air-line pilots or stenographers instead. But they will always benefit from having learned that human knowledge is expanding, and that its expansion is a stimulus to our will power, our brains, and our co-operation.

The type and the number of the problems outlined as challenges to future thinkers will obviously vary a great deal with the level of the students. The very young ones should hardly be told of them at all. It is difficult enough to learn to spell *cat* without being told that some propose it should be spelt *kæt*. Growing boys and girls should be told of very large-scale problems to expand their imaginations, and of very small-scale problems to test their ingenuity. It is at the age of twelve or thirteen that we lay the foundations for such imaginative lives as those of the astrophysicist and the international economist (someone asked them why the sun did not burn away to nothing, or what was the real meaning of a drawerful of inflation currency), as well as those of the precise professions like surgery and statistics (I once knew a boy of thirteen who passed a rainy afternoon by calculating $\pi = 3.14159$ . . . out to sixty places). Adolescents should be given critical problems which will bring them face to face with the hard surfaces and sharp corners called the facts of life. They should be dared to produce workable solutions which take in all the constants and allow for the variables. Now is the time to introduce them to the practical difficulties that will confront them throughout their careers: money (*how will you pay for it?*), manpower (*who will do the work and for what inducement?*), and authority (*who will direct it, and how can he be kept from abusing his power?*). But since it is also the time to form their critical standards in the arts, they should be asked what music is for (*is it only an amusement? if not, what?*), what makes a good picture and why, and what are the differences between a good movie and a bad one. (For most of the population nowadays, "the drama" means hardly anything more than the movies, and dramatic values must be discussed in terms of the screen rather than the stage.) Lastly, advanced students should be given a clear description of all the chief problems arising out of each subject they study. These problems concern them closely, and will help to see the pattern of their careers. The medical student who hears that the two most promising fields for research are psychosomatic activity and cell-changes in nutrition and destruction may become a general practitioner or a public health officer; but at least he will refine his own work by thinking specially hard about cases that involve either of these problems, and should he do any research of his own its impetus, if not its direction also, will come from that remark made to him at a critical time. The outline of these outstanding problems should amount to a succinct description of the state of knowledge on the subject, explaining what parts of the field are more or less static for the time, what areas are under dispute, where the biggest recent advances have been made, which problems have so far proved completely insoluble and which are partly solved, and where research is now most active. Students are nearly always interested, too, if they are told something about the chief advanced workers in their own field: a character-sketch of Oppenheimer, a description of Carcopino's career up to date, Toynbee's plans for completing *A Study of History*. The young often feel lonely and lost. Good teaching helps them to feel they are part of the larger world.

*   *   *

A good teacher with a good class will hardly need to plan how to complete his teaching by fixing the impression in the three ways which we have, perhaps rather artificially, distinguished. He need only be sure of the importance of applying the fixatives. Then, if he first explains briefly what he is doing, he and his students can go together over the ground, growing familiar with the features they now recognize together, asking and answering questions as they travel, and pointing out the peaks still to be scaled, the valleys unexplored. This is the best kind of teaching. On this level it stops being the mere transmission of information and becomes the joint enterprise of a group of friendly human beings who like using their brains.

IV

Great Teachers and Their Pupils

Some of the most important men in history have been teachers. Many of the biggest advances in civilization have been the chief work, not of politicians or inventors, not even of artists, but of teachers. Before we go on to look at teaching in modern everyday life—as it is done by editors and doctors, foremen and fathers, and many other types—let us see who the chief teachers of our world have been, and how they worked.

* * *

In Western civilization there are two lines of teachers from whom all modern teaching stems: the Greek philosophers and the Hebrew prophets. Outside the Jewish community the influence of the Greeks is far wider, stronger, and more varied—with the exception of the teaching of Jesus himself. In this book we are not concerned with what is taught, but with *how* teaching is done; yet in content, also, our schools and our universities are much more Greek than Hebrew. The Greek teachers claimed to be following the movement of Reason. The Hebrew prophets knew they were uttering the voice of God. We admire both, but we are apt to think that while a group of men who are in touch with God can change the world by a rare and miraculous intervention, it needs the steady work of reason to keep the place going and to train the young.

Apart from elementary schoolmasters, instructors of scribes and the like, the first professional higher educators in the Western world were the group of brilliant talkers and keen thinkers who appeared in Greece during the fifth century B.C. They were called "sophists." (The word means something like "professional wise men," and, because of its implication that these men sold their brains for money, fell into disrepute. After Socrates, the intellectuals preferred to call themselves "philosophers," which means "lovers of wisdom for its own sake.") We are still talking about many of the ideas the sophists worked out: for instance, it was they who first discussed whether there were any absolute standards of morality, or merely artificial conventions; whether justice is a constant, or simply means the will of the ruling class; and so forth. As thinkers—particularly as destructive critics—they were dazzling. As teachers, they were superficial.

They were exclusively lecturers. All that we hear of them shows them as phenomenally graceful and subtle talkers, usually to fairly large audiences. In that they are the direct ancestors of the modern "authority" who tours the large cities giving a carefully prepared speech in which his own personal power or charm is combined with well-spaced jokes and memorable epigrams, the whole varying very little from one repetition to another. Like him, they were highly paid and widely advertised and welcomed by a reception committee and entertained by ambitious hosts. But unlike him, some of them professed to be authorities on *everything*. They said they could lecture on any subject under the sun. Often they were challenged to speak on odd and difficult topics, and accepted the dare. However, they did not usually pretend to know more facts than others, but rather to be able to think and talk better. In that, perhaps, they are the ancestors of the modern journalists who have the knack of turning out a bright and interesting article on any new subject, without using special or expert information. The perfect example of the modern sophist would be Bernard Shaw, if he had only spoken his inimitable prefaces with his inimitable charm instead of printing them. Like him, the sophists dazzled everyone without convincing any-

one of anything positive. Like him, they argued unsys-
tematically and unfairly, but painted over the gaps in
their reasoning with glossy rhetoric. Like him, they had
few constructive ideas, and won most applause by taking
traditional notions and showing they were based on convention rather than logic. Like him, they demonstrated
that almost anything could be proved by a fast talker—
sometimes, as a stunt, they made a powerful speech on
one side of a question in the morning and an equally
powerful speech on the opposite side in the afternoon.
And like him, they never allowed anyone else to get a
word in edgewise.

The results of the sophists' method of teaching were
both good and bad. They were a strong disruptive force
in civilization, for they helped to blow up many sound
traditional values, and often blinded their pupils by the
temporary brilliance of the explosion, leaving them no
help in rebuilding their individual and social lives. Yet
they taught the Greeks what no other Mediterranean nation ever learnt, that thought alone is one of the strongest forces in human life. The respect for the thinker
which they created has lasted, off and on, until this very
day.

*　　*　　*

To some of his contemporaries Socrates looked like a
sophist. But he distrusted and opposed the sophists wherever possible. They toured the whole Greek world: Socrates stayed in Athens, talking to his fellow-citizens.
They made carefully prepared continuous speeches; he
only asked questions. They took rich fees for their
teaching; he refused regular payment, living and dying
poor. They were elegantly dressed, turned out like film-
stars on a personal-appearance tour, with secretaries and
personal servants and elaborate advertising. Socrates
wore the workingman's clothes, bare feet and a smock;
in fact, he had been a stonemason and carver by trade,
and came from a working-class family. They spoke in specially prepared lecture-halls; he talked to people at street-

corners and in the gymnasium (like public baths and bathing-beaches nowadays), where every afternoon the young men exercised, and the old men talked, while they all sunbathed. He fitted in so well there that he sometimes compared himself to the athletic coach, who does not run or wrestle, but teaches others how to run and wrestle better: Socrates said he trained people to think. Lastly, the sophists said they knew everything and were ready to explain it. Socrates said he knew nothing and was trying to find out.

The sophists were the first lecturers. Socrates was the first tutor. His invention was more radical than theirs. Speeches such as they delivered could be heard elsewhere —in the new democratic law-courts, where clever orators tried to sway large juries by dozens of newly developed oratorical tricks, and in the theaters, where tragic kings, queens, gods, and heroes accused and defied one another in immortal tirades, and in the assemblies of the people, where any citizen could speak on the destinies of Athens. And traveling virtuosi like the sophists were fairly common in other fields—touring musicians, painters, and sculptors, eminent poets like Simonides, were all welcome in Greek cities and at the rich courts of the "tyrants." It was not too hard, then, for the sophists to work out a performance of their own, as brilliant and sometimes as impermanent as a harpist's recital. The innovations Socrates made were to use ordinary conversation as a method of teaching, and to act on one society only, his own city of Athens, instead of detaching himself and traveling. He was not even a "brilliant conversationalist," in the style of Oscar Wilde and Madame du Deffand. He does not seem to have made memorable epigrams or thrown off eloquent paragraphs of improvisation like Coleridge. His talk was not "full of flowers and stars." He made the other fellow do most of the talking. He merely asked questions.

But anyone who has watched a cross-examination in court knows that this is more difficult than making a prepared speech. Socrates questioned all sorts and condi-

tions, from schoolboys to elderly capitalists, from orthodox middle-of-the-road citizens to extremists, friends and
enemies, critics and admirers, the famous and the obscure, prostitutes and politicians, artists and soldiers, average Athenians and famous visitors. It was incredibly
difficult for him to adapt himself to so many different
characters and outlooks, and yet we know that he did. (In
this one of his truest descendants was St. Ignatius Loyola,
founder of the Jesuits, who was different for every different person he talked to, and adapted his manner, indulgent or severe, gay or serious, to the character of the person he was interviewing.) Socrates looked ugly. He had
good manners, but no aristocratic polish. Yet he was able
to talk to the cleverest and the toughest minds of his age
and to convince them that they knew no more than he
did. His methods were, first, the modest declaration of
his own ignorance—which imperceptibly flattered the
other man and made him eager to explain to such an
intelligent but naïve inquirer; second, his adaptability—
which showed him the side on which each man could be
best approached; and, third, his unfailing good humor—
which allowed him always to keep the conversation going and at crises, when the other lost his temper, to dominate it. Some of the most delightful dramatic scenes in
literature are those dialogues in which we see him con-
fronted by a brilliant fanatic and drenched with a shower
of words that would have silenced most others, and then
emerging, with a humorous pretense of timidity, to shake
off the rhetoric and pursue the truth, until at last, under his gently persistent questions, his opponent is—not
forced, but led, to admit that he was wrong, and to fall
into helpless silence.

*   *   *

We know he was a good teacher, because he had good
pupils. The greatest was Plato, who founded a college,
named Academy, to pursue the studies on which Socrates
had launched him. As well as teaching and studying,
Plato wrote books on philosophical problems all his life.

Nearly every one is in the form of a conversation, and nearly every one is dominated by Socrates. There has rarely been a finer tribute to any master by any pupil. Plato's own character and his own philosophical ideas were strongly marked, but he seems to subordinate himself entirely to the personality and method of Socrates in every book but his last. He never appears in any of his dialogues by name, and mentions himself only twice. The dialogues were apparently meant to reproduce Socrates' own method of teaching by conversation, with the very accents of his voice. They show him to us as a young man, tackling the highly publicized sophists on their own ground; at a gay party in the prime of his life, surrounded by the best minds of his time, rising poets and scientists and statesmen, helping to bring the best out of them all and dominating the whole interplay of eloquence and imagination; in the gymnasium chatting with young athletes and their fathers; in the streets questioning passers-by; interviewing a touring celebrity; bringing geometrical proofs out of the mind of a little untrained slave-boy; speaking his own defense in his trial at the age of seventy, and still teaching the Athenians by the firmness with which he holds to his convictions; and, in the last hours before his execution, arguing for the immortality of the soul. In all these different situations he combines the steady unflinching aim, the pursuit of truth, with the most supple adaptability of approach to different people.

But the queerest thing about his teaching is that we do not exactly know what he taught. We know *how* he taught. We know that very well. But we do not know precisely what lessons his pupils and interlocutors drew from his questioning. His different pupils say he taught different things. Young Xenophon knew him before going out East to become a soldier of fortune, and wrote memoirs of him later. He shows Socrates as an inquisitive, pawky, charming but annoying eccentric, who inquired into everything and criticized everything more or less indiscriminately. Another of his pupils, Aristippus, thought he destroyed all moral traditions and all permanent spiritual values by his criticism, and encouraged men to live life without conventions, following only pleasure and the instincts. Plato himself began by writing conversations in which Socrates proved nothing except that no one knows anything; or, at most, that virtue must be knowledge. Then he went on to conversations where Socrates, after breaking down traditional theories, proceeded to build up elaborate theories of his own—still working on the question-and-answer principle, but reducing the other man to a mere stooge saying "Yes" and "No" and "Go on." Some of these theories are called Plato's by later writers. Were they Plato's, or did Socrates teach them?

Evidently the answer is "both." Socrates did not teach them in their fully explicit form, or his other pupils would have remembered them also. But Plato did not work them out entirely on his own. They were produced by the action of Socrates' teaching upon his mind. Also, we must remember that anyone who taught so well as Socrates and who used cross-examination as his method cannot have thrown out questions at random. He must have had some set of positive beliefs from which his questions flowed; and even if he did not explain them positively, his more brilliant pupils could reconstruct them. His teaching is therefore one of the great examples of the power of implication. What a teacher says outright sometimes goes unheard. What he stimulates his pupils to think out for themselves often has a far more potent influence upon them.

*　　*　　*

Plato himself taught more systematically and more exclusively than his master. More systematically, because he established a college instead of going about the streets: it had entrance examinations and disciplinary rules, and was apparently run rather like a monastery or a club of research workers. More exclusively, because instead of chatting with everybody he preferred specially selected pupils, and instead of falling into spontaneous conversations he gave lectures, which were sometimes very difficult to understand. But he was not a working man as Socrates had been. He was a nobleman, rich and gifted, a poet by his earliest inclinations and a mystic all his life, who felt it impossible to teach *everyone* and limited his efforts to highly trained, carefully chosen listeners. He was the founder of the examination system. His teaching therefore had a strictly limited effect. He had one outstandingly bad pupil, the young prince Dionysius of Syracuse, whom he tried to make into a philosopher-king, and who became a tyrant; and one superlatively good one, Aristotle, probably the best and broadest single mind the human species has yet produced. But besides these he has made many hundreds of pupils through his books, which are supreme masterpieces of the teacher's art.

In them he shows his master Socrates proposing a problem to one of his friends or pupils. Questions are asked, gently and almost casually. As the answers are given, Socrates draws them together and asks further questions about their apparent inconsistencies. Under his patient interrogation, irrational judgments are thrown aside and shallow ideas are plumbed and discarded and objections are raised and countered and slowly, slowly, under the guidance of Reason alone, we are carried through the labyrinthine paths of learning until we arrive at a positive result, which we could by no means have foreseen when we started and could not have reached except by cool rational discussion. At least, that is the effect which Plato wishes to produce. Every step of the argument is exposed. There are no appeals to higher authority. During the discussion there is no escape into windy words or mystical ideas. If you, as you read, think that the writer or the speakers are cheating, you are not intimidated or dissuaded from doing so. You are like a stranger who has walked up to a little group which includes Socrates, and who listens to the conversation without joining in it. At any moment, at any word, you can turn away and decide, if you wish, that Socrates is a charlatan

and that his pupils are stooges hypnotized into agreeing
with him. Some do. Many do. All do when they go beyond Socrates to Plato and read *The Laws,* a sinister doc-
ument which should stand on the same shelf as George
Orwell's *Nineteen Eighty-Four* but expresses admiration
of the bad state Orwell exposes.

Obviously what Plato taught was—as far as politics are
concerned—anti-democratic and narrow-minded and at
the end both sad and bad. But *how* he taught it is what
concerns us; and he taught it through these brilliantly se-
ductive conversations in which the reader, since he cannot identify himself with Socrates, automatically identi-
fies himself with the interlocutor, and so finds himself
saying "Yes" and "Certainly" to propositions which he
would never have thought of if he had been left alone.
In politics this is highly dangerous. In metaphysics and
logic and even in morality it is a very healthy and exer-
cising method of teaching. And certainly it is one of the
most powerful ever invented. As you begin to read a Socratic dialogue written by Plato, you relax under the
charm of the surroundings and the gentleness of the initial exchanges, and before you know it you are still thinking, yet thinking along the lines suggested—not laid
down, but suggested—by a teacher who died two thousand three hundred years ago.

There could not be a better example of the distinction
between the subject-matter of teaching and the method of
teaching. Few of us admire or believe the doctrines which
Plato taught. All of us must admire the methods by
which he taught them. From his master Socrates he had
learnt that there is no possible way to educate people, to
convert them and change them and convince them fully
and lastingly, except by calm, cool reasoning. Ask the
questions. Examine the answers. Go on discussing until
the reason is satisfied with the result. As you think by
yourself, all alone, you should converse with Reason almost as though Reason were another person, with claims
to respect at least equal to your own. When you argue
with someone else, the argument should not be a fight be-

tween you two, but a hunt after Reason, in which you both join, helping each other to detect and capture the truth you both desire. To read a dialogue in which Plato shows the work of his teacher is not necessarily to be convinced of the conclusions which are its end-product; but it always produces admiration of the men who could exhibit reasoned argument as the strongest and most permanent force in human affairs.

* * *

Aristotle—doesn't it make a magnificent series, Socrates-Plato-Aristotle?—was a rich doctor's son, and always preferred the scientific habit of thought. He came to Plato's Academy when he was seventeen, and stayed there until he was nearly forty. He left when Plato died, and after traveling and doing independent research for some years, founded a college of his own, called Lyceum. (Both Academy and Lyceum are only place-names taken from little individual shrines near the colleges, but they have now become generic names all over the Western world. If the obscure pagan saint Academus ever looks out from Limbo, he must be astounded to see his name perpetuated in the Royal Academy of painters, the Académie Française of intellectuals, the American Academy of Arts and Letters, the Accademia d'Italia, and many others, plus hundreds of schools of every kind, down to the newest Academía de Rumbas in Havana.) Apparently he thought of research and teaching as two sides of the same coin. So had Socrates, who taught by persuading friends and acquaintances to join him in the search for truth. So, in a different way, had Plato. Aristotle organized his teaching very thoroughly. His Lyceum resembled a modern research institute: the vast numbers of specimens for his biological work which he collected from many parts of the known world must have been examined by squads of research students; and his masterly political treatises were the distillation of important analyses of numerous existing constitutions made by his assistants under his supervision.

Much of Aristotle's teaching, then, was the sort of very high-level discussion which goes on in similar institutions today wherever they exist. They are not common. They need a great deal of money to support them, and complete political freedom (Aristotle was eventually hunted out of Athens because he had supported the imperialist monarch Alexander), and high standards of achievement already established, and an expanding horizon. Much of his teaching also was done on a slightly lower level, to less advanced students who were still much more highly educated than the average citizen. Many of the works handed down under his name are not books he wrote, but collections of lecture-notes taken down by his pupils, and perhaps later corrected from his own notes. We see from them that he combined lecturing with class discussion, but put the emphasis on the lecture. That is, he set out a series of topics, which linked together to form a complete survey of a subject. He took each topic separately, broke it down into a number of problems, and then examined each of these. How, we do not exactly know. The notes show him talking on continuously, analyzing one suggestion after another, explaining where each falls short and why, and finally working his way to the solution. But we do not know whether he asked the class to make the suggestions and then helped them to discuss each one in turn, or merely talked out the analyses himself. We do know, though, that like all experienced lecturers he had a number of standard illustrations, which appear in potted form in his notes, and that he used people and things in the classroom to explain his arguments. Some people think that he did a certain amount of teaching while walking about the grounds of his college—the name Peripatetic, given to his philosophy, simply means "strolling." This implies that he was careful to keep it informal. Many thinkers since Aristotle have found that they thought best and talked best while walking up and down. Body movement seems to keep the mind from standing still. But it is only an affectation to walk if one's teaching is all cut and dried and if one does not intend to change or develop or improvise. Aristotle was never accused of affectation, and we know from the state of his extant books that he kept developing his own doctrines. It is ridiculous that both in the Middle Ages and in the baroque period he should have been considered as a pundit whose utterances composed an unalterable system of truths, when what he wanted to show was that knowledge was a constant process of discovery.

* * *

One of the hardest jobs in teaching is to train leaders of men. Socrates had thought a great deal about this, but had failed miserably in doing it. Plato failed too, on the whole. His rival Isocrates, who ran a "school for princes," had more success. Now Aristotle attempted it with the young prince Alexander, whose father, by treachery and aggression, was making himself ruler of Greece, and who was to fight his way clear through to India and become the greatest of Greek monarchs.

This was an exceptionally difficult assignment. Alexander and his family were not pure Greeks, but Macedonian highlanders with a strong strain of ferocious barbarism in them. Unbounded courage, aggressive energy, a vastly adaptable and inquiring mind, rocklike resolution—these are good qualities for a pupil, and these Alexander had; but he also had inherited a tradition of savage cruelty, violent pleasures, and primitive coarseness. Like the Anglo-Saxons and the Germans of the Dark Ages, the Macedonians drank heavily night after night. Once at a drunken dinner Alexander speared his best friend to the wall of the officers' mess for making jokes about him. We see the same boisterous violence in the Icelandic sagas and the stories of the Vikings; it goes with good fighting spirit, but for Aristotle it was five or six hundred years behind the times. He must have felt like Sir Francis Bacon trying to educate Eric Bloody-Axe, or Newton teaching Peter the Great. He could never have done it if he himself had been a pure Athenian. But he was a Macedonian, his father was King Philip's doctor, he knew the northerners, and he judged the limits of the possible, very cleverly.

We know scarcely anything about his methods in teaching young Alexander, but we can infer them from the results. What could not possibly be changed, he left alone. Alexander learnt more from his father and mother than from anyone else, and this, together with his Macedonian manners and temperament, was unalterable. It was both good and bad. That heritage made him destroy the entire city of Thebes, selling nearly all its citizens as slaves, after it tried to regain its freedom from him by a short revolt. It also made him a superb cavalry officer, a general unequaled in history, and an able far-sighted monarch. Aristotle determined to leave his temperament and family inheritance untouched and to create counterweights to diminish their bad and increase their good effects.

First and most important, he taught him to respect and love Greek culture. He began with Homer. This was a splendid choice, for the original heroes of Homer were very like the Macedonians, and Homer idealized them so skillfully that they became fine patterns for the young prince to follow. Naturally Alexander most admired the northerner Achilles, said to be his ancestor. He visited the old mound believed to be Achilles' tomb outside Troy and held a memorial service at it; he took with him everywhere a copy of Homer revised by his tutor, and once he said he envied Achilles for having such a poet to write of his adventures; he evidently thought of himself as a new Achilles conquering the rich old cities of Asia. (Long afterwards another young northern prince, Charles XII of Sweden, was brought up in the same way on Quintus Curtius' life of Alexander: he carried it everywhere with him, and thought of himself as a new Alexander.)

From Homer, Aristotle went on to instill in Alexander an admiration for other Greek poets and other aspects of Greek culture. Even when Alexander made Thebes into a Lidice, he left the house of the princes' poet Pindar standing as a memorial. Later, as he got more political experience, he realized that his enormous conquests of the amorphous Middle Eastern lands and peoples were meaningless and would be ephemeral unless they were bound together by a permanent bond of unification that was above law and politics. He found this bond in Greek civilization. Wherever he went he founded cities on the Greek model, and spread the knowledge of Greek arts, sciences, language, literature, manners, and trade—not as an extension of the Greek nation, but as the best way to establishing a world-wide civilization. His favorite Alexandria was not an Egyptian city at all, but a cosmopolitan megapolis based on Greek culture—as to some extent it still is.

Nearly four hundred years later the Christian gospel was preached in Greek and written in Greek, and the Roman empire's strongest and longest survival was in the Greek-dominated Near East, because of the cultural mission which Aristotle helped to teach Alexander the Great.

Personally, Aristotle could not do much with Alexander. The youngster was hunting or fighting a good deal of the time, and then became a serving soldier. Even if Aristotle had believed that the democratic type of man was the best, he could not have taught Alexander to practice the democratic virtues: he would have failed ridiculously and lost his post. Instead, he taught him something of the virtue most important in a monarch—generosity, which Aristotle himself called greatness of soul. It was this that made him repent bitterly after killing his friend Cleitus. Later, when he was told that his personal doctor had been bribed to poison him, he called the man in, asked him for his medicine, and, while drinking it, handed him the accusation to read. His father, Philip, would have had the doctor tortured on suspicion. It was this also which made him treat the harem of the conquered king of Persia with scrupulous courtesy, although it was a painful effort to restrain himself in the hour of victory. Something of the magnanimity taught by Aristotle survives in the fine portraits of Alexander in coins and sculpture, and made him a pattern hero for the age of chivalry.

* * *

The most famous teacher of the Western world was Jesus of Nazareth. He taught in the tradition of the Hebrew prophets. In some books of the Old Testament we hear of "the sons of the prophets"—groups of men who gathered round some great visionary like Elisha living in a place apart, who gathered his sayings, followed his routine of life, and shared his inspiration; and we know of Eastern thinkers like Gandhi who have an *ashram,* a community dedicated to living with the master. Such was the group of pupils which attached itself to Jesus. Earlier, others had left their homes and joined John, the purifier or baptist. Jesus himself passed through John's influence before becoming an independent prophet.

And he was also a teacher in the newer Jewish sense—an authority on the meanings of Jewish literature and law. He did not speak Hebrew at home, for it had become only a literary language some centuries before his birth, as it remained virtually until this present century. But like most talented Jewish children he was taught the holy books in the original Hebrew, and then he was instructed in the immensely complicated system of interpretations and analyses which Jewish scholars had erected on the foundation of the old tribal laws and prophecies. The first time we meet him after his birth, he is in the very center of Jewish cultural life, the Temple at Jerusalem, where, at the age of twelve, he is discussing varieties of interpretation with the shrewd professors of Hebrew law and ritual; and, as he said himself, he felt that was his real duty, more important than going home with his family. Later he was to transcend this difficult science, but first he had to learn it and think deeply about it. "Wonder children" like that are encouraged by the intense educational tradition of the Jewish people.

Many of them have had wonderful careers, but none like the teacher Jesus.

His teaching had two aspects, both vitally important and closely connected. He taught his own pupils, whose names we know; and he taught the Jewish people, as many of them as would listen. His pupils were with him all the time. They listened to him and watched him and tried to understand and imitate him. They sailed with him in the storm. They went to Jerusalem with him and celebrated Passover as orthodox Jews. They were not arrested and executed with him, evidently because the Jewish authorities thought that such a school soon breaks up when its teacher is removed. They attended his execution, and handed on the tradition of his resurrection afterwards. It was they who founded the Christian church in Jerusalem, and preserved the story of his life. They were all poor, ordinary men, simple and good. If he had chosen, he could easily have had rich and highly educated pupils, skilled in Hebrew scholarship, fluent in Greek, expert in historic ritual, wells of traditional lore. Nicodemus and other such men became his followers. But he chose simple pupils because his teaching was meant for ordinary people, and particularly for the poor and the misguided, since there are so many more of them.

He also taught the general public. We hear of his doing this in the synagogue. Like a traditional scholar ("scribe"), he read out a piece of the scriptural books and then explained it to the others. When a modern Christian clergyman takes a text from the Bible and preaches a sermon analyzing its meanings, he is following the tradition of Hebrew scholarship which came into Europe and America from Christianity. But more often Jesus delivered short speeches in the open air. Huge crowds gathered to hear him. They would follow him for a long time, forgetting about food sometimes, and simply hoping he would say something, or do something. Apparently he did not always speak. There was no fixed program, nothing like a preaching tour—no arrangements so carefully organized, for instance, as those of the Greek sophists five hundred years before, or of modern evangelists. Once he spoke from a boat to a crowd on the shore. He made his most famous speech sitting on a little hill, with his pupils grouped beside him and the public spread out all around. His teaching in the traditional manner given in the synagogue is not so carefully recorded, and was not always successful. Apparently it was felt to be a more direct attack on the orthodox doctrines of Judaism. After one of his addresses, in Nazareth, the congregation tried to lynch him. But his teaching to the crowds gathered in the open was overwhelmingly effective. His influence was increasing rapidly right up to the time of his arrest, for when he entered Jerusalem to celebrate Passover he was met by enthusiastic crowds who greeted him as a representative of God.

The reason for his growing reputation is given in the gospels. People came to hear him because he spoke like an original thinker and not like the professional scholars. That means that he did not spin out endless interpretations of difficult texts and solve artificially complicated questions of casuistry (like the one the Sadducees asked him, about the woman who had seven successive husbands and met them all in heaven), but gave them positive advice, on which they could remake their lives. He knew the canonical books intimately, quoted them often, and was never caught in ignorance of them or misunderstanding. Yet he had apparently gone out beyond them to build up a new doctrine, which he conceived as *completing* the teachings that had guided his nation till then.

* * *

His methods of conveying this teaching, as far as we can know them from the gospels, were four in number.

First, his speeches. Not very many of these are recorded, but we hear that he gave many, all over Palestine. The most remarkable thing about those we have is that they are not organized. They have hardly any plan. They have no continuous argument. They do not connect and develop a single series of ideas into a logical structure. The Sermon on the Mount begins abruptly with a single mystical assertion, for which an equally mystical reason is given. This pattern is repeated seven or eight times, and then dropped. The rest of the speech is made up of equally mystical and even more disjointed sentences, some of which cohere into brief paragraphs. The speech stops as abruptly as it started.

If we read it carefully, we shall find it impossible to imagine it as a speech in the real sense, a speech which is planned and delivered as a continuous whole in order to have a cumulative effect. In the usual translations it is split up into separate units called "verses." As we examine it, we become convinced that that is how it was delivered. Jesus sat down. His pupils came round him because they knew he was going to say something memorable. The crowd watched. He did not stand up and fix them with his eye and embark on a carefully rehearsed propaganda oration. There was a silence, a timeless silence. Then he spoke "and taught them," sitting like a teacher among little children. He said: "Blessed are the humble in heart: for theirs is the kingdom of heaven." After that, it is hard to believe that he spoke right on continuously. More probably there was another silence, while this utterance sank in. It was remembered for many years before it was written down. Then he taught them again, saying: "Blessed are those who mourn: for they will be comforted." Then another silence; and so, slowly and thoughtfully, Jesus uttered the sentences which he had worked out in his mind during the many years of preparation for his mission as a teacher.

This method of teaching is strange to us. It is sometimes called gnomic, because *gnomé* in Greek means "a wise saying." It exists here and there in the European tradition, but it is much commoner in the East. We can see it elsewhere in the Bible. For instance, when Job's friends come to see him in his disaster, they first of all remain silent for a week. Then they speak alternately and discuss his responsibility for it with him. Although

Job and his three friends each speak for a considerable time, what they say cannot be brought into any logical construction. Instead of arguing, each of them repeats one point of view over and over again, driving it home with a series of poetic images and vivid phrases. We imagine them not as pouring out angry streams of words, but rather as uttering each of these sentences slowly and weightily, with long pauses between. The same is true of many of the utterances of the Hebrew prophets. The denunciations of Ezekiel, the lamentations of Jeremiah, the sublime aspirations of Isaiah, gain most force when they are read as they were uttered—slowly, slowly, like the movement of the hand which wrote upon King Belshazzar's palace wall:

MENE

MENE

TEKEL

UPHARSIN.

Biblical scholars point out that, since it is unlikely that Jesus' teaching was written down until many years after his death, we can scarcely tell now whether its separate elements were arranged in any larger structure, and they believe, many of them, that it could only be transmitted in fragments. This may be true. But it has been shown (from studies of oral transmission of literature and wisdom in others countries) that it is quite possible for long continuous poems to be passed on from one generation to another in their original order and emphasis. Jesus' words as we have them are partly fragmentary (the separate sayings discussed on pp. 173-4) and partly organized in groups like the Sermon on the Mount. It would seem probable therefore that the Sermon and continuous preachments like it are the closest approximation to his continuous teaching which could be made by the memory of his pupils. His hearers remembered the structure of his parables very well. If his longer speeches really had a comprehensive structure, it is unlikely that they should have forgotten it entirely, when they remembered so much else.

This reconstruction of the manner in which Jesus spoke is supported by the work of recent scholars such as Professor Torrey of Yale and Professor Burney of Oxford, both of whom emphasize the fact that he used the Aramaic language. Professor Burney retranslated his most famous sayings into Aramaic and found that they often fell into rhythmical patterns, like our own versified proverbs:

> Red sky at morning
> the sailor's warning—

and like the poetic utterances of the Hebrew prophets and teachers. Some of these sayings, he suggested, not only scanned rhythmically but had an echoing rhyme. If this is true, then Jesus composed his sayings in the form which would make them most memorable. To be given their full value, and to be memorized by their hearers, they must have been spoken slowly and rhythmically, with long pauses. Therefore Jesus did not make a speech or preach a sermon, as we should understand it. By uttering half in speech and half in song the phrases over whose compressed wisdom and memorable form he had labored for long years, he taught his people and the world.

His second method of teaching was allied to the first. It was to utter one single important piece of wisdom, and then fall silent again. Such a remark struck his pupils as important because he had evidently thought over it for a long time or because it expressed his character very completely. They felt that no one else could possibly have said it: so they remembered it. We can see three or four typical situations in which these remarks were made. Sometimes they were answers to hard questions. His pupils would ask him to solve a problem that they had vainly tried to work out from their knowledge of his teaching; or outsiders who were sorely perplexed asked him about their difficulties; and he would reply. We hear of many Eastern sages who taught almost entirely by this method. Kung, whom we call Confucius, preferred answering an inquiry to making a positive statement. Sometimes again the critics of Jesus tried to show him up by the competitive method of the Jewish scholars— asking him complex and tricky questions in the hope of proving that he did not understand the Jewish law or was breaking it. Many of his answers to these questions are recorded. For instance, the legal experts brought him a woman who had been caught in the act of committing adultery. "Now," they said, "Moses in the law ordered us to stone such women to death. So what do you say about her?" At first he gave no answer. They pressed him. He answered: "The man among you who is without sin is to throw the first stone at her." Sometimes also Jesus would comment on a human situation, showing his hearers the right interpretation of it. Often these comments sound very teacherish, for Jesus corrected people firmly and unequivocally. For instance, his pupils scolded parents for bringing babies to Jesus and asking him to touch them. Jesus then scolded his pupils, corrected them, told them that it was impossible to receive the kingdom of God unless by becoming like a child, and took the babies in his arms and blessed them.

Sometimes again Jesus would give a lesson by telling a story. The story was usually interesting for its own sake, and it always illustrated a religious and moral lesson. But he did not always explain the exact application of the lesson: sometimes he told only his pupils, sometimes he left it all for them to work out themselves. And the lesson was usually either quite complex, having several different levels of meaning, or quite difficult and unexpected. There are only two ways to teach such lessons —either by prolonged discussion, with argument and objection and amplification and qualification, which reduces their force, or as Jesus taught them, in a single brilliantly clear and memorable likeness. (In this Jesus was using a technique similar to that of Plato, who in-

troduced poetic stories and images to make points that
could not be completely proved or fully driven home by
argument alone.)

This takes us to Jesus' third method of teaching. Like
all great teachers he knew that a picture is worth a thousand words and that people learn most quickly by doing
something or seeing something done. Therefore he punctuated all his teaching by performing a number of acts
which meant something. They were symbols, or they
were rituals. For example, he said little about marriage,
and little about drink. But the first miracle told of him
in John's gospel was the creation of wine to help the
festivities at a wedding. He could not have said more
plainly that he approved of both marriage and drinking.
And the last lesson he taught his pupils before his arrest
was the ritual of sharing a meal of bread and wine, to
which he gave a deep and deathless meaning. There are
many of these gestures in his life. Remember how he
drove the money-changers out of the Temple with a
whip; and when the adulteress was brought to him and
was accused, how he wrote with his finger in the dust.
Many of them are as clear to us as though we had seen
them; and the ritual of Jesus' last supper is celebrated
every hour, somewhere in the world.

His fourth method of teaching was propaganda. After
his pupils had learnt what they could, he sent them out
to travel all over Palestine and spread his teachings. Not
many teachers do this, even when they have a religious
message. Instead, they tend to teach every class by itself,
and to treat every class as a little closed community. Socrates went about teaching everyone who was willing to
answer questions; he had pupils who used his methods
and his doctrines; but we never hear of his sending out
agents to spread a Socratic creed. Plato had a college;
pupils came to it for education and left again, sometimes
to form their own colleges. Aristotle too had a college;
like Plato he distinguished the "esoteric" learning which
its advanced pupils commanded from the "exoteric" teaching open to the public. Neither of them encouraged

teachers to disseminate his ideas. But we know Socrates, and Plato, and Aristotle chiefly because of the dialogues and lecture-notes which have survived from their work with their own pupils. And the enormous effect of Jesus' teaching is largely due to his training teachers to spread it and to teach other teachers. The pastor thinking over next week's sermon, the nun reading to a sewing-class in the Philippines, Schweitzer writing in his jungle hospital, and the mother teaching her child its prayers are all connected by a direct, unbroken tradition passing through seventy generations back to Jesus teaching his first chosen pupils.

* * *

One of Jesus' twelve chosen pupils was Judas Iscariot, who helped the Jewish authorities to carry out his arrest. Jesus knew it, too. At the Passover supper he spoke of it without mentioning the name of the traitor: although we do not hear that he said or knew anything of it until the last few hours.

This is a memorable case of one of the most important and difficult questions in teaching. Why does a good teacher have bad pupils? Jesus was one of the best teachers, and he had one of the worst pupils. Why?

It was not that Judas simply fell short of the best in Jesus. He did not try to understand the teaching of Jesus and then fail in all good will, as the others sometimes did. He did not break down in a crisis, like Peter. He turned his back and went the other way, resolutely and effectively. To prove this, think of the method he chose to single Jesus out for the police. His master's chief lesson was that all men should love and trust one another. So Judas, instead of pointing to him with his hand or standing beside him, went up and kissed him.

Spectacular as the Judas case is, it is only one of many. Socrates had a number of outstandingly bad pupils. The best known is the most brilliant—Alcibiades, who loved Socrates dearly and admired him fervently, and who also betrayed his country, went over to its enemies the Spartans and then betrayed them, returned to Athens and left it once more, and was killed after a career which included such other exploits as the seduction of the Spartan queen and blasphemy against his country's religion. But there were others—such as Critias, who became one of the Thirty Tyrants put in by Sparta after the defeat of Athens and who tortured and murdered hundreds of his fellow-citizens in a savage attempt to crush out the rule of the people. The real impetus behind the condemnation of Socrates was the people's hatred for the men he had taught to hate democracy. He had other pupils, certainly, but the revolutionaries were among the most brilliant. We cannot be quite sure how Socrates himself regarded them. Plato tells us that he thought they were potentially good young men who had been misled by other influences; and of course once they were fully embarked on their bad careers, he had little to do with them. But he seems to have been closely associated with them for a long time. Why did they go so very far wrong? Was he the best teacher in Greece, as Plato and others believed, or was he a man who, as the accusation read, corrupted the young?

The history of education is dotted with such terrible failures, as the chart of a difficult channel is starred with wrecks. Move on into the Roman empire and you will find others. Nero is one. He was the son of a princess who managed to get him adopted by her second husband, the reigning emperor, Claudius. As an heir to the throne, he was educated with great care. He was handed over to Seneca, a brilliantly clever talker and writer and an experienced courtier, who was also a philosopher attached to Stoicism—which means that he upheld a stern moral code based on the primacy of Duty, but was not unrealistically rigid about it. Seneca, assisted by an experienced soldier and administrator, worked over the young prince for years, with all the care and subtlety he could command. He gave him a thorough grounding in

moral philosophy, and a considerable knowledge of literature and art. It was not all hard work and ethical principles either. After the old emperor died, Seneca wrote
an outrageously funny skit about his trying to get into
heaven and being kicked out, which was apparently
meant to be read at Nero's coronation party; and he
wrote nine blood-and-thunder tragedies which (according to one theory) were specially designed for the stage-
struck young emperor to produce in his private theater,
with himself as a star. The results of all this care were
very good, to begin with. The first five years of Nero's
reign were universally admired. Social justice, sensible
financing, big public works, and much else were due to
Nero's own enthusiasm and the guidance of his advisers.
Then he began to deteriorate. From the age of twenty-
two or so he got worse every year. He retired his tutor
Seneca. He divorced, and then executed, his wife. He
executed, or murdered, his mother. He started a career of
absurd and foul debaucheries. He threw off every good
influence, neglected his duties, ruined the empire, pro-
voked it to revolt against him, and even then had
scarcely the courage to commit suicide. And Seneca, his
tutor? Several years earlier, Nero had condemned Seneca
to death, like everyone else who had ever benefited him.

But why did he go wrong? Was it simply that the limitless power of an emperor was too much for anyone to
bear? No, because others used it sanely. Or did it come
too suddenly upon him? No, because he had been carefully trained for it by experts for years. Or was he badly
trained—did Seneca perhaps encourage him to loose living so that he would be easier to handle? No, we do not
hear that he did. On the contrary, all the evidence is that
Nero was well educated, on a high moral standard.

There are many more like him in history, on a smaller
scale: hundreds; thousands; tens of thousands of young
men and women who had talent, and health, and security, who were trained by teachers who understood them,
who were surrounded by people who loved them, and

who threw the whole thing away. The mediocrities do not matter so much—the expensively educated girls who turned out to be bumpkins or bridge-fiends, the privately tutored and hand-tailored youths who went on the Grand Tour and returned without an idea in their sleek narrow heads. Chesterfield's son is a good example of that sort of unimportant failure. They are simply bald patches, thin and sandy gardens, depressed areas. No, the important problem is why really talented people with the best of teaching should turn out fatally, damnably bad: like Nero, like Judas.

This is a very hard problem for teachers, and for parents. To solve a question so tough as this, there are two devices that we can use. One is to find out what answers have already been suggested, and to think them over, comparing them together and filling up one by the help of others. The second is to ask whether the same problem appears in any other shape, to see what answers are given to it then, and to apply them.

Not many useful answers are given to our question. Why did Judas betray Jesus? Why did Nero kill his own teacher? Why did Alcibiades destroy so much that Socrates admired—integrity, purity, patriotism? Judas himself did not know. After he had finished, he knew he had done wrong. He knew it could not be put right; and he knew it had nothing much to do with the bribe he was paid; but he could not tell why he had done it.

As for Nero, he said Seneca was mixed up in a plot against him, but did he believe it in his heart? When he forced Seneca into retirement and disgrace, was he only safeguarding himself against assassination—against a plot made by the old man who could have killed him at any time for years?

Alcibiades has left no record except his acts. But his fellow-pupil Plato gives a valuable explanation of the problem, evidently written with him in mind. He says in effect that all sorts of pupils go wrong, including many mediocrities. But, he adds, philosophy is an exceptionally difficult type of education. It takes unusual talent to be a good pupil of Socrates. Therefore, when such a pupil goes wrong, he goes spectacularly wrong, by applying his unusual gifts to bad purposes. Remember that Plato was not thinking only of brain-power, but also of the other strengths that make up an exceptional personality—physical and spiritual energy, rapid and strong will-power, social adaptability and charm, bodily dexterity and beauty. When a young man or woman so richly endowed goes wrong, he or she goes very far wrong.

Plato adds another solution, which is certainly true in part. It is, he says, fearfully difficult to teach such a gifted pupil efficiently, because evil influences compete much harder for his attention. This is certainly true, so far as it goes. Obviously if Seneca had been able to train Nero under laboratory conditions he would have made a better thing of it. But he could not watch the young prince all the time. Even if he could, it would have been ill-advised to do so. And how can you teach self-control when every pretty slave-girl in the palace contrives to catch the master's eye and brush against his hand? How can you repress his extravagance when the rooms are full of courtiers anxious to sell everything they possess and procure whatever the master fancies? Can anyone learn clemency, even from Seneca, when vile whisperers slander every decent man at court, suggest confiscations of great wealth, describe the pleasures of inflicting torture?

True in part . . . but is this the only explanation? Is it all the truth? Do we feel that it explains everything?

No, we do not. We feel that men like Judas and Nero who turn against their teachers are not merely led aside by other influences. They do not simply wander off the path. They turn right round and go in the direction opposite to their guides. They do not merely drop their teachers, forget lessons and personalities. They deliberately attack their teachers, trying to annihilate them and all they stand for. And the problem we have to solve is: why does this so often happen to teachers of exceptional brilliance and goodness?

* * *

Perhaps we can solve it by asking if it appears in any other shape. As soon as we consider it, we find that it does.

We have already noticed the peculiar fact that the best schools, with the oldest and noblest traditions, produce some of the most complete scoundrels. This is the same pattern. They do not simply turn out stupid and mediocre, these failures. Instead, they turn out brilliant but bad. Usually they retain something of what their school taught them. It may be only a set of intonations, a social technique, a haircut and a style of dress; it may be a whole intellectual attitude as complex as that which the Jesuits gave to their pupil Voltaire. But in everything else they are rebels. All that the school tries to teach, they deny and pervert. Sometimes they hold it up to ridicule by caricaturing its customs and personalities with a plentitude of detail which is positively boring for outsiders though evidently necessary for themselves. Sometimes, when they cannot write, they try to shock and disgrace the school in other ways. All their conduct is marked by a compulsive reference to the school, a strong emotional link which, it seems, they both love and hate, like a dog playing with and worrying the chain he cannot break.

This begins to look like a problem which is rooted somewhere below the level of ordinary rational behavior. Lots of people dislike their old schools and schoolteachers. When they remember their school adventures, perhaps once or twice a year, they think: "Well, thank heaven that's over." But they do not go on and on having dreams about Public School 97, remembering what Frog-eyes said in P.S. 97 after the incident with the ink, writing poetry based on the slang of P.S. 97, becoming a dervish in order to wipe P.S. 97 out of their souls, going specially to live in Tierra del Fuego or the slums of Naples because these are the extreme reverse of P.S. 97, or planning new social systems in which there

will be nothing like P.S. 97 and all the schools will be
its 180° opposite. They just forget the whole thing. It
does not alter their way of living from day to day. But
to suffer such an extreme and powerful set of obsessions
as seems to afflict the bad or rebellious sons of certain
schools and colleges—that is a kind of spiritual illness.
Does it appear in any other form?

We have seen it in two forms: the pupil revolts against
the good teacher, the student rebels against the ancient
school. Now, are these not minor variations of a much
more difficult and fundamental conflict, the revolt of the
son against the father? Surely it would be wrong to discuss them without also discussing the many cases in
which a boy, well brought up by a wise and good father,
has wasted his life in trying to bring disgrace on himself
and his family, trying hard and repeatedly, again and
again committing actions which are perfectly ridiculous
in themselves and can be explained only as expressions
of the wish to belittle his father and destroy him. That
also is a problem of education. It is not the most serious,
but it is certainly the most painful, because it is one of
the hardest to understand.

If it were only revolt against authority, it would be
simple. All the young hate authority. They feel it as tyr-
anny. If it actually is tyrannical, they often take action
to escape it. If the father is a proud cruel domineering
man who believes his son should be his slave or his carbon copy, his son will either become slavish and imitative, or else break out violently, kick over the traces,
leave home, knock the stick out of the father's hand and
thrash him with it. Such a father deserves what he gets.

But the sad cases are much more complex and difficult.
In these, the father is not cruel and tyrannous. He is
gentle and considerate. He does not try to impose his
will on his son. He tries to guide him, rather than to
drive him. He wants his son to be happy and successful
—not necessarily in the same line as himself, but in any
line the boy can usefully follow. When there is a conflict
of wills, the father does not always win. Often he wins

only half the arguments. More often there are no real conflicts, above the surface. The family atmosphere is not tense with constant dueling. Usually it is calm and reasonable, and, from the outside, charming. And yet now and then such a family has a son who, apparently without provocation, without even a semblance of reason, chooses to make a career of thwarting and disgracing his parents. That becomes his aim in life. Other young men may go wrong because they cannot get accustomed to hard work or monotonous duty, because they like women or gambling. This youth has no such simple guiding principle. He merely wanders through life wrecking his prospects and himself. The débris looks as ridiculous and pathetic as a chapel or a schoolroom after a gang of naughty children has invaded it, breaking up the seats, throwing ink at the walls, turning everything movable upside down, and staining everything else. The wreck appears to have no design whatever. But it has. It has a purpose. And the apparently random, unreasonable, and even unenjoyable aberrations of the young man are not meant to shape a life for himself, but to wreck his father's life, or the life which he shares with his father. Usually the boy does not understand what is happening to him. The father almost never does. They both suffer, that is all. Their talents and their lives are wasted.

Shakespeare, who thought a great deal about the relations of fathers and children, makes this problem the subject of several of his best plays. He shows us a father who, with vast dexterity and energy, has won himself a great position. The father loves his son, and hopes that he will share the rewards and responsibilities of power. The son is talented and charming, brave and energetic. It would be easy, one would think, and pleasant for him to join his father. There is no compulsion. He can do whatever he likes. He may sit at home playing shove-ha'penny if he chooses; or hunt all week during the season; or waste time harmlessly in other ways. But he chooses to become a gangster. He is only an amateur, but he is on the fringe of the professional crooks. His best friend is a broken-down old ruffian who has drunk almost all his gifts away and is living by the remainder of his wits. He sees far more of Falstaff than he does of his father, King Henry IV. He makes Falstaff into a sort of substitute father, laughing with him as he cannot with his father, tricking and befooling him as he would like to belittle his father. As the play goes on, it is harder and harder to understand what is wrong with Hal. Why should he throw away his chances? Why does he want to hurt his father? He *says* he is doing it so that he can get more praise for reforming later; but that is not the real reason, and it never comes up after his reform takes place. The real reason appears when his father is in genuine danger and when Hal himself is challenged by a rival of his own age. Then he rushes to help the king's cause, and kills his challenger, Hotspur. Immediately afterwards, when his father is gravely ill, Hal goes in to see him, finds him unconscious, and—as though he were already dead—picks up his crown and puts it on. That is what he could not do before. That is what he has always wanted. In default of that, he has done the extreme opposite. In order to *be* something, he has had to be something totally unlike his father: for he could not be his father while his father was still alive. The moment King Henry IV dies, Hal becomes king. He is a model king, strong, chivalrous, wise, energetic. And he rejects Falstaff, his substitute father, the false staff he had used to prop him for a while: doing so with such coldness and cruelty that the old man dies of it. Now both Hal's fathers are dead, and he can be himself.

Yet we are left to feel that he might never have reformed. If his father had lived another ten or fifteen years, if no war emergency had arisen, would Hal have broken with his bad life and his dissolute companions? Would he not have been in danger of becoming a perpetual wastrel? He would have grown older, more set in his silly protest, until it grew into an end in itself enjoyable for its own sake. Or, even worse, he might have decided to make the protest more pointed, to do something which would hurt his father more grievously, over-throw him or destroy him. *Henry IV* and *Henry V* are happy plays. But often in life this conflict ends tragically. After these dramas, Shakespeare wrote *Hamlet* and *King Lear*.

* * *

We have suggested, then, that the revolt of some pupils against good teachers and of some students against good schools rises from the same conflict which is expressed in the revolt of some sons against good fathers. If so, it is a permanent conflict, rooted very deep in the human soul. Freud, who named it the Œdipus complex, de-scribed it as based on the sexual competition between son and father for the undivided love of the mother-wife. But it looks as though Freud had, here as elsewhere, exaggerated the importance and pervasiveness of sexual drives. Many subtle observers of the human soul have traced the same conflict between sons and fathers (or father-substitutes such as teachers) without discovering any sexual basis for it. Some, like Shakespeare, have seen the conflict sometimes as emphatically sexual (in *Hamlet*) and sometimes as quite divorced from sex (in *Henry IV*). Certainly in the revolt of pupils against schools and teachers there are some sexual overtones, but the main emphasis is elsewhere.

Although we have tried to describe the conflict, it is still difficult to understand. And it is terribly hard to see it as a frequent, almost inevitable conflict in which nei-ther side is to blame. We see only the grieving father; we can scarcely spare a glance for the son. We read of the painful death of Seneca, and spurn Nero as a monster. Jesus was betrayed and executed. Who thinks of Judas except with hatred? Yet the clash is a disaster in which both sides lose. If we are to understand it, we must be sorry for both. Jesus was crucified, and the world weeps at his agony. But we should spare a tear for Judas, mad with remorse and hopeless regret, hanging alone on a tree in the field of blood.

If the conflict is no one's fault, what causes it? Is it merely a misfortune for the father and son, as when the boy is born blind? Does it strike by chance, like death in a traffic accident? Or is it regular but governed by laws still undiscovered, like the incidence of Mongoloid births? Or are both father and son, teacher and pupil, partly responsible?

We do not know. Psychologists have their hypotheses, but none of them has yet been accepted as a law. Teachers can only guess, and their guesses are irregular and unreliable. In fact, there are some eminent teachers who have had loyal pupils and disloyal children. Parents never know. There are some fathers who have had four or five sons, all of whom turned out well, and one other who, with the same treatment, turned out a coward, a liar, a traitor, a sponger, anything that would hurt most. They have done their best with all. They cannot see why they failed with only one. No one knows. All we can do at present is to try to understand what goes on in the mind of the rebellious pupil and the bad son.

He is trying to be himself. He does not know what that is. Like all the young, he has hardly any idea of his own powers and weaknesses. His spiritual growth is even more mysterious to him than his physical development, and far more erratic. He feels as though he were driving a car very fast, without knowing which are the brakes, where the steering-wheel is, and whether the road-signs are telling the truth. He knows he must keep going, but he does not know where. He knows he must grow, but into what?

Now, if he has an unusually good and admirable father, or a teacher who seems to have no weaknesses, he is led to believe that he must follow his father or his teacher. He must copy them in everything. He must try to *become* them. Yet he feels that if he does so, he will have lost something, he will not be himself. And he also feels that he *cannot* become them, because they are so much better. The boy of eighteen cannot reproduce the calm wisdom and self-control of the man of forty-five.

The hot young emperor can never be as poised as an elderly Stoic. Therefore, rather than be a weak and inferior copy, he decides to be a bold original. My father is king? Good. Rather than be an imitation kinglet, I shall be king of the rascals, monarch of the underworld. Some Christian theologians say that the first sin ever committed was the same action, when the creature rebelled against the creator, when the prince of angels made himself the king of devils, saying:

> Better to reign in hell than serve in heaven.

But usually the revolt is less systematic. The young man wanders about doing disgraceful things with the maximum of publicity, so that they will make him as real as his father and as important. Meanwhile, he wastes his substance. Sometimes he kills himself, or undertakes a symbolic suicide. Even then he is both punishing himself for being unworthy and killing the image of his father.

In this conflict, as in all conflicts between father and son, or between teacher and pupil, more weight of responsibility rests on the father and the teacher. He knows more, and can plan better. But it is very hard for them both.

One method of minimizing the conflict is for him to allow his son, or pupil, to differ from him. He should encourage him to differ. He should suggest new paths along which the boy can move freely without treading in his father's footsteps. Even then there will be a danger. The boy may be torn between the desire to be his father's image and the need to be something different. It is the father's duty to try to help the two parts of his son's personality to harmonize and grow together.

Another method, which is even more difficult, is to diminish the distance between father and son, and to make the boy understand that achievement is quite possible. Tell him the mistakes you made. Describe your early struggles and conflicts, not as titanic battles which only a superman could have won, but as anxious skirmishes similar to his own. If you beat him hollow in some areas of competition, allow him to beat you in others, and praise his wins. When he emerges successfully from some trial you have never faced, make much of it and show him how it has strengthened him. It is awful for a young man to feel his father or teacher has no human weaknesses. To show him yours will actually help him in conquering his own.

This conflict is not altogether suffering and loss. Its other aspect is growth. For a conflict challenges both parties to show the best in them. The pupil who questions and criticizes every statement made by his teacher learns far more than the nestling who absorbs everything with a gaping mouth. The son who knows that it will be difficult to rival his father will, if he thinks he can succeed, put out energies he never knew he could command. Therefore the wise father and the good teacher will challenge their sons and pupils to equal them, and help them, where it is wise, to differ and even to excel. The best proof of the educational genius of the Jesuits is that many of their best pupils were not Jesuits. The best proof of Plato's genius as a teacher is that Aristotle worked with him for twenty years, and then founded a mighty school of his own, based partly on his criticisms and refutations of Platonic doctrine. The aim of good teaching is summed up in Aristotle's own remark about these differences: "Though both truth and Plato are dear to me, it is right to prefer truth."

*　　*　　*

We have mentioned some of the most famous teachers of the ancient world. There were hundreds and thousands more. Even to name them would fill this page, and to describe their work would fill books. The world of Greece and Rome was a world of vast power and wealth, but it was also pre-eminently a world in which things of the mind meant much. Its long tradition of culture was built up, developed, and transmitted by admirable teachers.

When the barbarians flooded in, when the social structure of western Europe and north Africa collapsed, the broad river of education dwindled to a thin trickle. Among the ruined cities and the débris of schools and libraries, filtering on precariously from monastery to monastery, it made its way through the Dark Ages, emerged into the light with Charlemagne, and then, slowly, from the year 1000 or so, began to spread again, and grow deeper and wider, and fertilize the neglected territories of the mind, many of them silted over with new deposits of tough virgin soil. But although in the Middle Ages there were many great individual teachers, the technique of education was still far behind that of the Greeks and Romans: teaching was slow and cumbrous, learning was difficult and rare.

A new group of great teachers appeared in the schoolmasters of the Renaissance. All over western Europe from about 1450 onwards, there sprang up new schools founded and staffed by enthusiastic believers in the civilizing powers of education. They were outstandingly successful, when judged by the hardest and the safest test—the pupils they produced. In Italy, in France, in England, hundreds of splendid names shine out during the next century or so, all or nearly all of them owing their inspiration and much of their knowledge to good teachers. All sorts of books on education were written, translations of Euclid and manuals of horsemanship, guides to teach people how to pray and guides to teach them how to become social successes, manuals of geography and handbooks of speechmaking. From Poland to Spain, from Scotland to Sicily, eager students looked for men who could teach them how to read, to talk, to think, to know, to act, to live.

Some of the greatest writers of the time wrote vividly interesting stories, plays, and meditations about the processes of education. In Shakespeare's *Henry IV* we watch Hal getting a peculiar, but evidently necessary, kind of princely education. In *The Tempest* Prospero is a teacher, who has educated his daughter and then educates his future son-in-law. He too has had a Nero-like failure. One of the villains of the play is his bad pupil Caliban, whose temperament was too brutish to be trained, and who turns against his master with the savage words:

> You taught me language, and my profit on't
> Is, I know how to curse.

Rabelais's *Gargantua* begins, after the birth of the giant child, with a careful description of the bad education which nearly ruined him by teaching him only to misuse his talents, and of the good education that made him a super-prince; it ends with a description of an ideal school for young men and women, the Abbey of Thelema, where they did what they should do because they wanted to (Thelema means "Will"), not because they were compelled. Rabelais's *Pantagruel* takes another giant prince through an equally careful education, in which he visits all the French universities and spends a long time in the University of Paris. His chief courtier, Panurge, although he is a joker like Rabelais himself, is also a scholar like Rabelais himself: he speaks German, Italian, English, Basque, Dutch, Spanish, old Danish, Hebrew, Greek, Latin, and three nonsense languages with bewildering fluency. (Rabelais makes us feel in these chapters that it is actually *fun* to know a great deal fluently, just as it is fun to be able to climb a rock chimney or break 80 on a golf-course.) Montaigne's *Essays* are the by-products of his own self-education. After spending twenty years as a soldier and diplomat, he retired and set to work to complete his character. He did this not merely by analyzing his own mind, which is usually as sterile a task as taking your own pulse and blood-pressure every hour, but by reading a huge list of great books, discussing their contents with himself, and applying their teachings wherever he could. As he wrote down his discussions, they became his "attempts" or essays at finding out the truth. They are road-maps of his own explorations. As part of his self-education he wrote three or four essays on the teaching of children, describing his own and offering suggestions drawn from it; they are still valuable documents. But the most valuable thing for us in his whole life is to see how a very carefully planned, varied, and stimulating education, applied to a French boy who was nothing out of the ordinary, equipped him to be the founder of a revived branch of literature, encouraged him to continue the enlargement and refinement of his mind throughout his life, and made him what Sainte-Beuve called "the wisest of all Frenchmen."

These are only a handful of the noble educational books written in the Renaissance, when western Europe was re-educating itself. Why they interest us here is because they show that education was not thought of as a matter for children and their teachers, but as a process which continued active throughout life. The best kind of education is that in which the young are taught something they continue to use and to learn and to appreciate all through their lives.

The subjects taught in the Renaissance do not concern us in this study. The methods of teaching do. Their success is proved not only by the men and women they produced but by the enthusiasm with which most of their pupils speak of them.

The first point is that teaching began early. Children were sent to school almost straight from their mother's knee, and from school they went on to college four or five years earlier than we do. You may say that this simply means that they were still doing high-school subjects although they were called university students, but that is not really true. They did learn more, earlier, and more concentratedly than we do. When the child went to school it was not given colored blocks to play with and supervised in bodily co-ordination (*Subsection 4—Skipping the Rope*). It was given a copy of the alphabet and taught how to read and write. It began to learn foreign languages and to study the Bible soon after it could read. Shakespeare, who got an average small-town middle-class education, began Latin about the age of seven. Milton (who became a schoolmaster himself after being forced out of politics) was put into Latin by his father at seven and into Greek at nine. Queen Elizabeth, Ariosto, Erasmus, Luther, Lope de Vega, Galileo—almost any distinguished figure you can think of in that great age started learning very early, and had a richly equipped mind by the time adolescence started. (One of the exceptions is St. Ignatius Loyola, founder of the Jesuits, who was a brave but ignorant soldier when he was converted; one of his chief trials was the humiliation of putting himself to school at the age of twenty-five or thirty to learn ordinary subjects among a group of children.)

Next, the subjects were more limited in number, so that the energies of the pupils were not dissipated. But, at the same time, teaching was not rigidly departmentalized, as it tends to be nowadays. In our schools the boys and girls study French, say, from ten to eleven, and history from eleven to twelve. In Renaissance schools, if there was a master who taught French, he would not treat the language as a "subject" in itself. He would talk about French manners and customs (i.e., "sociology"), history, geography, literature, and anything else he felt important. Instead of teaching "French," he would teach France. This throws a great deal on the teacher. It means he must be a man of wide culture. It means he must be creatively interested in everything about his "subject" and be ready to discuss it. But teachers can do this. Again and again the men of the Renaissance praise their schoolmasters as "universal minds," "eloquent as Cicero, wise as Socrates," "fountains and treasure-houses of knowledge." By these affectionate exaggerations they mean that, when they were young, they admired the completeness and versatility of their teachers rather than their accurate but limited knowledge of one speciality. They would have said that a teacher who knows *only* biology or *only* French is not fit to teach at all.

This leads naturally to the third point, which is that the better teachers used very little compulsion. Yes, there was a good deal of flogging and driving and loud-roaring brutality in inferior schools. Montaigne complains bitterly about it. But he never says he experienced it himself, and he, like all other writers discussing education in the Renaissance, says it is inexcusably bad and ought to be abolished. The good schools, the successful teachers, used none of it. What did they use instead? How did they get the young to study difficult subjects? First of all, we are told, largely because they themselves loved the subjects so much and talked so interestingly about them that their pupils were fascinated. Nowadays we should think that the analysis of a complex and obscure passage of Greek lyric poetry was a serious but rather tough and effortful theme. Yet teachers like Jean Dorat did it in such a way that their pupils called them "magicians," spoke of "gathering up every word like jewels," said their hearers begged them to go on and on, as though bewitched by their charm and vitality. Interest of this kind, when implanted by good teachers, always lasts all through the lifetime of the pupil.

Perhaps it follows from this that they were not very accurate. Sketchy, sometimes. Bold and inventive, very often. Wrong, badly wrong, often enough to surprise us. They did not attach so much importance to being literal and correct and supported by evidence as we have done since the early nineteenth century. The spirit of Scientific Method had not yet emerged from the test-tube. There were very few indexes, lexicons, reference books, and other such aids. In the excitement of discovering books that had been lost for a thousand years, and translating and explaining them in their own languages for the first time in history, the teachers sometimes forgot about accuracy, as a gang of gold-miners forget about preserving the beauty of the landscape when they start burrowing into a vein. Shakespeare is full of allusions to Greek myths which he read, or heard about, in school. Sometimes he gets them wrong, and often he alters them with nonchalant freedom—yet he uses them in such a way as to show that he loved them. Important translations were made at tremendous speed, by inexperienced young men with a fluent style and a lively imagination: Chapman prided himself on finishing half the *Iliad* in less than four months. Prominent teachers committed blunders which shock us as our own ignorance of psychology will shock the men of 2350 A.D. Poets like Spenser boasted of knowing books which they had never read, and stole their quotations from intermediate authors. But on the whole they knew far more about literature than we do, because they were taught in school that it was interesting and shown how to discover its interest. There is a dichotomy here. Scholarship must be accurate, whether it is interesting or not. But teaching must be interesting, even if it is not one hundred per cent accurate.

Lastly, the best Renaissance teachers, instead of beating their pupils, spurred them on by a number of appeals to the play-principle. They emphasized the fact that learning is a pleasure. Vittorino da Feltre called his immensely successful school Jollity House, *La Casa Giocosa*. They encouraged the boys to compete with one another, rewarding the winner with prizes and praises. They invented difficult tasks, challenging their best boys to complete them. They wrote plays for the boys to act. (These were sometimes very nearly literature. The first full-length comedy ever written in English was *Ralph Roister Doister*, an adaptation of a Greco-Roman comedy made by Master Udall of Eton College and acted by his boys. A good deal of the English drama of the Renaissance developed from school plays.) They made games out of the chore of learning difficult subjects—Montaigne's father, for instance, started him on Greek by writing the letters and the easiest words on playing-cards and inventing a game to play with them; and others taught mathematics in the same way. All these methods, when applied by strong and charming personalities, made the process of learning perfectly delightful. The most famous teachers of the Renaissance are spoken of by their pupils with sincere enthusiasm, admiration, and love, as benefactors of humanity and as personal friends.

It was their work which prepared and advanced that noble age in the history of Western man, an age which, although its general level was lower, produced far more great men and far finer works of art than our own.

*   *   *

Next in the line of famous teachers, the Jesuits. I have already praised Jesuit education so much that it must be obvious I am not a Jesuit myself, or even a Roman Catholic. The Jesuits themselves would not make the mistake of heaping praise on their own system. They are too good psychologists. They know that the effect might be to turn people against it; and indeed I hope I have not done so, for it is an admirable system. Or, perhaps it was an admirable system until the Order was dissolved by the Pope in 1773. Since it was re-established in 1814, it does not seem to have done so well or to have produced quite such brilliant results.

The best thing about its methods was the thoroughness with which they were planned. Planning is not a merit in itself. Many an outrageously bad school has been run like clockwork. But it helps to avoid some deadly faults which schools often contract. It keeps the pupils and their masters from wasting time. Wasted time is not free time, it is not recreation and rest. Usually it is a week, or a month, or a term, or a year in which neither the teacher nor the pupils really know what they are doing. They are working on some subject they have already done, in a boringly similar form; or they are filling in until June comes round, so as to start afresh next year; or they are taking some examination for the second year in succession in default of any other goal to aim at. The educators who drew up the Jesuit Plan of Studies arranged the entire schooling of their pupils as a continuous career, with plenty of free time but no duplication or waste.

As well as avoiding waste, planning gives the young an unusual sense of purpose. They know where they are going, whereas very often in less systematic schools the boys feel they are shunted from one class to another like cattle in the loading-pens. It is terrible to feel chained when young, but it is painful and humiliating to feel one's life is meaningless and purposeless, or, in the old Scots phrase, "like a knotless thread." The Jesuit regulations made sure that the pupils realized what they were doing, and why. It is noticeable that very many of their pupils have turned out to be men of very strong will-power and long vision. A good modern example is the Irishman who spent seven years on writing a book about the events of a single day, and then spent seventeen more on writing about the dreams of a single night. You may not admire *Ulysses* and *Finnegans Wake,* but they are monuments of æsthetic planning and perseverance, and it was the Jesuits who taught Joyce how to make such plans.

Still, planning and purpose can be very inhuman. They can stifle independence and originality. Sometimes they are admired because they do just that. The Jesuits avoided this fault by their insistence on the complementary principle: adaptation. Again and again and again they repeat that pupils differ, classes differ, ages differ, and that the teacher's duty is to teach, not an abstraction, but the particular collection of boys he has in front of him. To begin with, he must allow for their youth. He is accustomed to learning and to using his mind: they are not. Remembering this, he will adapt his teaching to their age. In a vivid image, Father Jouvancy says that the mind of a schoolboy is like a narrow-necked bottle. It takes in plenty of learning in little drops, but any large quantity you try to pour in spills over and is wasted. Patience, patience, patience.

Then the teacher will adapt his teaching to different classes, and treat different pupils differently. To do this he must be a good psychologist. The boys look pretty much the same. He must detect the real character concealed by their appearance. In another vivid image (notice how the Jesuits teach in pictures), Father Possevino says they are like salt, sugar, flour, and chalk, which all look pretty much alike and which have vastly different natures and uses. Having discovered the different capacities of his pupils, the teacher will—as far as possible within the plan—adapt his teaching to their differences.

The Jesuits went to unparalleled lengths and showed unbelievable patience in adapting themselves to the people they had determined to teach. For instance, they sent out a small expedition of ten or twelve priests to Christianize four hundred million Chinese. This almost impossible task they started by studying China. It was an empire, ruled from the top by comparatively few men. Good. If the few men could be converted, the rest would, in due course, follow. Now, how could the few men be converted, the emperor, the courtiers, and the mandarins? Not as a Dominican priest with Pizarro had tried to convert the ruler of Peru, by giving him the Bible untranslated, but by approaching them through something they already admired. What did they admire? What interested them most? Chinese culture—philosophy, art, literature; and science—particularly astronomy and geography. Good. The Jesuits therefore spent several years learning Chinese philosophy, art, and literature, making ready to meet the Chinese on their own level. After the imperial officials had, slowly, reluctantly, admitted them, the Jesuits at once flattered them by talking to them in their own tongue, and attracted them by displaying specially prepared maps and astronomical instruments. Instead of being rejected as foreign barbarians, they were accepted as intelligent and cultivated men. One of them, who became a painter in the Chinese style, is now regarded as one of the classical artists of China.

The next stage, which they approached very, very delicately, was to make the mandarins willing to learn from them. They did this by discussing astronomy with the Chinese scientists, constructing maps of the world with the place-names shown in Chinese characters and the Chinese empire at the center, presenting sun-dials and astronomical instruments to the high officials whom they met, and ultimately by assisting the Imperial Board of

Rites to correct its calendar so as to forecast eclipses and calculate celestial phenomena more accurately than any Chinese had ever been able to do. Their intention was to move forward again, with both Jesuitical and Oriental patience, to discussing more fundamental problems of science and philosophy with the rulers of that vast and sluggish empire. You see, they had reached the point at which conversion could—very, very gradually—begin. The stars; the laws that govern the movements of the stars; the nature of God as creator and lawgiver of the universe; God's relation to the inhabitants of this planet . . . it would all have followed in due time, gently, slowly, but unhesitatingly, and it might well have succeeded. The failure of the Jesuits in this magnificently ambitious enterprise was caused by opposition within the church and by dynastic changes in China, and not by any failure in their educational powers of adaptation and penetration.

Planning and adaptability were two of the pillars of Jesuit education. The third, equally important, was the high standard of the books which were studied, and, consequently, of the achievement demanded from their pupils. The Jesuit schools were established largely to counteract the Protestant Reformation, and their founders went on the excellent principle that they would do this best by producing Catholics who were not only devout but brilliant. To do this, they must teach them the most exacting and most rewarding subjects, superlatively well. They worked out, therefore, a curriculum of the finest things in classical literature, on the assumption that "we needs must love the highest when we see it." This book is not concerned with the subject-matter of education, but here the form and the material are virtually impossible to distinguish, for, as the Jesuits themselves said, they used the classics as "hooks to catch souls."

The success of Jesuit education is proved by its graduates. It produced, first, a long list of wise and learned Jesuit preachers, writers, philosophers, and scientists. Yet if it had bred nothing but Jesuits it would be less important. Its value is that it proved the worth of its own principles by developing a large number of widely different men of vast talent: Corneille the tragedian, Descartes the philosopher and mathematician, Bossuet and Bourdaloue the orators, Molière the comedian, d'Urfé the romantic novelist, Montesquieu the political philosopher, Voltaire the philosopher and critic, who although he is regarded by the Jesuits as a bad pupil is still not an unworthy representative of their ability to train gifted minds. The Company of Jesus has many enemies, but none of them has ever said that it did not know how to teach.

* * *

In the nineteenth century there were several revolutions in education. The most important was the introduction, in certain western European countries, in certain American republics, in some of the British dominions, and in Japan, of universal education. For the first time in fifteen hundred years the majority of people in such countries became able to read and write. Most of the townsfolk and city people in the Greco-Roman civilization, and numbers of the farmers, had been literate, as we know from the wide distribution of literature and the many inscriptions put up all over the empire. But illiteracy came in with the barbarians, and settled down for centuries. It was almost universal in the Dark Ages. It was widespread in the Middle Ages, as we can see from shop-signs and coats of arms. If your soldiers cannot read, you put up a shield azure with three roses gules upon it, to tell them their master's name and descent. If your customers cannot read, it is useless to put up a sign saying PAWNBROKER: you hang out three golden balls, borrowed from the coat of arms of the Medici bankers. Then in the Renaissance reading became commoner, especially after printing was discovered by the Western nations; but literate people remained in the minority. In the modern world, it is only since about 1870 that the majority of the citizens of civilized countries have been able to read and write. But most of the world's population is still illiterate.

However, we are talking here of the Western nations. In them and in their dependencies the movement for universal education covered the nineteenth and early twentieth centuries. It grew constantly. It succeeded. It has been a noble and peaceful revolution. Although its effects are too vast to be clearly defined at this stage, an obvious one was that it filled the Western countries with schools and colleges. Places which were only villages in 1820 had become good-sized cities by 1920, and provided big schools and elaborate school-systems for their young citizens. Boards and Ministries of Education spread their control over entire nations.

We might expect to find the nineteenth and early twentieth centuries a time of wonderful teachers: pioneers, enthusiasts, apostles. But they were not. Certainly there were many distinguished teachers, and certainly a great deal of hard work was done in education. But relatively there was more poor teaching, there were more bad and hateful teachers, than at any time since the Middle Ages. Many causes contributed to produce this depressing fact. Partly it was the result of the grim quasi-religious moral attitude of the early nineteenth century, which thought that important subjects could only be treated in a deadly serious way, which admired the discipline of floggings and harsh examinations as a preparation for life, and which believed the aim of education to be the collection of large masses of useful facts, as the aim of life was the collection of large masses of stocks, bonds, and landed properties. Partly it was created by the mistaken parallel between science and the other subjects which are part of education. This misled A. E. Housman, although a sensitive poet and critic, into spending his life lecturing about beautiful Latin poetry without ever, except occasionally under protest, mentioning the fact that it was beautiful poetry. And it misguided thousands of teachers into meeting every class and discussing every subject with the same expression of icy detachment as a surgeon conducting a major operation. There are several other reasons, social as well as cultural, which we cannot discuss here. But the fact remains that in the nineteenth century more complaints, in proportion, came from intelligent and interested men about the bad teaching which had hurt their minds and characters at school than ever before. Run-of-the-mill teachers increased in numbers, probably not in proportion. Bad teachers rapidly multiplied, and almost wrecked several important subjects by teaching them repulsively. Good teachers were fewer than we should expect, or hope.

Remember, this does not mean good scholars. For scientific discovery, in medicine, astronomy, geology, botany, chemistry, physics, it was an age of unparalleled achievement. For the exploration and refinement of other subjects—literary and historical criticism, sociology, history, ethnology, æsthetics—it was a time of wonderful industry and energy and organization. The men who made these discoveries and explorations were brilliant thinkers, powerful and capacious minds. But often they were not good teachers.

Sometimes they were actually afraid of their pupils. Gauss the mathematician hated teaching, and told each individual student who enrolled that his course would in all probability not be given at all. More often they were out of touch with the young. They themselves were constantly pushing forward into unexplored territory, and saw everything behind them as uninterestingly clear. They could not understand the elementary difficulties of their pupils, or realize that connections between distant areas of the subject, obvious and exciting to themselves were inconceivable for beginners. Helmholtz the physicist, for example, would not even answer his pupils' questions in the laboratory. When one of them asked him anything, "he would promise to think it over, and would bring in the answer several days later. Then it was so distant from the pupil's situation [because it was so broad and general] that the young man could hardly ever see any connexion." Lord Kelvin once recommended a manual of astronomy to his pupils, saying that they could easily get through it at fifty pages a day; and when he lectured he would sometimes let his subject run away with him until "his audience, understanding but little of what he was saying, were fain to content themselves with admiring the restless vivacity of his manner." Mommsen the historian did not commit this kind of error, for he prepared his lectures very carefully and accurately, but he seems to have discussed what interested him rather than what his hearers could assimilate, so that his lecture-room was half-empty long before the end of term.

*   *   *

Still, the nineteenth and early twentieth centuries did produce a number of great teachers, whom their pupils remembered with gratitude and honor. It is hard to describe them, scattered as they were through many countries and several generations. And since they did not form a compact group like the Jesuits and the Renaissance teachers, it is hard to pick out more than a few general characteristics which appeared in their work. But five or six are common to them all.

All their pupils agree that they were knife-sharp critics. Where the Renaissance educators had been bold and slapdash, where the Jesuits had been suave and encouraging, the teachers of this period were ruthless and sometimes cruel in their exposure of faults and flummeries. Jowett of Oxford, though not a first-rate scholar, raised the standards of Balliol College higher and higher by jabbing his little stings into the young men until they deflated and moved faster. Many of his remarks are still preserved. They don't seem very bright. Yet we know, from the accounts of those who suffered and profited, that they were effective. And, taken all together, they have a crisp astringent flavor which is still refreshing. For instance—

To the young idealist who said his life was a search

for the Holy Grail: "And what will you do with the Holy Grail when you find it, Mr. Bowen?"

To the young atheist who told him: "I cannot see any signs of God in nature, and when I look into my own heart I fail to find him there," Jowett's command: "You must either find him by tomorrow morning, or leave the College."

To the young thinker who declared it was his idea to dedicate his life to the pursuit of Truth: "You can get it up to £900 a year, perhaps, but no more than that."

Jowett's portrait still looks down from the walls of his college. An unpleasant little man, with a beady eye and a pursy mouth, like a blend of Queen Victoria and Mr. Tulkinghorn; but as you meet that bright little stare you still feel that it would be very difficult indeed to get past it with a second-rate piece of work. The Berlin philologist Wilamowitz-Moellendorff once received a first visit from a young student whom he did not know. The young student is now a world-famous scholar, but he still remembers the tall, powerful, commanding figure of Wilamowitz coming downstairs at eight a.m. and opening the conversation with the brisk question: "What are you reading?" No long speech could have so powerfully taught him the lesson that a scholar's duty is to keep reading, reading, reading.

Again, the historian Fustel de Coulanges, who spent the zenith of his career in the École Normale, refused to listen to any of his pupils' theories unless every step in the argument could be supported by documents to prove it. "Have you a text?" he would ask. If they had none, then their theories were merely guesses. In America the same function was performed by James Harvey Robinson, historian, philosopher, trainer of philosophical historians. He revolutionized the accepted idea that history could be learnt out of textbooks. They were only predigested material—previously digested, distorted, and weakened. Instead, he compelled his pupils to examine the original evidence as minutely as possible. A fourteenth-century charter, an eighteenth-century pamphlet, is worth more by itself than anything a twentieth-century expositor writes about it. His critical attitude was reflected both in his lively and informal seminar discussions (one of his pupils recalls little of their content, except that they gave him personally "an abiding interest in learning why people think as they do think") and in his brilliant lectures, delivered with what looked like cold detachment (he stood perfectly still, looking at the ceiling), but in fact filled with the keenest and gayest sallies of wit and paradox.

On a lower level there is Kipling's tribute to the master who taught him English and the classics. We have already questioned the wisdom of "King" in using bitter sarcasm, but his criticism when applied to literature was excellent. Kipling best remembered his way of teaching Horace. "I wish," he says, "I could have presented him as he blazed forth once on the great Cleopatra Ode. . . . I had detonated him by a very vile construe of the first few lines. Having slain me, he charged over my corpse and delivered an interpretation of the rest of the Ode unequalled for power and insight. . . . [He] taught me to loathe Horace for two years; to forget him for twenty, and then to love him for the rest of my days and through many sleepless nights."

From a modern French author, André Maurois, we have an even warmer tribute to the critical powers of the man who taught him philosophy at the Lycée de Rouen. This was Émile Chartier, who wrote eloquent essays under the pseudonym of Alain. Maurois still remembers his first lesson. A tall, vigorous young man walked in, looked at the class, and wrote on the board a sentence from Plato in Greek:

> We must go towards truth with our whole soul.

He made Maurois translate it. Then, leaving this on the board to occupy their eyes, he sat down and began a stimulating but difficult critique of the idea of perception. His teaching was a perpetual challenge. He would an-

nounce an incredible paradox as truth, and support it by
keen logical arguments. Then he would either break it
down himself by counter-arguments or make the boys
do so. Maurois says that next to his father he owes more to
his teacher Alain than to anyone in the world.

* * *

In spite of being such relentless critics, the good teachers of this period had another quality which ineffective
teachers, however brilliant as discoverers, lacked. It gave
them that power over their pupils which extended to all
kinds of young men and women, from different countries
and classes, and which continued to work long after they
were dead. It is difficult to describe. Indeed, many people,
after feeling it, have complained of being unable to describe it. It is still more difficult to acquire. It cannot be
taught at teachers' colleges, and not always developed by
meditation and practice. Yet it is invaluable for a successful teacher; it is the core of a successful man or woman.
Roughly speaking, it could be called largeness of heart.

It contains generosity and love of mankind. Poor teachers like Housman might have a soft heart and might be
very generous to a few chosen individuals, but they hated
—or, more probably, feared—the majority of the human
race. Others were so intensely absorbed in their own
work that they regarded the students as a cook regards
flies—hungry nuisances to be brushed away and kept
from interrupting the job in hand or polluting it with
their inquisitive feet. The good teachers liked most of
their pupils and most of the rest of the world, and
showed it. Some of them, like Osler, the Canadian who
was professor of medicine at Toronto, then at Johns
Hopkins, then at Oxford, were jolly high-spirited fellows,
always cracking jokes and bringing students out as the
sun brings out zinnias. Others were grave and almost
owlishly solemn, like Arnold of Rugby. One of his pupils wrote a famous educational novel, *Tom Brown's
Schooldays,* about Rugby as he ran it. Arnold is the least
real figure in Hughes's book. He appears as the dreadful

Doctor, a personage halfway between one's father and God, and it is never quite clear what he has actually been doing for the school. To get a true picture of Arnold one must read Hughes's eulogistic chapters, then Lytton Strachey's amusing caricature in *Eminent Victorians,* then his real life in the *Dictionary of National Biography,* then his biography and letters by A. F. Stanley, and lastly his son's idealization of him in *Rugby Chapel.* But all these in different ways convey the same impression, that Arnold loved his fellow-creatures, even when they were boys. Once when he was a young tutor, at Laleham, he scolded a slow learner. The boy looked up at him, saying: "Why do you speak angrily, sir?—indeed I am doing the best that I can." Arnold was deeply moved by this incident, and never forgot it. Thenceforward, even although austere, he was fundamentally kind.

Even a bad teacher can be made into a good teacher if he has this warmth. (Of course, it is also necessary to have a brain.) Some clever and unsystematic men have taught well almost in spite of themselves because they so liked their pupils. Often it is very difficult to find out, from reports of their work, how they managed to do it. Everything looks messy and self-contradictory and half-finished and unsatisfactory. The musician Leschetizky trained Paderewski and Schnabel and Brailowsky and many other remarkable pianists; yet he said himself: "I *have* no method and I *will have* no method," and a verbatim description of one of his lessons leaves no clear impression on us except charm, metaphors, cigar-smoke, and enthusiasm. Evidently he knew that art is partly spontaneous and must always retain the improviser's touch.

In philosophy the most notable teacher of this type was surely William James—or should we say *perhaps* William James? "In his classroom he was precisely what he was everywhere else—just as unorganized, just as stimulating and irresistibly charming." He found it impossible to make a long, sustained, orderly, authoritative speech and to unfold, stage by stage, argument by argument, proof by irresistible proof, a philosophical theory. He felt that any such speech would stiffen and cripple the essential flexibility of thought, and that any such theory must misrepresent the infinite complexities and novelties and inconsistencies of reality. It was wrong, he felt, to *tell* people things. He would rather add *if* and *maybe;* he interrupted himself to catch a fleeting suggestion and come back saying "What was I talking about?" He created objections to his own proposals, he preferred discussion to straight oratory, and he made jokes on the most solemn subjects, very much as life itself does. Once he read out Spencer's definition of evolution:

Evolution is an integration of matter and concomitant dissipation of motion; during which the matter passes from an indefinite, incoherent homogeneity to a definite, coherent heterogeneity.

And then he translated it:

Evolution is a change from a no-howish, untalkaboutable, all-alikeness to a somehowish and in general talkaboutable not-all-alikeness by continuous stick-togetherations and something-elsifications.

He even projected the grimmest problem of all, the problem of evil, with impish realism rather than professorial logic, by telling a class:

This universe will never be completely good as long as one being is unhappy, as long as one poor cockroach suffers the pangs of unrequited love.

And we can imagine what horror he aroused in Harvard by remarking: "God is certainly no gentleman." Yet everyone knew that through his naughtiest flippancies as through his most puzzling incoherences there pulsed the genuine warmth which comes from the heart of life.

This quality which we have called largeness of heart also involves energy, physical and psychical. Even when good teachers are thin dry ladies like Mrs. Angela Thirkell's Miss Bunting, or little wiry men like Vittorino da

Feltre, they have remarkable vitality. They do not flag, falter, miss on one cylinder. When they work by routine, they use the system as a sail, not as a hammock. Some really first-rate teachers who speak in a calm gentle voice appear for the first twenty minutes to be taking things very easily—until you transcribe what they say and endeavor to compress it, or until you have heard them complete a course on a difficult set of problems with the same effortless ease: you realize then that they have been drawing on underground reservoirs of vigor, which you have been sharing. Sometimes these energies are startlingly physical. Plato knew that, and he was a powerful fellow himself. At the end of the *Symposium,* early in the morning, he says only the host, Agathon the playwright, and the hard-drinking comedian Aristophanes were still awake—together with Socrates, who argued a literary and philosophical point with them until they too passed out. Socrates then covered them up where they lay, had a bath, and spent the next day as usual. Boissier the historian was a perfect dynamo. Even in old age he rose before six to prepare his daily lecture, gave it and attended the inevitable committees in the morning, read and wrote in the afternoon, and spent the evenings dining out and telling stories and making epigrams in his gay southern voice.

Some of the stories told about the teaching of Jesus look like descriptions of an energy which may be comparable. People used to crowd around him trying to touch him—which means they thought that if they could tap the current flowing through him, they would get new strength. And he himself felt the same thing, because once, when a sick woman touched his clothes without his knowing, she was cured; and he at once noticed that he had lost some energy. The traditional translation of his remark is: "Virtue has gone out of me," but what he really said was: "I felt power going out of me."

It is a strange thing, the energy of great teachers. We do not know much about it yet, and there is still a great deal to be found out. It seems not to be purely physical, or mainly physical, in origin. Comparatively frail people command it, and so do people who take very little thought for their health. But it undoubtedly can have physical expressions and effects. Another point about it is that it does not often seem to flourish, or even to exist, when its possessors are alone: meditating, writing, in prison, on journeys. It rises to its full force and seems to renew itself and refresh itself, as if it were powered by Niagara, when its possessor is surrounded by a number of other people—not a random crowd, as in a railway station, but people who are being taught by him, receiving something from him. Some of those who command it say that its strength depends largely not on themselves, but on the others, the men and women around, the listeners, the watchers, the pupils. Jesus himself was surprised that when he went back to Nazareth and taught there, most of the townsfolk did not believe in him; and that (it is implied) was why he was not able to do any deed "of power"—that is, any of the miracles he had performed among crowds elsewhere. Perhaps, therefore, this power will in future be explained as the spiritual energy, not of one individual, but of a group led and controlled by him, energy which he is able to canalize and use in ways that astonish them, and may even surprise him. Perhaps it will be seen as a parallel to the "inspiration" felt by a great orator when, after a struggle, he has dominated his audience and made himself its voice: he feels its energies pressing upon him for utterance like an inarticulate shout, to which he can give form and meaning.

As well as friendliness and vigor, the best nineteenth-century teachers had minds large enough to take in many different subjects and to relate them to their own lives. The specialists were often marvelous discoverers, but seldom good teachers. Their world narrowed with the growing intensity of their gaze. The teachers who had most influence usually worked in three or four fields at once and combined their professional duties with a vivid and active private and public life. As well as being a physician, Osler was an amateur of the classics, a bibliophile, and a host of other things. The research scholar can feed himself, but the teacher has to nourish many others: so he must draw his vigor from many different sources.

* * *

Much of the work done by these teachers was in guiding their advanced pupils through research in the laboratory and seminar. But here their methods differ widely, not only by subjects but by individuals: so that it is scarcely possible to discuss them under any common scheme. But they exercised an even wider influence by their lectures, and here we can easily distinguish and examine some characteristic methods.

Their styles of lecturing fall into two boldly different types. One was cold and dry. The other was warm and rich. One was like etching, the other was like painting. Both, when done by good teachers, were effective and memorable.

The first was the manner of the historian Fustel de Coulanges, the physicist Rutherford, and the philosopher Dewey. Fustel used to bring in a few books, carefully arranged to give him his illustrative quotations, and a short outline of his lecture. Then he spoke continuously, in a sharp penetrating voice, for an hour and a half, with no digressions, no relaxations, and no graces. Although it was a historical discussion, one of his pupils says it was really more like a mathematical demonstration (notice the influence of the scientific ideal), and Fustel himself was proud to write: "For twenty-five years, not one eloquent phrase has ever passed my lips." He meant "eloquent" in the sense of "showy" and "spellbinding." Yet he was always strikingly clear. Similarly Rutherford in speaking as in writing "used simple and direct English, combining clarity with power." He objected to the habit some scientists have of spending months on a piece of research and then grudging hours on putting it into understandable language; and once he told his friend Tweedsmuir that "he did not consider a discovery complete until it had been described in simple and correct English."

So again one of Dewey's pupils, the philosopher Irwin Edman, describes his lecturing technique in these words:

He sat at his desk, fumbling with a few crumpled yellow sheets and looking abstractedly out of the window. He spoke very slowly in a Vermont drawl. He looked both very kindly and very abstracted. He hardly seemed aware of the presence of a class. He took little pains to underline a phrase, or emphasize a point, or, so at first it seemed to me, to make any. . . . He seemed to be saying whatever came into his head next. . . . The end of the hour finally came and he simply stopped; it seemed to me that he might have stopped anywhere. But I soon found that it was my mind that had wandered, not John Dewey's. I began very soon to do what I had seldom done in college courses—to take notes. It was then a remarkable discovery to make . . . to find that what had seemed so casual, so rambling, so unexciting, was of an extraordinary coherence, texture, and brilliance. I had been listening not to the semi-theatrical repetition of a discourse many times made—a fairly accurate description of many academic lectures—I had been listening to a man actually *thinking* in the presence of a class.

Perhaps Professor Edman is too kind to his old teacher. Surely he cannot believe that Mr. Dewey thought his way through every problem from beginning to end in public, every time he gave his course of lectures. If so, he is paying a remarkable tribute to Mr. Dewey's histrionic powers, which although not semi-theatrical were evidently convincing. What he means is that, as Mr. Dewey spoke, his hearers were made to feel that he *had* thought his way through all these problems, with just the same patience and sincerity. What he was doing as he lectured was reporting the process step by step, and its results. He had noted down the steps and the results, it would seem, on the "crumpled yellow sheets" and was now retracing the journey.

But there is another description of Mr. Dewey's teaching which implies that he was not thinking out his problems during every lecture, but was rather trying to find words to express the results of his thought.

The difficulty of utterance in his lectures, like the tortuous style of his technical writings, results from over-conscientiousness. When he misses the right word he does not pick any one at hand and go on but stops talking until he finds the one he wants, and he is so anxious to avoid a misunderstanding that he sometimes fails to insure an understanding.

What his hearers admired most in this was intellectual honesty. Pupils sometimes distrust teachers who are never baffled. They like now and then to see a tutor puzzling over a problem, a lecturer groping for his words. Ralph Waldo Emerson knew this well. Even when he had his entire speech written out, he would scarcely seem to read it, but would contrive to make his hearers forget that he was delivering a rehearsed address. He would pause at complex thoughts as though to invite the audience's help in grasping and expressing them. Just before delivering his most dazzling epigrams (although they had been shaped long before and polished for days), he would hesitate—and make a visible effort—and then seem to catch at a fleeting idea just before it vanished, improvising brilliant words to hold it and solidify it—as though—with difficulty but with success—he were creating out of the very air a perfectly cut diamond.

However, the most effective lecturers in this, the etcher's manner, are those who give their pupils clear continuous undiluted thought, 100 proof. Logic, pure logic, has a sovereign power over young minds. T. H. Huxley, the biologist, thought the finest lectures he ever heard were given by Wharton Jones, whose career had been darkened by his connection with the body-snatchers Burke and Hare, but who, speaking without notes in a dry, even voice and never looking at the class, gave a perfectly luminous explanation of the most difficult physiological problems. This kind of lecturing may be called light without heat.

* * *

The other type of lecturing is warmer. It is eloquence. Eloquence needs logic. The lecture and the speech must have a well-built substructure of reason. But to it the eloquent lecturer adds other powers—a varied and attractive delivery, graceful and memorable phrases, striking illustrations, a personal relationship with the audience. Instead of merely exposing the truth for the pupils to assimilate, this type of lecturer offers it to them in such a way that they are encouraged, moved, captivated by it. T. H. Huxley, one of the finest lecturers of the nineteenth century, used this method. Characteristically, he was always nervous. He had miserable nervous indigestion for fifty years, and felt sick with anxiety even when entering the College of Surgeons, where his subject was familiar and his hearers sympathetic. His lectures were masterpieces of logical arrangement: for instance, when giving a course he began each lecture by recapitulating the points covered in the previous one; but they were dramatically set out. "He gave you in 50 minutes striking analyses of two or three phenomena in nature which did not seem quite cognate. He glanced at the clock, and in the remaining 10 minutes put them all together, showed their analogies, and left us with a sense that nature was 'not without a plan.'" All his pupils add that he was a brilliant sketcher, and drew while he was talking, "his rapid, dexterous strokes building up an organism in our minds, simultaneously through ear and eye."

Huxley's closest parallel in America was Louis Agassiz, the little Swiss who founded the teaching of zoology and geology at Harvard, and thence throughout the United States. Agassiz loved teaching; and he loved people. He would teach anyone: "a sailor on a fishing schooner or the captain of the *Hassler,* a legislator in Massachusetts or the president of Harvard University, the newsboys on the street or the young collegians in his parlor, the originator of the Concord grape or the professor at the Jardin des Plantes, all were equally fascinated by his words."

But he had two widely different methods of teaching. One was through lectures. Here he was nearly as eloquent as Huxley, and quite as vivid. (Like Huxley too, he was always nervous. He told Longfellow that before beginning a course he invariably felt "terrible fright.") Instead of talking in abstractions and generalities, he brought in specimens to describe. He would display a tank of shark embryos, or hand round a fossil, or give each of his hearers a grasshopper to hold and examine while he talked. When he could not show specimens, he would draw, vividly and beautifully, on the blackboard. For instance, when he described how an insect's egg changes into a larva, then into a pupa, and finally into a full-grown insect, he would draw the metamorphosis stage by stage on the board, "until suddenly the winged creature would appear as if it had burst from its chrysalis."

Agassiz's other method of teaching is better known. He used it, not like his lectures to instruct the general public, but to train professional scientists. A scientist, he thought, is first and foremost a man who sees things which other people miss. So he trained his laboratory pupils to see. One of them has left a fine account of this training.

I had assigned to me a small pine table with a rusty tin pan upon it. . . . When I sat me down before my tin pan, Agassiz brought me a small fish, placing it before me with the rather stern requirement that I should study it, but should on no account talk to anyone concerning it, nor read anything relating to fishes, until I had his permission so to do. To my inquiry "What shall I do?" he said in effect: "Find out what you can without damaging the specimen; when I think that you have done the work I will question you." In the course of an hour I thought I had compassed the fish; it was rather an unsavory object, giving forth the stench of old alcohol. . . . Many of the scales were loosened so that they fell off. It appeared to me to be a case of a summary report, which I was anxious to make and get on to the next stage of the business. But Agassiz, though always within call, concerned himself no further with me that day, nor the next, nor for a week.

At first, this neglect was distressing; but I saw that it was a game, for he was . . . covertly watching me. So I set my wits to work upon the thing, and in the course of a hundred hours or so thought I had done much—a hundred times as much as seemed possible at the start. I got interested in finding out how the scales went in series, their shape, the form and placement of the teeth, etc. Finally, I felt full of the subject and probably expressed it in my bearing; as for words about it then, there were none from my master except his cheery "Good morning." At length, on the seventh day, came the question "Well?" and my disgorge of learning to him as he sat on the edge of my table puffing his cigar. At the end of the hour's telling he swung off and away, saying "That is not right."

It was clear that he was playing a game with me to find if I were capable of doing hard, continuous work without the support of a teacher, and this stimulated me to labor. I went at the task anew, discarded my first notes, and in another week of ten hours a day labor I had results which astonished myself and satisfied him.

After this arduous assignment was over, Agassiz did not praise his pupil. At least, he did not emit words of admiration. Instead, he gave him a gallon tank full of bones and told him to see what he could do with them. The young man examined them, and found (from the jaws) that they came from a number of fish of different species. So he started to fit them together so as to reconstruct the skeletons. After two months or more, he succeeded. Once more Agassiz did not praise him, but gave him a more difficult task of observation and comparison. This was all the praise the pupil could expect, for it meant: "You are becoming a more competent scientist."

Admirable, this training. No one who had gone through it could ever forget that the scientist's duty is to observe; and no one who had been so arduously disciplined would fail to observe carefully. Another of Agassiz's boys was told to look at a grunt. A grunt is a small and unprepossessing fish, whose character is reflected in its name. But the boy looked at it for some hours, then began to draw it. Agassiz approved of this. "Good," he said; "a pencil is one of the best eyes." Yet Agassiz scolded him when he left something out of the drawing. It took him four days to see all that could be seen, just looking at the grunt.

This was the challenge of difficulty and intensity, which only the best teachers can use without remission. It can be applied in any field. We have seen it used by the eighteenth-century singing-master who kept his pupil on one page of exercises for years. It is often used as a selective process, to filter out unsuitable pupils. One of the most brutal apprenticeships I have ever heard of was endured by a Russian boy who took a machinist's course arranged in the German manner. On the first day (this was in the 1900's) he was given a chunk of steel and a couple of files and told to file the steel square. This took him a month—four hours a day, five days a week. When he had done that, he was given a hammer and a cold chisel and told to cut parallel grooves in the block of steel. This took a week, at the end of which his thumb was bloody from badly aimed hammer-blows. Then it was the file again; and then the chisel; and so it went for three months. "At the end of that time," he says now, "I felt on fairly familiar terms with a file and chisel." *
However, he is now a talented designer and adapter of machines. His scars have healed.

The same arduous type of challenge, without compulsion but with all its difficulty, was given to one of the most distinguished of American educators, Mr. Abraham Flexner. His adviser, Professor Morris of Johns Hopkins, told him that if he wanted to master Greek, he should get a compact little shelf of Greek books and read nothing but Greek for five years. "Read the daily papers to

* Reprinted by permission from an article by Robert Rice in *The New Yorker*.

keep up with the world," he said, "but don't read books in any other language. Read Greek only." The ambitious young student took this hard advice, and, like the pupils of Agassiz, he gazed at the intricate subject until he really felt at home in it. Just as they could take a new specimen and see a thousand things which would escape the untrained eye, so he could pick up a book (an immortal book, a permanently valuable book) in Greek, and read it through with ease and pleasure. Such efforts are painful; but without effort there is no reward.

*　　*　　*

Osler the pathologist was a teacher equal to Agassiz. He too insisted on vividness above all. Before he went to Johns Hopkins, American medical students studied textbooks and heard lectures, but were not shown how to connect theory and practice. Osler introduced the technique of teaching medicine by using the patients as texts. Instead of discussing an illness in theory, he explained it at the bedside of a man who was suffering from it. If he had not been so invariably kind and good-humored, perhaps this might have become a callous and cruel practice; but he inspired both patients and students with his own vitality. He specialized in equally vivid epigrams: a certain type of bloated crimson face he described as "the Bardolphian facies," the result of "worship at the shrines of Bacchus, of Venus, and of Circe," who turns men into beasts. I imagine that he was able to give this description with a grave expression and a twinkling eye while the Bardolphian patient stood by him uncomprehending and unoffended. And he would always make facts memorable by casting unexpected lights on them—for instance, when a pupil used the name Graves' Disease for exophthalmic goiter, Osler made him look up Graves and write a paper on his work.

*　　*　　*

It is not possible for us to survey the work of all the other fine teachers who worked during the nineteenth

and early twentieth centuries; nor would it be generous
to speak of those who are still active, as though their careers were over and done. But we may pick out a few
more of the greatest, to show the heights to which, in a
period suffering from far too many pedants and bores,
the best teaching rose.

These were all writers, and most of them brilliantly
original thinkers. Yet their work as teachers was an essential part of their careers, and it would be wrong to
estimate any of them by his books alone, without trying
to hear his voice. And the techniques they used in lecturing differed as broadly as their personal characters.

The first group strides to the front of the platform,
fixes the audience with a glittering eye, dominates it by
forceful gestures and the commanding tones of aristoc-
racy. Such was Kittredge, who taught English literature
at Harvard for nearly fifty years, from 1888 to 1936. Tech-
nically, his method was explanation of the text. He
would take a scene from one of Shakespeare's tragedies
and go over it word by word, analyzing the precise meaning of every speech, discussing the dramatic values of
every shift in the plot, bringing out new psychological
undertones, and setting the whole episode in its place
until his hearers, finally and unforgettably, understood
what the poet had written. But such detailed dissection
is not possible unless the class has already read the scene
and thought well over it: so Kittredge's pupils had heavy
assignments of preliminary reading to do, and could expect to be closely questioned on what they had read. His
class usually began with five minutes of queries ad-
dressed to him by the students, on points still obscure
from the previous lecture—a very sound practice for establishing the confidence necessary in continuing an
analysis of constantly increasing difficulty. Then Kittredge took over. Anyone present was liable to be called
on, and if he could not answer, Kittredge made no effort
to conceal his fury. He had a violent temper and an un-
disguised contempt for the average student. White-
bearded, cigar-puffing, loud-voiced, he commanded their

respect rather than attracted their affection. They laughed at him once when he strode too far and fell off his platform. He glared at them, and said: "This is the first time I have ever reduced myself to the level of my audience." If one never heard Kittredge, one finds it difficult to read of him without a certain antagonism. Nevertheless, that antagonism was one of the responses he wished to provoke. He intended to challenge his students with the difficulties of good literature, and to make them humble in the pursuit of greatness.

Such in Germany was Ulrich von Wilamowitz-Moellendorff, who taught Greek literature in the same spirit. As his name shows, half-German and half-Slavic, he came of a Junker family whose estates lay on the frontiers of Poland and Prussia. His *Recollections* opens with descriptions of the double world in which he was brought up, a few haughty squires dominating a mass of ignorant, dirty, and serflike peasants. To the end of his life he retained much of that confident air of authority, and it was surely symbolic that his career began in a violent conflict with Nietzsche, who was himself Polish by ancestry. His teaching, like his writing, had the ring of command; but that was part of its effectiveness. Even his lectures to the general public in Berlin were carefully prepared and always filled the hall.

* * *

Turn now—if you dare—from these dynamic teachers to the second type, the persuader and charmer. Whatever qualities join to make an actor admirable and a teacher lovable, this type unites. A beautiful voice; a distinguished, mobile face, reflecting the sensitive play of emotions in the speaker's mind; graceful gestures which do not seem like affectations but like expressions of the genuine wish to convey a thought or define a fancy; and an obviously sincere love of the subject, love of people, love of himself. His aim is not to challenge but to attract, not to oppose and outface but to give delight.

Such was the Cambridge don A. W. Verrall. He could

read Greek poetry, Latin poetry, and English poetry so sonorously and melodiously that new meanings emerged from every line. He could lecture for an hour with closed eyes, leading his students in pursuit of a result which they might have rejected as nonsense if they had met it abruptly face to face, but which, after a long and exciting hunt, they seized with an eagerness largely created by the charm of their delightful guide. Such also was Burckhardt, the Swiss historian of the art and culture of the Renaissance. His lectures were not prepared speeches, but rather the overflow into talk of a brimming love for painting, for poetry, for Italy, and for the warm centuries when modern man was still young and hopeful. So much loved were they that they were often encored, and he was compelled to repeat them on the same evening. Such in America was William Lyon Phelps of Yale. One of his pupils, who won the Nobel Prize for literature, called him the best teacher of literature in America, adding that he was also "a great actor." His character was so winning and the volume of his journalistic output so huge that observers sometimes thought him shallower than he was. But his teaching was based on very hard and careful preparation. During his first important course of lectures (on nineteenth-century poetry) he distributed guide-sheets which (a) gave full outlines of every lecture, (b) advised books to be read concurrently, and (c) invited written or spoken questions. That is the mark of a man who genuinely wants to teach, not merely to charm. At the height of his career he was reading and marking a hundred and fifty papers every week. He was an actor, but more than an actor: he was an interpreter.

*   *   *

Above both these complementary types stand a few men who were able, through the richness of their personality, to unite the virtues of both. If the others were great teachers, these were great men who happened to teach. They had no special technique. They simply communicated their greatness. The philosopher Henri Bergson is now, of course, known through his astonishing revaluation of our ideas of time and consciousness; but during his lifetime he was the most distinguished lecturer in France. His hall in the Collège de France was crowded by professional students of philosophy and literary men and fashionable Parisian ladies and visitors from abroad. He spoke without notes, slowly and musically, forming each sentence into a perfectly cadenced expression of his daring and subtle thought; the sentences grew into a planned whole, not an artificial structure but a living organism; and both speech and thought were marked by the personal imprint of genius.

Those who only know the bony face and toothy smile of Woodrow Wilson from old photographs and caricatures are apt to forget that he was really a tall, noble, and commanding man. When he rode through Rome beside King Victor Emmanuel of Italy, it was he and not the king who looked the true Cæsar. Those who only think of him as an idealistic President who failed are liable to forget that he was one of the greatest teachers of this century. Almost without exception, his pupils describe him as "the finest lecturer I have ever heard." His career began at Princeton University, where he taught jurisprudence and political economy. Dry subjects. Necessary, but repellent. Wilson spoke on them with such energy, such conviction, such wealth of ideas and warmth of words, that his students often broke into cheers at the end of a lecture—a phenomenal gesture which can only have been spontaneous. Long afterwards, when he had passed from the presidency of Princeton to the governorship of New Jersey and thence to the Presidency of the American Union, he became the teacher of the world. Yes, he failed. He was outmaneuvered, perhaps, by more cunning diplomats; or else he expected too much. Yet he taught the human race how to strive for the grandest ideal on the planet, the creation of universal peace. Perhaps such a lesson was too mighty to be learnt in a generation. Perhaps he was wrong in hoping for results too soon. But he was right in trying to teach it;

and when at last we learn it, one of the greatest of teachers will have his reward.

*   *   *

The last group of teachers to discuss is one of the most important and effective. However, it is not really a group, but a collection of individuals, hardly any of whom knows or cares anything about the others. It exists now. It is self-perpetuating. It is given far less credit than it earns. Usually it is forgotten altogether by the public and sometimes by its pupils. But its work has been invaluable, and ranks as teaching of the very finest type.

These teachers are the fathers of great men, who taught them much of what they needed to become great. The idea that a "genius" is a human being of a superior species who creates himself like a ghost materializing is a poor oversimplification. So is the opposite mistake that every eminent man is nothing but the product of his social environment, as brass is the product of zinc and copper, or diabetes the result of a pancreas deficiency. Individuals differ far more widely than their environments. All great men do a good deal of work on themselves. By their long exertion of will, their disregard of others, and their development of slowly maturing plans, certain existentialists would say that they really create themselves. And obviously their social life affects them very deeply. But the first influences upon them, which often create the most lasting impressions, are received from their own families. When the parents deliberately set out to teach them, these impressions are deeper and certainly more systematic. Many distinguished men were produced not only physically but also spiritually by their fathers.

For a woman the physical act of producing a child is a long, tremendous enterprise, which fills her (whether she likes it or not) with purpose and responsibility and vitality. For a man it is brief and, in feeling, almost purposeless. The rest of his share in the child's life before birth is auxiliary at best. But after it is born he can begin to share equally with the mother in helping it to live and learn. As it grows able to think and talk, he will share that job more and more, whether he knows it or not, whether he wants to or not. Large numbers of fathers do not know this, do not care, and hope it is not true. They try to live as though the child had never been born. They leave it to its mother, or to the schools, or to the other children. Sometimes they try completely ignoring it. Nearly always they refuse to adapt themselves to it when it brings in new ideas and lets loose new forces in their home. Yet by doing all that they are teaching the child just as carefully and emphatically as though they were concentrating on it several hours a day. They are giving it ideas, patterns of emotion and thought, standards on which to base future choices. A child cannot make up its own mind with nothing to work on. It has to see how people behave. For this, it watches other children, and people in the movies, and characters in books; but the people who bulk largest and whose acts have most authority, in the time when its formless mind is being shaped, are its mother and its father. Enormous in size, terrible in strength, unbelievably clever, all-seeing and all-knowing, frightful in anger, miraculously bountiful, unpredictable as a cyclone, cruel even in kindness, brave and impressive, mostly incomprehensible even when they speak, a child's mother and father are its original King and Queen, Ogre and Witch, Fairy and Giant, Mother-Goddess and Saviour-God. It obeys them and makes itself to suit them, it watches them to copy them, and, often without knowing it, it becomes them—or else it becomes an opposite of them in which their power is still expressed.

Whatever the father does, his child will learn from him. It is far better then for him to decide what to teach it, and how. As he does so, he will be giving up some part of his own personality, and some of his time and energy. But afterwards, when the results begin to show, he will be astonished to see that the sacrifice is repaid: his character (when he was perhaps becoming a little tired of its inadequacies) reappears with new strength and new originality in his child. Then he will really be able to say that he made it, and that he is its father.

It would be interesting to write a book on the fathers of great men: those who educated their sons by neglecting them, those who educated their sons by bullying and thwarting them, those who educated their sons by being their friends. These all taught their sons something about the world, for the world gives us all these treatments. It would be interesting, too, to write a book on the last of these three groups. It would not mention the fathers who taught their sons badly, like Chesterfield, and Cicero, and Pope Alexander VI (Borgia), and Coleridge. It would spend some time on those families in which many talents have been kept flowing through several generations, not only by heridity, but by the activity of successive fathers maintaining a tradition of excellence in their sons: the Bachs, the Medici, the Este, the Churchills, the Adamses, the Lowells, the Coelhos, the Montmorencys. It would study the psychological links between brilliant well-taught sons and their fathers, so often based on rivalry and conflict, acknowledged or unknown; sometimes built on genuine selfless affection and forming part of a rich happy family life; occasionally expressing the father's bitter frustration, which the son *must* grow up to compensate, to avenge. Here we can point out only a few of the fathers whose sons, through their teaching, became great and famous.

* * *

The first group looks at us, out of the picture-frames, with a steady, rather frowning gaze, firm lips, neat clothes, and an expression of cold competence. Their sons sometimes stand near them, looking much more like diminutive copies of their fathers than the independent geniuses we know from their own later portraits, wearing similar clothes, and ready to perform in the same way as their parent-teacher. These are the professional fathers who had talented sons and taught them their specialty. Out of a hundred thousand such families only one reaches eminence—but that is rather good odds compared with Nature's usual wild gamble in the game of birth and survival. Usually the fathers had no thought of training world-famous artists whom future generations must admire. They thought merely of giving their children a good living by starting them early in a profession; and sometimes of training an assistant who could take some of the work off their own shoulders.

A number of these fathers are musicians. For music is a language, and no one can be fluent in it, far less write works of art, unless he begins to learn it early. Mozart's father was a musician with a considerable reputation. Both his daughter and his little son took to music under his tuition so well that he also became their manager. He taught them so kindly and efficiently that the boy was writing sonatas at the age of seven and operas at the age of twelve, that he not only played the harpsichord exquisitely but toured Europe giving infant-prodigy concerts, that instead of becoming bored with the whole business (like so many child virtuosi) and composing facile but empty pieces, he continued throughout his life to write sweeter and richer and nobler music. Even in his hours of personal tragedy, it speaks with an angelic serenity that is a fine tribute to the father who taught him that art is an infallible consolation for the worst of life, and the very voice of the best.

Not all musical fathers formed the character of their sons so well. Beethoven's father was a brutal drunken beast. The boy had to go to the bars and pick him up when he was too drunk to get home, then to help him through the streets past the censorious looks of the other boys' parents, then to get him into the house and if possible dodge the kicks and slaps with which his father rewarded him. If Beethoven saw the world afterwards as a society in which life was possible only through tremendous exercise of will-power, if he admired heroes who rebelled against their powerful masters (Fidelio, Coriolanus, Prometheus), if his own manners were coarse and violent, and if he ruined his own and his adoptive son's life by giving the boy too much care and love, he learnt all this from the sot who shut him in the cellar when he was a boy and whom he had to rescue from the police when he was a young man. Still, his father did teach Beethoven music. He taught him to play the violin and the clavier beginning at four, and when at nine he could learn no more from his father, the man was wise enough to hand him on to better teachers; and he gave him much of the animal energy and drive which had been perverted and drowned in himself.

Bach was himself the grandson of a competent musician, and the brother and the cousin and the great-grandson. The Bachs had all been musicians for three generations or more. He was well taught himself by his elder brother, and he taught his own children very well. We still have a little book of progressively arranged first exercises that he wrote out for his son Wilhelm Friedemann, and another little clavier book he made for his young second wife. Of his twenty children, five became competent musicians, and three showed superior talent. You can see his interest in teaching coming out in several of his best works. For instance, the Forty-eight Preludes and Fugues, two each in every major and minor key throughout the twelve-note scale, are conceived and described as exercises to help musicians to grow familiar with all the possibilities of the new keyboard instrument. As he said himself, "I have had to work hard: anyone else who works as hard will get as far ahead." If Bach has a fault, it is occasional dryness and solemnity. Therefore he had one son who was a wonderful improviser and ruined his life with drink.

One could go through the other professions in the same way, noticing that the chief interest of professional fathers is not to build character but to build technique. This is one of the main reasons for what is sometimes called "the instability of genius." Many an artistic father will teach his son how to plan a quartet, but not how to control his expenses; how to choose words, but not how to avoid drugs. One peculiar example of this we have already met. Alexander the Great was an amazingly fine soldier and statesman. By the age of twenty-five he had mastered complex problems of supply and tactics, conquest and administration, propaganda and morale, which taken separately would need years to study. This was because he was his father's pupil. King Philip of Macedonia came of an astute and ruthless family, which had climbed to power among the north Greek highland clans over the bodies of many opponents. Philip learned "the hard way" how to divide his enemies and lie to them, when to attack them and when to make peace with them and when to invite them to a conference, how to keep an army in good training when it was not fighting, how to study the opponent's tactics and outthink him, where to get money and how to spend it, what to do and what to delegate. The young prince rode with him, fought under him, became his aide and his lieutenant and leader of his best troops, heard him explain his problems and argued about them, even, in defense of his mother, quarreled with him. Alexander's achievement was improbable enough. It would have been impossible without his father's teaching. But Philip also taught him his personal failings, cruelty and debauchery and vanity, a brutal streak which we sometimes see in the horns Alexander wears when he is pictured as a god. Aristotle, his other teacher, tried to counteract it but could not quite outweigh his father's influence.

*　　*　　*

The second group of fathers who taught their sons are quite different from these competent technicians. We do not know their faces as we know the faces of Bach or the elder Mozart. They do not appear in portraits with their sons. They are neglected in biographies. Quite often they would have been well content with this, for they were happy men whose life was its own reward. They are the fathers who taught their sons well because they them-

selves were overflowing with ideas. With no idea of
training their sons to any special profession, they simply
wanted to share with them the wisdom and beauty
achieved by the human race. They enjoyed culture themselves. They would not deny it to their sons any more
than a passionate Alpinist would forbid his son to climb
hills. Sometimes we see them saying to the boy: "I missed
this happiness until I was about thirty, because nobody
told me of it. Let me show it to you." Sometimes they
tried terribly hard to teach their sons one set of lessons,
which the boys rejected; and yet the lessons which the
boys finally learnt were also learnt indirectly from their
fathers. There is a fine biography which shows the beginnings of this, Edmund Gosse's *Father and Son*. Gosse was
the only child of a rather staid and elderly Victorian couple who belonged to a very pious, very limited religious
sect. But they were charming people, who loved each
other and their son very dearly. The mother was a writer
in a small way. The father was a biologist, whose profession was to study, describe, and teach the public about
the animal life of England, and particularly the fish and
shellfish of the coastal waters. The two parents made
little Gosse completely a part of their lives. He was even
inducted into their tiny church at an age which would
have been impossible for other children, because he had
learnt so much about its doctrines. He really lived almost
wholly on their level. There is a delicious account of
how he went to a children's party where the other boys
and girls recited *Casabianca* and similar "sweet stanzas."
When he was asked if he could say any poetry, he stepped
out quite cheerfully and began a passage of stern baroque
moralization from one of the devout works his family
admired. It was Blair's elegy *The Grave*. Off went Gosse,
aged twelve:

> If death were nothing, and nought after death,—
> If when men died at once they ceased to be,—
> Returning to the barren womb of Nothing
> Whence first they sprung, then might the debauchee . . .

At this point his hostess said: "Thank you, dear, that will do. We won't ask you to repeat any more," and, to Gosse's inexpressible surprise, stopped his recitation.

Now, what Gosse's father tried to teach him was (a) the religious beliefs of the Plymouth Brethren, and (b) marine biology. The boy drew hundreds of specimens for his father, and colored them with the bold simple tints of a primitive or a scientist; he even discovered a new species of mollusk. In his book he describes with great delight the long hours he spent with his father looking into the rocky pools of the Cornish coast and learning the habits and appearance of tiny but beautiful creatures living in a different element from ours. You will note, though, that in spite of the grim limitations of the family's life, literature was taken very seriously. The mother wrote; all read—not trash, but good though stodgy books; and the father had once, before giving up "profane things," known and loved even better literature. Gosse tells how once his father, hearing him at his first Latin lessons, took down his own favorite Vergil and read a few lines—their melody was so exquisite, even without meaning, that they enchanted the boy: he learnt them off by heart for sheer delight. As Gosse grew up, he went through the usual struggle to free himself of his father's influence—more severe in his case because they loved each other genuinely. After a painful break, he became something his father could scarcely have guessed, and would not have approved: the leading literary critic in England, a dandy, and a snob. Yet he was a complete personality. The best and the worst in him flowed from his father's teaching. His industrious habits, his refinement of taste, his eager sincerity, his admiration for beauty, his love for literature itself were his father's lessons; his worldliness and distrust of religion and epicureanism were reverse products of his father's teaching. Proust could have written an amusing page comparing, in one single sentence as fluid and iridescent as those seaweed fringes through which the biologist's apprentice once conducted his minute safaris, the bright crowded rooms of his home, bustling with visitors, whether familiar neighbors or bewildered strangers washed up by the tide of success, to the rich pools in which he had once entertained and examined his favorite curiosities; the poets and prosateurs whom, after discovering, he explained, with equal enthusiasm whether they were small, obscure, and difficult like shy rock insects or large, opulent, and insubstantial as anemones and nautili, to the biological specimens collected by his father and himself through many an exciting morning and drawn and colored as brightly as life through many a laborious evening; and the formidably large output of books which he poured out through his critical career to the illustrated catalogues of fauna which his father, with scientific completeness, filled up year after year, rather than to the bolder, more cohesive work of a constructive critic of literature.

In spite of Gosse's tribute to his father, their relationship was rather sad. A much gayer one was that between Robert Browning and his father. Obviously his father taught him an energetic attack on life's problems; gaiety and optimism; versatility; open-mindedness; much else. But in a fine little poem written when he was about seventy-five he crystallizes all his debts into gratitude to his father for teaching him Greek—and poetry in general. When he was five, he says, he saw his father reading and asked him what he was reading about. Looking up from his Homer, his father said: "The siege of Troy." "What's a siege?" said the little boy, "and what is Troy?" Now, at this point most fathers would reply: "Troy is a city in Asia, now run off and play with your train." Browning's father was different. He leapt up and began to build Troy, there in the living-room. He built a city of tables and chairs. On top he put an armchair for a throne and popped little Robert into it. "There now," he said, "that's Troy, and you're King Priam, and let me see, here's Helen of Troy, beautiful and sleek," and he pointed to the cat beneath the footstool. "Outside, you know the two big dogs in the yard, always trying to get in and catch Helen? They are the fighting kings, Agamemnon and Menelaus, and they are making a siege of Troy so as to capture Helen." And so he told the child as much of the story as could interest him, in just the terms he could understand. Sometimes I laugh when I read the poem, and think of the boy's delight and astonishment at his cheerful energetic father jumping up and slamming the book and piling an armchair on top of a table and popping him into the chair—like a magician in a fairy-story, changing him into a king and the familiar room into a city with a siege. Browning goes on to say that later, when he was seven or eight, his father gave him a translation of the *Iliad* to read, encouraging him (as soon as he could) to start it in Greek. And he judges his father a wise teacher for giving him not only an amusement for a day but a possession for all his lifetime, and choosing the right stimulus for each age in his growth.

Tennyson's father was a less happy and successful man. We hear that he taught his son carefully but badly. He made him learn off by heart all the lyric poems of Horace, in Latin, with all their complex meters and difficult ideas. The result was exactly the same as was produced on Byron ("Then farewell, Horace—whom I hated so, Not for thy faults, but mine"), on Swinburne, on Kipling, and on many others. It was a ridiculous and cruel "overdose." None but a great poet like Horace could have retained any appeal after it wore off. Years later Tennyson said that, although it was the wrong system, he was grateful for knowing Horace—the poet whose subtle art of word-placing and high sense of duty are often like his own.

Making the boy learn his poems *by heart* was the mistake. At most that might have been made tolerable as a game with other boys: not all alone. Pitt, the statesman who organized the resistance to Napoleon, was well educated by his father, who got him to translate passages from the great orators of the past, aloud, and at sight. That was not done as a task, however. It was done as a competition, a display in which his father was both trainer, rival, and audience. It was to his training that his friends attributed those amazing powers of oratory which he developed so early, which contained such a wealth of vivid imagery and powerful phrases, and which astonished, delighted, overpowered even his most durable opponents. That was not only a training in languages: it was a training in oratory, in the command of ideas, in greatess of soul.

* * *

I wonder how much the word "heredity" really means. Physically it probably means a lot. Mentally and spiritually, what do we inherit? Does it make any sense to say "Your son has inherited your knack of handling machines" or "Your daughter inherits your love of sports"? Is it not truer to say "You have taught your son to handle machines" by constant example, stimulation, and practice, and "You have taught your girl to love sports" by praising her golf-swing and giving her a new tennis racket for her birthday and chatting to her about games and taking her to matches? Do we use the words "inherit" and "heredity" to cover up our feeling that parents ought to think very carefully about how and what to teach their children, although most of them do not? Do we wish to imply that it will be all right without planning, that what we wish our children to learn will get into them somehow, through their pores perhaps? If so, we are wrong. We know that the world is full of people who are unhappy because they are vague and confused. Yet we often miss the priceless chance of teaching our own children something sure and reliable. The commonest answer to this charge is that we don't know ourselves what is sure and reliable. But that is not true. By the time we have reached the age of thirty-five or forty, and our children are becoming old enough to be taught the difficult questions, we have found answers which satisfy us as a working basis. Good. Let us teach them to our children. They will criticize them, attack them, and discard them, for a time at least. Good. We have done our duty. We have given them a basis to work on for themselves. They can come back to it, or find something better. They can accuse us of teaching them wrongly (although usually not of deliberately cheating them), and of trying to thrust our opinions down their throats (however gently we teach them, they will say that); but they cannot say we neglected them, wasting forty years of our own experience and fifteen years of their lives. Juvenile courts and mental homes are full of youngsters who were taught nothing useful by their fathers and mothers. It is not that they were badly brought up. They were not really brought up at all. They were never told how to behave. School meant practically nothing to them. The other children whom they knew were equally ignorant. The movies taught them that life meant excitement and daring. Their fathers never told the boys how to control their powers and arrange their lives. Their mothers told the girls nothing about the real pleasures and satisfactions of life. Nothing. When we look at the pouched and bestial face of such a boy or girl, ruined at seventeen, and instinctively feel that he or she looks worse than a savage, we are right. A Sudanese tribesman, a Jivaro Indian, a Borneo highlander trains his children far more purposefully and far more successfully than many fathers in the mightiest cities of the civilized world.

V

Teaching in Everyday Life

W̲ᴇ ᴀʟʟ teach and learn, all our lives. What I have
been saying about fathers as teachers, at the end of the
last chapter, is only about the few whose sons became
great men. But every father and mother do an astonishing amount of teaching. Their lessons cover the entire
universe, from "Where is God?" to the use of soap, and
have a lifetime effect. Thirty years from now, an eminent
politician will be surlily refusing an important invitation
because his parents did not teach him table manners, and
a playwright will be going to sleep with veronal and wak-
ing up with benzedrine because his family encouraged
him in bad sleep habits. The disciplinary kind of parental
teaching is tiresome to do, although necessary. But there
is another kind which is so interesting and exciting that
it is hard to see why anyone misses it or cuts it down.
Children ask thousands of questions, because their world
is all new, all strange and bright. If they ask at the wrong
time, when we are fishing out the laundry or trying to
get them to sleep, they should—no, they should not be
shut up, they should be told: "Ask me again, at break-
fast-time, will you?" When they ask at the right time,
they should always be answered. It is hateful to hear a
little boy in a train asking, as he looks out of the window: "What makes the wires go up and down?" and receiving a reply which would be downright rude from one
grown-up to another, and is anyhow stupid and stupe-
fying for a child. "Never mind" and "Don't bother me
now" and "Sthespeedofthtrain." What good is that? It
merely makes him (a) decide that all grown-ups are
stuffy and ill-tempered and unable to enjoy wonderful

things, (b) become a little less hopeful about understanding the world, slower, a little stupider, less interested in learning, (c) draw a little away from his parents, so that the family group feels more strain and has less of the easy communal life which is natural to it. Of course it is difficult to answer all their questions. It is impossible to answer some of them completely. But an answer should be given, if only to keep them interested in learning and friendly to their parents, for that is what all children are naturally, and anything else is a distortion. When they ask "Where does the rain come from?" tell them. If you don't know, tell them that too, and promise to find out. It is hard for them to think you know everything. It is good for them to think you like learning: that you find the world a place to enjoy, and not a mere factory to work in.

Fathers and mothers might do a great deal more talking about central subjects, when the children get older. Boys and girls in their teens are sometimes very distant, hard to talk to. But if you talk to them about the subjects which worry them, like war and money and love, or the subjects which they foresee will worry them, like getting a job and holding it and getting married, they ask very sharp questions and talk without any sign of boredom. Not enough fathers talk to their sons about their own jobs. Many a boy finds out with astonishment that his father holds a post which is important and interesting, and about which the two have never exchanged a sentence. Or he learns too late that he could have profited from his father's experience in a career he thought quite unconnected with his own.

And in general the relation between parents and children is essentially based on teaching. Many of us forget this. Some think it is based on Love, others on control. But you can give a child as much love as it can absorb and still make it an idiot unfit to face the world; while the best and surest way to control your children is to explain the rules you intend to enforce. And there is a great quantity of learning which can never be acquired

outside the home, unless the family is abolished altogether and twenty-four-hour-a-day schools are set up. It is
ridiculous that schools should be asked to teach children
how to brush their teeth, or save money, or organize
their personal lives. Parents can, if they try, do all that
more wisely and effectively than any school-teacher.
Long afterwards the children will remember such teaching and see that it has become part of themselves.

* * *

Husbands and wives also teach each other and learn
from each other. Many of the angers and sorrows of married life arise because they forget this. A wife sees her
husband making a fool of himself with his pay. She has
her own ideas about how it should be spent. Usually she
sets out to break his will and impose her own will upon
him. The obvious results follow. Either he resists, and
breaks hers; or he yields, and hates her for dominating
him; or there is a fifteen-round draw, leading to a continuous series of grudge-fights. A husband finds his wife
lazy and untidy. Usually he complains, and then shouts.
Either she resists, and makes a point of being lazier; or
she yields under protest, and rapidly and reluctantly
clears up the house they both live in; or the result is another draw in which neither is satisfied. Yet, looked at
from outside, one of the two is more right than the other,
and instead of being a trial of will-power the problem
should be one of persuasion and education. Every young
husband and wife can realize, when they think, that they
are not equally competent in all subjects; but uncountable quarrels break out because one of them is unwilling
to acknowledge his or her inadequacy and learn from the
other. In this book we are looking at the art of teaching,
but it is hard to teach if the pupil is unwilling to learn.
Men, we can still learn, even from our wives. Ladies, . . .

* * *

Looking about, we find that there are a great many re-
lationships in ordinary life that depend on teaching and

learning. For instance, a well-run office always has an efficient manager. And the efficient manager always spends most of his energy explaining what he knows should be done and persuading people to do it. So many efficiency systems have broken down because they were based on the assumption that people could be used like machine parts. But when the people, instead of being treated as "hands" or "units" or "bodies" or even "personnel," were told what they were doing and why—*sincerely*—they worked efficiently. Foremen, secretaries, shop-stewards, production-managers, department heads, all these essential persons have been taught, and have learnt, and are teaching others. One good sergeant is worth fifteen men, because he can teach the fifteen men with him so well that their effectiveness doubles.

Doctors can cure people by chemical and surgical interference, but they can only keep them well by teaching them. After correcting the throat condition, they say "You must cut down on your smoking. You must avoid abrupt changes of temperature. You must be careful about sources of infection." That is teaching. Not every doctor does it well. Often it is done by authority without persuasion, the worst method of teaching. That is why modern medicine is so efficient in curing diseases and sometimes so inadequate in averting them. That is why the legend has grown up that doctors are willing to stop illnesses, but not unwilling to see them start. Or perhaps the recent shift in proportion has deceived us, and they have merely been concentrating more upon the more urgent problem, which is to stop diseases; and now they are going to turn to the preliminary job of educating their patients not to catch diseases. More and more we are beginning to see how the mind affects the body and can make it ill or well. A man does not simply "contract" stomach ulcers as a car "contracts" a smashed fender. He gives them to himself by eating and digesting wrongly. He cannot be prohibited from making these blunders. He can be frightened; or he can be taught. The good doctor will teach him what mistakes he has been making, why they are mistakes, and how to avoid them. There are still some people who will continue to make the mistakes even after that, just as there are people who will smash up their cars by passing on a turn, although they have learnt the traffic rules; but these types suffer from a deeper psychological illness, which the ordinary doctor cannot cure. The ordinary man will accept the lessons, and learn.

The ordinary doctor cannot minister to a mind diseased. The specialists who can are the psychiatrists. And they are essentially teachers. To begin with, they did not think of themselves as teachers. They thought of their job as analogous to that of the chemist who analyzes an obscure substance, slowly and patiently, until he has measured all its components, discovered the cause of their interactions, and explained its peculiar powers, instabilities, opacities, and resistances. They hoped that once their patients saw the hidden components of their minds exposed, they would become able to conquer the weaknesses from which they had suffered. But experience has proved this to be wrong. The psychiatrist's patient usually does not sincerely thank him for the exposure of his hidden weaknesses, but proceeds to build up another set of concealments to preserve them. Analysis is only half the doctor's job in these cases. The other half is teaching. After finding the weaknesses, he must start a process of education designed to complete and correct the education which his patient's father and mother bungled. Because of her mother's cruelty, a girl is convinced that no man will ever love her normally, that she can never marry and have a home like her mother. This conviction, which she may never put into words, makes her behave strangely, foolishly, badly. If she goes to a psychiatrist, his first duty is to find out why she is misbehaving. With patience, he will discover the conviction, which she may have hidden away by "forgetting" or obscuring it. But he must then start to substitute a new and healthy conviction for it, explaining to her that she is an ordinary girl, that her chances are as good as those of all her friends, that the world is full of normal healthy marriages, and so on, gently and patiently for many hours. If he effects a real cure, he will have done it by discovering the faults in her education and teaching her to correct them. He will be like the orthopedic surgeon who gets a patient with distorted muscles, diagnoses the cause of the distortion, and then prescribes and supervises a set of exercises to correct it. The teaching is as important as the analysis.

Clergymen and priests have something of the same responsibility. Their congregations see them as friends and as fellow-workers, and listen to their teaching in the form of sermons; but it is when something really goes wrong that they are called upon for help. The help they give is largely in the form of teaching. Guidance, it is called, and consolation. A great deal of it consists in talking over problems which have always existed, but which some sudden crisis has made urgent. An only son is killed, a husband deserts his wife, a woman is told she has only a year to live. The sufferers ask "Why?" They ask "What am I to do?" They ask "How can I bear this?" Sometimes they make violent threats which they themselves know to be wrong, which they want someone to overcome by persuasion. A minister of God can do a great deal by merely being there. Company is sympathy. (After Job had lost all his sons and daughters, his friends came to comfort him. What they said is in the Book of Job; but their best consolation was given before they spoke, when they sat down with him upon the ground seven days and seven nights, in silence.) But after silent sympathy has done all it can, consolation still has to be given in words. If these words are to have any permanent effect, they must have some content. What content can they have, except advice, explanation, teaching? The Christian church has been best in those periods when it took its mission of teaching most seriously, and its priests still show their noblest side when they teach us how to bear what must be borne.

In public life, on a larger but shallower scale, there are

many men who use the techniques of teaching although they may not think of themselves as teachers. Advertising men have grasped some of these essential methods more firmly than many professional educators:

(1) *Make it vivid:* every package has a symbolic design, every poster has a picture.

(2) *Make it memorable:* the name of the product must be clear, crisp, and attractive, easily pronounced and remembered; slogans must be devised to cling to the slippery mind of the public.

(3) *Make it relevant:* this is the advertiser's chief difficulty, for how on earth can he persuade millions of people that their lives will be improved if they use one kind of toothpaste rather than another? However, he solves it, partly by association (Toothpastium supports a favorite radio comedian, and so it is attractive; Soapium always has a picture of a girl with a pretty smile, in bridal dress), and partly by persuasion in double-talk, heavily controlled by the Pure Food and Drug Laws (Cleanium contains that New Magic ingredient, Cleano, which 1,589 doctors say makes every one of your 32 teeth Cleaner.)

However debased—and however lucrative—this is still teaching.

Commercial advertising is only one branch of a large activity which is growing larger all the time. In politics this is called propaganda. (The word, by the way, means "spreading," and comes from the name of one of the Roman Catholic church central committees, De Propaganda Fide, for the Spreading of the Faith.) It is a mistake to believe this new. Nearly all states and statesmen have always been trying to get the people to support their policies: the only exceptions are a few of the secret-police oligarchies, like Venice and Sparta. The only thing that is new about it is the scale on which it can now be done, because of the invention of printing and of instantaneous communication over distances, and the introduction of universal education and adult suffrage. And I believe in the long run we shall find that the difference in scale has not made any important difference in kind. It seems to me that the Reform Bill agitation of 1831-2 in Britain and the abolitionist propaganda of the fifties in America stirred these nations more deeply than equally important causes which have been more heavily propagandized in recent times. In our own lifetime we have seen a number of propaganda lines, after being heavily plugged and widely accepted, fade away into nothing— for instance, the idea that world wars were fomented by private armament firms. Yet on its highest level political propaganda is a very honorable, necessary, and useful form of statesmanship. We believe, and others profess, that good government is built on the consent of the governed. The governed cannot consent fully to any course of action unless they know what it is. It is therefore the duty of every good government to tell them what is being done for them and in their name. They may refuse their consent because they do not understand it. If so, the government will explain more fully and simply. They may withhold consent because they do not approve. If so, the government will try to persuade them more convincingly. And this is where the distinction between explaining the truth and embroidering it begins to fade away. A government easily assures itself that if it tells a lie, it does so to bring about a great truth; if it conceals a fact, it is doing so for tactical reasons only; if it distorts the whole nation's view of history, it is acting in the service of the people rather than for its own self-perpetuation.

Is there any hope, then? Must all governments corrupt themselves and then the people they govern? Is all political propaganda bound to teach lies and to encourage lying?

The answer is *Yes, unless*— Yes, certainly, if only one group holds power and permits no opposition or contradiction. Yes, unless every government's tendency to lie itself into success is checked by the criticism of its opponents. Yes, unless the governors realize their responsibility to their people. The wisest of the Greeks used to say that a politician was bound to be a teacher. He is not, they thought, merely bossing the people, but educating them as he goes along. By each law he sponsors, he encourages them to behave in a certain way—to be saving or extravagant, to be brave or cowardly, dutiful or irresponsible. By the general trend of his policies he makes the people shape their lives in one direction rather than another. It is his duty, therefore, to choose such policies as will make the people develop good qualities rather than bad ones. If a statesman, however powerful, leaves the nation more silly and lazy and vicious than he found it, then, Plato says, he has been a bad statesman. If that is true, the real danger of political propaganda is that it is a powerful instrument which stupid and irresponsible men may use; and the best check on it is the intelligent distrust of the citizens.

*   *   *

The Communists in Russia have recently been attempting an ambitious scheme of political teaching, by taking prisoners of war and training them in Communist principles. At the time this is written, one batch of Japanese soldiers has been returned to Japan after indoctrination, and an entire German army under General von Paulus is reported to be learning Communism in preparation for its return to Germany. It is too early to tell how effective this teaching will be, and indeed it is too early to write anything very definite about Communist systems of teaching. But since we ourselves attempted to teach democratic principles to war prisoners and have made endeavors to teach them to Germans and Japanese in the occupied territories, it will be worth while to look at a few of the methods the Communists use.

First, patience. They have plenty of time. They are apparently resolved not to release healthy prisoners until they have converted them to Communism, or gone part of the way by imbuing them with Communist habits of thought. From the prisoners' point of view, this acts as a strong incentive to learn. It is the same fact that makes boys learn more at a boarding-school than at a day-school: they have nowhere else to go, and fewer things to do. And if you know that a rigid refusal ever to listen to a single Communist lecture will keep you in prison until you are decrepit or dead, while willingness to listen might get you released, you are very apt to go to the lectures.

Second, planning. As far as we can see, the education of the prisoners in Marxist theory has been carefully worked out, adapted to the different intelligence levels of the troops, built up slowly, piece by piece, and designed to produce a completely finished article. It would be possible to teach democratic principles in the same way, but only, perhaps if its teachers felt democracy was a difficult and revolutionary idea. Most of us think it is the most natural and easy way to live. Most of us admire it because we feel it does not go with careful planning and the production of special types of men, but rather allows for free improvisation and the relatively unchecked growth of character. Perhaps it will only be in countries where democracy has been overthrown and has to be re-created, or where it is so gravely threatened that all its supporters are really aware of all it means, that it will be formulated as a compact set of doctrines and taught by plan.

Third, completeness. The theory of Communism claims to provide answers to all problems. It offers standards for judging art, religion, morals, literature, history, science, politics, and of course economics. It is not a set of economic plans, but a world in itself. Now, if a complex of theories so complete as this is taught to any audience for long enough, it will impress them by its coherence and completeness whether it is true or not. The less highly educated they are, the more this will impress them. Those who are quite impervious to it will be those who have a larger or richer set of answers in their own minds, and those who have another equally coherent body of doctrine to which they are already attached. Both the Germans and the Japanese had such a doctrine, but their defeat made it seem far weaker and less reliable. Prisoners from a victorious German army could never have been taught anything. The men who were beaten at Stalingrad must ask "Why?" The Communists offer a complete answer. The completeness of the answer is of course very greatly helped by lack of competition in the prison-camps. If the men, after hearing a lecturer explain that Hitler was the tool of the German capitalists, were to march back to barracks and hear another lecturer explain the falsity of this opinion, they would take years and years to make up their minds. But the Communist lecturers apparently have no organized criticism to combat. And the questions and objections of their audiences actually help their propaganda when they come, as they usually will, at random. For an experienced Communist lecturer is always ready with an orthodox answer, true or false. In debate, with free access to facts and impartial citation of evidence on both sides, he is often at a difficulty. Against only the puzzled questions of homesick soldiers who almost *want* to accept any positive teaching, he is well armed and confident.

Such evidence as we have seen about this educational plan shows that force is not used on the majority of the pupils. We do not know what would happen to a strong Japanese nationalist and emperor-worshipper who organized opposition to all the lectures, though we can guess; but the average Communist pupil is not even threatened; he is persuaded. The chief difficulty Communists have had to face since 1917 has been the enormous discrepancy between their theories and the real facts. We shall see in the next ten or fifteen years how the prisoners sent back by Russia as converted will assimilate the shock of the discrepancy. It depends on how well they were taught.

* * *

Like politicians, authors and artists are teachers, because they persuade their public. There are a number of reasons which make this difficult to believe at first hearing. For instance, how can it be applied to music? Do artists not merely copy what they see? Do they not merely make decorative patterns? Is a novelist not supposed to tell the truth rather than to persuade? Does propaganda not spoil any art it invades?

Yet to these and other objections there are good answers. For instance: music appeals to the emotions and can strengthen or weaken our control of them; painters do not copy what they see, but select very carefully, and the elements which they choose to select carry a meaning, all the more powerful for being sometimes irrational; novelists usually claim to be telling the strict truth, but that means one set of truths out of the million million possible sets; and therefore that one set, told vividly, acquires a special power of persuasion; and propaganda does not necessarily spoil art, or else all the medieval cathedrals, from their † shape to the stained-glass pictures in their windows, would be bad art, and so would Dante's *Comedy,* Tolstoy's *War and Peace,* Shelley's *Prometheus Unbound,* Beethoven's Ninth Symphony, and many another mighty work of imagination.

But every artist knows in his heart that he is saying something to the public. He does not want merely to say it well. He hopes that it is something which has not been said before. He hopes the public will listen and understand, either at once or, at worst, after his death. That is, he wants to teach them something and he wants them to learn from him. What visual artists like painters want to teach is easy to make out but difficult to explain. They can hardly ever explain themselves, because they put their experiences into shapes and colors, not words. Basically, they seem to feel that a certain selection of shapes and colors, out of the countless billion possible, is exceptionally interesting for them and worth showing to us. But for their work, we should never have noticed these shapes and colors, or felt the delight brought by them to the artist. Most artists have taken their shapes and colors from the world of nature and from human bodies in motion or repose; from animals, buildings, food, and furniture. They mean that these aspects of the world are worth looking at, that they contain beautiful sights. Contemporary artists would say that there was nothing more in it, that they merely choose subjects that provide an interesting pattern. But they do not choose entirely without reference to the character of the things they paint. If one painter chooses to paint a gangrenous leg and another to paint a lake in moonlight, each of them, as well as showing us shapes and colors, is directing our attention to a certain aspect of the world. He is telling us something, he is showing something, he is emphasizing something: which means that (often unconsciously) he is trying to teach us. When Piet Mondrian spends his life on constructing pictures made purely of straight lines and rectangles of color, he is (a) making interesting patterns in the same way as a designer of carpets and pottery, and (b) saying that a certain world of pure mathematical shapes is more valuable, for him at least, than the world of people, animals, and nature. It is possible to admire the patterns without accepting the judgment for ourselves, if we think over the pictures carefully. But usually approval of the patterns made by an artist brings acceptance of the judgment they imply: the people who like Chinese scroll-paintings do in fact often prefer a calm contemplative life from which extreme emotions and violent colors are banished.

In books the problem is much easier. Books are about people. People act in a moral world. As we read the books, we hear the voices of the characters, and see their actions. Behind both we hear the voice of the author himself, implying praise of this action, making fun of that, omitting a cruel consequence here, inserting a detailed description there. All this adds up to a series of judgments about life which he wishes us to accept. Any author who heard a stranger praise his latest book by saying: "It was beautifully written, and admirably constructed, although the way he made the characters behave was quite unreal and their standards were ridiculous," would be deeply wounded, because it would mean that his judgments about life were rejected and nothing was praised but the pattern they made. Yet many writers will not admit this. They will not say they are trying to persuade us. They will not say they are teaching. They say: "I am trying to put down the truth as I see it," and if we ask: "Why?" they shrink from the obvious answer, which is "To communicate my view of the truth to others" and means "To teach them what I believe." All books contain persuasion. All books communicate a selection of judgments about life. All books try to teach. The differences are between those which teach well and those which teach badly, and between those which teach valuable things and those which teach bad or trivial things. Criticism deals with these important differences. They should never be forgotten, and they cannot be denied. If style alone mattered, and content were irrelevant, it would be possible and desirable to write a book describing, in exquisite prose, with the finest sensitivity of phrasing and the most vivid and attractive detail, the pleasures felt by certain criminals who experience life very keenly: for instance, the delights of setting fire to a stranger's house at night, making sure that the doors and windows catch first, the gorgeous colors of the flames, the blend of the crackling wood and crashing brick with the shrieks of the family, the godlike pleasure of the "gratuitous action" (as an eminent French immoralist has named it), the sense of power, the assertion of the individual above society. It is easy to imagine similar perversions which could be made the subjects for very fine writing. But society would not admire such books, or any society which did would soon extinguish itself. Therefore the judgments which are implied in a book are the lesson that it teaches; and that lesson is one of the criteria on which the value of the book will be judged. It is not by any means the only criterion, but it exists and it must be recognized by the author as well as by his readers. An author who does not care what he teaches is just as likely to be a bad author as one who does not care how he writes. Confused and shallow judgments or vicious and stupid ones spoil a book as surely as a bad style; and if an author is to defend himself against critics of his ideas, he will do so more effectively by justifying the ideas than by saying he did not mean to teach them. For teaching is a serious responsibility.

* * *

Fathers and mothers, husbands and wives, managers and foremen, doctors and psychiatrists, clergymen, advertisers, propagandists, politicians, artists, and authors: all these, in one way or another, are teachers. Their methods will vary as widely as their jobs and characters, so that we can point out only a few general principles to make their teaching more effective.

The first is *clarity*. Whatever you are teaching, make it clear. Make it as firm as stone and as bright as sunlight. Not to yourself—that is easy. Make it clear to the people you are teaching—that is difficult. The difficulty lies partly in subject-matter, and partly in language. You must think, not what you know, but what they do not know; not what you find hard, but what they will find hard; then, after putting yourself inside their minds, obstinate or puzzled, groping or mistaken as they are, explain what they need to learn. And you must be sure they understand your words. A strange name, a phrase only vaguely understood, will blur an explanation badly. Abstract words mean little on first hearing. Illustrate them. Give pictures and examples. And whenever possible, make sure you have been understood, by talking over what you have been trying to teach. A good pupil is seldom silent.

The second is *patience*. Anything worth learning takes time to learn, and time to teach. It is a mistake often made by great scholars and distinguished statesmen, to assume that their audiences have thought deeply about their problems and are only a few steps behind them in any discussion—so that they treat as partially solved problems which the majority of their audience have scarcely envisaged, or dart rapidly from one obscure question to another without attempting to show the connec-

tion. Real teaching is not simply handing out packages
of information. It culminates in a conversion, an actual
change of the pupil's mind. An important change takes
a long time to carry through, and should therefore be
planned carefully and approached in slow stages with
plenty of repetition disguised by variation. It is particularly important to keep out emotion, or rather to control
it carefully. Fathers and mothers, husbands and wives,
and people in authority very often forget this. When
they explain, they shout. Their faces become distorted
with anger or urgency. They make violent gestures. They
feel that they are explaining things more forcibly. But
in fact their emotion makes them difficult to understand.
A wife screaming at her husband, a sergeant roaring at
a platoon, a father bellowing at his son, create fear, and
even hatred, but they do not manage to explain what
they want done and persuade their hearers to do it.
Whenever we sink to believing that the more emotion we
display, the more effect we shall produce, we are revert-
ing to our animal ancestry and forgetting that conscious
reason is what makes us men.

The third principle is *responsibility*. It is a serious
thing to interfere with another man's life. It is hard
enough to guide one's own. Yet people are easily influenced for good or evil, particularly when they are young
or when their teacher speaks with authority. The effects
of bad teaching, of glib and shallow advice, of money-
grubbing or publicity-hunting declarations to a trusting
public are quite incalculable. Every now and then the papers mention that a man has been arrested for selling a
Cancer Cure composed of bread pills flavored with sac-
charin. He gets ten years; but how can that compare
with the tortures he has inflicted on his "patients"? In
the same way, it is hard to see how any politician who
has once offered to teach the public what was right on a
vital issue, and who has been proved wrong, can ever
venture to open his mouth again. But such men are seldom
punished, and sometimes praised as versatile and constructive thinkers. It must be a fearful thing to write a

series of plays or novels, rapidly and irresponsibly, in order to gain a reputation and make money; and then, late in life, to realize that they express foolish or wicked ideas, and to be ashamed of your own words. The surest safeguard against that is to ask how your ideas could possibly be misused or misunderstood, and to think, not of yourself, but of your friends and brothers whom you are trying to teach.

Notes

CHAPTER I: INTRODUCTION

p. 5 *Dr. Johnson.* See Boswell's *Life* (Oxford, 1953) 327.

CHAPTER II: THE TEACHER

24 *La Pieuvre!* Victor Hugo: *Les Travailleurs de la mer,* part 2, book 4, chapter 1.

24 *Je suis hanté.* Mallarmé: *L'Azur.*

25 *Waterloo!* Victor Hugo: *L'Expiation: Les Châtiments,* 5.13.2.

25 *Mark Hopkins.* "Give me a log hut, with only a simple bench, Mark Hopkins on one end and I on the other, and you may have all the buildings, apparatus and libraries without him."—General Garfield, at a dinner of Williams alumni, 28 December 1871, quoted in H. Peterson's *Great Teachers* (Rutgers University Press. New Brunswick, 1946), p. 75.

28 *"expiated in tears and blood."* Lytton Strachey: "Dr. Arnold," in *Eminent Victorians.*

30 *snatching a book from his hands.* This incident, along with others equally revolting, is reported from a New York school by Bradford Chambers, in "The Boy Gangs of Mousetown" (*Reader's Digest,* August 1948), p. 148.

35 *"If I had remembered all your faces . . ."* A. S. F. Gow: *A. E. Housman* (Cambridge University Press, 1936), p. 18.

38 *Sheldon's* The Varieties of Temperament. Harper & Brothers, New York and London, 1942.

40 *an old and oily clay pipe.* A. Conan Doyle: *A Case of Identity.*

46 *"pulling books out of a thousand shelves . . ."* Thomas Wolfe: *Of Time and the River* (Charles Scribner's Sons, New York, 1943), chapter 7, p. 91.

53 *pinnacled dim.* Shelley: *Prometheus Unbound,* 3. 4.204.

54 *he says he enjoyed it.* "To be made the butt of one's companions in full form is no bad preparation for later experiences" (e.g., being hissed at the age of twenty by every member of his club because of an editorial written by his chief): see *Something of Myself* (Macmillan, London, 1937), pp. 31–3 and 112.

58 *"It is the cause."* Shakespeare: *Othello*, V, ii, 1.

CHAPTER III: THE TEACHER'S METHODS

67 *"so given to insistence."* N. M. Butler: *Across the Busy Years* (Charles Scribner's Sons, New York, 1939–40), 1. 65 f.

67 *about fourteen hundred lines.* There are exactly 1,419.

70 *the White Rabbit,* Lewis Carroll: *Alice's Adventures in Wonderland,* c. 12.

72 *"The instructor never changed."* W. L. Phelps: *Autobiography with Letters* (Oxford University Press, New York and London, 1939), pp. 136 f.

74 *"Longinus."* On the Sublime, 9.13.

76 *Walter Headlam.* E. F. Benson: *As We Were* (Longmans, Green & Co., London, 1930), pp. 117–19.

82 *"Some books are to be tasted."* Bacon: "Of Studies" (*Essays,* 50).

84 *Always read sources.* Karl Lehrs: *Immer Quellen lesen, daraus ergibt sich alles von selbst.*

89 *A great orator.* Demosthenes: see pseudo-Plutarch, *Vit.X orat.,* 845a-b, Philodemus, *Rhet.,* 1.195.

90 *He who has ears to hear.* Matthew xi, 15.

91 *"Professor Murray."* A. Conan Doyle: *The Lost World,* c. 5.

94 *Mishnah.* See H. Danby: *The Mishnah* (Oxford University Press, 1933), introd. xiii, n. 1.

95 *proofs of the existence of God.* See James Hastings's *Encyclopædia of Religion and Ethics* (Charles Scribner's Sons, New York, 1951) under Cosmological, Ontological, and Teleological Arguments.

102 *Merlin.* Tennyson: *Vivien.*

107 *St. Luke.* Acts xvii, 21.

110 *Socrates' carbon copy.* Aristodemus (Plato, *Symp.* init.; Xen. *Mem.* 1.4) and Chærephon (Plato, *Charm.* 153b, *Apol.* 21a; Xen. *Mem.* 1.2.48, 2.3).

111 *Logan Pearsall Smith.* "Yet I cannot but feel that this

system of personal tuition involved an intolerable waste of fine material, and that it was a fantastic, almost a wicked thing that hours and hours of time of men like Nettleship and Abbott and the other Greats tutors should have been devoted to the culture of an intellect so raw and crude as mine." L. P. Smith: *Unforgotten Years* (Little, Brown & Co., Boston, 1939), p. 179.

112 *Caffarelli* (1703–83). His tutor was Porpora.

113 *The American statesman:* Garfield. See note on Chapter II, p. 25.

116 *Mrs. Battle.* C. Lamb: "Mrs. Battle's Opinions on Whist," in *Essays of Elia.*

117 *Montaigne.* 1.26: *To the Lady Diane de Foix, on the Education of Children.* This remark did not appear in editions of Montaigne until 1802, but it is now printed in the genuine text; e.g., in Villey's big edition.

122 *Tiberius.* Browne: *Urn Burial,* c. 5, quoting Suetonius: *Tiberius,* 70.3.

127 *Arabian Nights tale. The Young King of the Black Islands.*

128 WHAT IS THE PROBLEM? *De quoi s'agit-il?*

143 *Housman. Last Poems* 35.

144 *Tom Jones.* Book 7, c. 12.

144 *David Copperfield.* C. 4.

145 *Stephen Dedalus.* J. Joyce: *A Portrait of the Artist as a Young Man,* c. 1.

148 *Winston Churchill. The World Crisis, 1916–1918,* pt. II (Charles Scribner's Sons, New York, 1931), p. 392.

150 *quodlibets.* See P. Glorieux: *La Littérature quodlibétique de 1260 à 1320* (Bibliothèque Thomiste, Paris, 1925).

CHAPTER IV: GREAT TEACHERS AND THEIR PUPILS

154 *the first professional higher educators.* See H. I. Marrou, *Histoire de l'éducation dans l'antiquité* (Éditions du Seuil, Paris, 1948), c. 5: "*saluons ces grands ancêtres, les premiers professeurs d'enseignement supérieur.*"

165 *Alexander as a Macedonian.* See W. W. Tarn: *Alexander the Great,* 2 (Cambridge University Press, 1948) 106–7, 137, and especially 295, quoting Plutarch: *Alex.* 51.

166 *Alexander and Achilles.* Tarn: *Alexander the Great,* 2.
     52–3, quoting Arrian, 1.12.1.

167 *Alexander and Aristotle.* Tarn: *Alexander the Great,* 1.
     54–5 and elsewhere, thinks that Alexander passed
     definitely beyond Aristotle, which is an even greater
     tribute to Aristotle's teaching. Aristotle wrote two
     treaties for his pupil, of great political significance:
     On Kingship and *On Colonies:* see E. Barker's trans-
     lation of Aristotle's *Politics,* introd. xviii–xix. Tarn:
     Alexander, 2.368–9, shows he also taught Alexander
     geography, which Alexander later investigated for
     himself.

168 *Jesus in the Temple.* Luke ii, 42–50.

169 *Nicodemus.* John iii, 1–21; vii, 50–2; xix, 39.

169 *synagogue.* Matthew iv, 23; ix, 35; Mark vi, 2; and
     especially Luke iv, 15–32. There is an interesting out-
     line of this custom from the Jewish point of view in
     Zunz: *Die gottesdienstlichen Vorträge der Juden* (ed.
     N. Brüll, Frankfurt, 1892²), pp. 342–6.

170 *lynch.* Luke iv, 28–30; and see Matthew xxi, 23–7; Luke
     xx, 1–8.

170 *representative of God.* Matthew xxi, 9.

170 *an original thinker.* Mark i, 22.

170 *seven husbands.* Matthew xxii, 23–30.

173 *Professor Torrey and Professor Burney.* C. C. Torrey:
     The Four Gospels (Harper & Brothers, New York,
     1947); C. F. Burney: *The Poetry of Our Lord* (Ox-
     ford University Press, 1925).

173 *answers to hard questions,* Mark x, 17–22.

174 *questions on the Jewish law.* Luke xi, 53–4.

174 *the woman in adultery.* John viii, 3–11.

174 *Jesus and the babies.* Mark x, 13–16.

175 *wine and marriage.* John ii, 1–11.

175 *last supper.* Matthew xxvi, 26–9; Mark xiv, 22–5; Luke
     xxii, 19–20. John xiii, 3–20 gives another symbolic
     act at the last supper.

175 *his pupils sent out.* Matthew x; Mark iii, 14–19, vi, 7–13;
     Luke ix, 1–6; and especially Luke x, 1–20.

176 *the kiss of Judas.* Matthew xxvi, 48–50; Mark xiv, 43–5;
     Luke xxii, 47–8.

187 *Better to reign in hell.* Milton: *Paradise Lost,* 1.263.

188 *Aristotle on Plato.* Nicomachean Ethics, 1.6.1096a 16; cf.
     Plato: *Rep.,* 10.595c.

189 *Renaissance schoolmasters.* See W. H. Woodward: *Studies in Education during the Age of the Renaissance* (Cambridge University Press, 1924).

190 *Caliban.* Shakespeare: *The Tempest*, I, ii, 363–4.

190 *Gargantua.* Rabelais: *Gargantua,* 14, 21–2; 15, 23–4, 52, 57.

190 *Pantagruel.* Rabelais: *Pantagruel,* 5, 7, 8, 9.

191 *Shakespeare's Latin.* T. W. Baldwin: *William Shakspere's Small Latine and Lesse Greeke* (University of Illinois Press, Urbana, 1944), v. 1, c. 25, pp. 557–8; and cf. p. 565.

194 *Montaigne's father.* Montaigne: *Essays,* 1.26, calls the pastimes "table games"; and cf. Rabelais: *Gargantua,* 23: "Cards, not to play, but to learn 1,000 pretty tricks and new inventions which were all founded upon arithmetic."

196 *Father Jouvancy.* J. de Jouvancy: *Christianis litterarum magistris de ratione discendi et docendi* (Paris, 1691), quoted by F. Charmot: *La Pédagogie des Jésuites* (Éditions Spes, Paris, 1943).

196 *Father Possevino.* A. Possevino: *De cultura ingeniorum,* quoted by Charmot (see previous note).

197 *a Dominican priest.* Fray Vicente de Valverde (Prescott: *Conquest of Peru,* 1.465).

197 *a classical Chinese painter.* This was Giuseppe Castiglione, S.J. (1698–1766), whose name among Chinese connoisseurs is Lang Shih-ning. W. Cohn: *Chinese Painting* (Phaidon, London, 1948) gives reproductions from one of his paintings on pp. 96–7 and some information about him on p. 98. Details of the mission in C. W. Allan: *Jesuits at the Court of Pêking* (Shanghai, 1935).

201 *Gauss.* W. Ostwald: *Grosse Männer* (Leipzig, 1910), quoted by C. G. Jung: *Psychological Types* (tr. H. G. Baynes, Harcourt, Brace & Co., New York, 1926), pp. 408–10.

201 *Helmholtz.* W. Ostwald, cited in the preceding note.

202 *Kelvin.* J. D. Cormack: "Lord Kelvin," in *Cassier's Magazine,* 16 (May-October 1899) 151; obituary in *The Times,* 18 December 1907, p. 8.

202 *Mommsen.* L. M. Hartmann, in *Biographisches Jahrbuch und Deutscher Nekrolog* 9 (1904) 503–4.

202 *Jowett.* L. Pearsall Smith: *Unforgotten Years* (Little,

Brown & Co., Boston, 1939), p. 172; L. A. Tolle-
mache: *Benjamin Jowett* (E. Arnold, London, 1895),
p. 127. The Grail story I have been unable to trace,
but it is current in Balliol.

203 *Fustel de Coulanges.* P. Guiraud: *Fustel de Coulanges*
(Hachette, Paris, 1896).

203 *Robinson.* His seminar: C. Becker: "James Harvey Robinson," *Nation,* 144 (9 January 1937) 48–50. His
lectures and his insistence on documents: L. V. Hen-
dricks: *James Harvey Robinson, Teacher of History*
(King's Crown Press, New York, 1946), p. 15; H. E.
Barnes: "James Harvey Robinson," in *American Masters of Social Science* (ed. H. W. Odum, Henry Holt
& Co., New York, 1927), c. 10, especially pp. 376–7,
384–5.

204 *Kipling on "King." Something of Myself* (Macmillan,
London, 1937), pp. 31–3. "King" was apparently
based on W. C. Crofts of Brasenose College, Ox-
ford, who won the Diamond Sculls twice (G. C.
Beresford: *Schooldays with Kipling* [Victor Gollancz,
London, 1936], c. 14; and *The Kipling Journal* 1
[1937]); but he also contained something of H. A.
Evans of Balliol, on whom see *The Balliol College
Register* (ed. Elliott, Oxford University Press, 1934),
1865–6.

204 *Alain.* A. Maurois: *Mémoires* (E.M.F., New York, 1942),
pp. 74 f.

206 *Arnold at Laleham. Arnold of Rugby,* ed. J. J. Findlay
(Cambridge University Press, 1897), p. 75.

206 *Leschetizky.* A good note on him by Houston Peterson,
and a play-by-play description of one of his lessons
by his pupil Ethel Newcomb, in H. Peterson: *Great
Teachers* (Rutgers University Press, New Brunswick,
1946), pp. 289–99.

206 *James.* C. H. Grattan: *The Three Jameses* (Longmans,
Green, & Co., London and New York, 1932), pp.
155–6. "Remarks" by Henry James in *In Commemo-
ration of William James* (Cambridge University Press,
1942), p. 4. D. S. Miller in *The Letters of William
James* (ed. Henry James, Atlantic Monthly Press,
Boston, 1920) v. 2, pp. 11 f. R. B. Perry: *The
Thought and Character of William James* (Harvard
University Press, Cambridge, Mass., 1948), especially

pp. 123 and 326–7. J. R. Angell: "William James" (*Psychological Review* 8 [1911] 82), asserts that James seriously overestimated his students, but adds that this put them on their mettle.

208 *Boissier. Discours de réception de René Doumic: Séance de l'Académie Française du 7 avril 1910* (Perrin, Paris, 1910), p. 27.

208 *Jesus and the sick woman.* Luke viii, 43–8. Cf. Matthew ix, 20–2; Mark v, 25–34.

209 *Jesus in Nazareth.* Mark vi, 1–6; cf. Luke iv, 16–30.

210 *Fustel on eloquence.* P. Guiraud (see note on p. 229), p. 90 f.

210 *Rutherford.* A. S. Eve: *Rutherford* (Cambridge University Press, 1939), p. 406.

211 *Dewey.* I. Edman: *Philosopher's Holiday* (Viking Press, New York, 1938), pp. 138–43; E. E. Slosson: *Six Major Prophets* (Little, Brown & Co., Boston, 1917), pp. 265–8.

212 *Emerson.* J. R. Lowell: "Emerson the Lecturer," *Literary Essays* 1 (Houghton, Mifflin Co., Riverside, Cambridge, Mass., 1890) 359–60.

212 *Wharton Jones.* H. Peterson: *Huxley, Prophet of Science* (Longmans, Green & Co., London, 1932), p. 28.

213 *Huxley.* His nervousness: Sir W. H. Flower: "Reminiscences of Professor Huxley," *North American Review* 161 (1895) 279–86. His recapitulation and his sketching: St. George Mivart: "Some Reminiscences of T. H. Huxley," *Nineteenth Century* 42 (1897) 985–98. His synthesis of disparate phenomena: F. Harrison: *Autobiographical Memoirs*, 2.110, quoted in H. Peterson: *Huxley, Prophet of Science* (Longmans, Green & Co., London, 1932), p. 161.

213 *Agassiz.* His lecturing: J. D. Teller: *Louis Agassiz, Scientist and Teacher* (*Ohio Graduate School Studies* 2, Ohio State University Press, Columbus, 1947), pp. 38–9, 80–4; B. G. Wilder: "Louis Agassiz, Teacher," *Harvard Graduates' Magazine* 15 (1906–7) 603–7. His art of training laboratory workers: Teller, c. 4; N. S. Shaler: *Autobiography*, quoted in H. Peterson: *Great Teachers* (see note on p. 232).

216 *The eighteenth-century singing-master.* Porpora, see p. 112.

216 *The Russian apprentice.* Mr. W. Rabkin of New York,

whose story is told in R. Rice's article, "Penny-Arcade Philanthropist," *The New Yorker*, 16 October 1948.

216 *Mr. Flexner and Charles D'Urban Morris*. A personal reminiscence of Mr. Flexner, summarized in his *I Remember* (Simon and Schuster, New York, 1940), p. 55.

217 *Osler*. His new technique: J. M. T. Finney: "A Personal Appreciation of Sir William Osler," *Journal of American Medical Association* 77 (24 December 1921) 2033–9, and A. McPhedran: "Sir W. Osler's Influence on Medical Education in the U. S.," *Canadian Journal of Medicine and Surgery* 47.3 (March 1920) 151–3. The "Bardolphian facies": L. F. Barker: "Osler at Johns Hopkins," ibid., 141–6. Graves' Disease: W. R. Steiner: "Reminiscences of Sir William Osler as a Teacher," *Transactions, American Clinical and Climatological Association*, 1935.

218 *Kittredge*. R. W. Brown: " 'Kitty' of Harvard," *Atlantic Monthly* 182 (October 1948) 65–9; G. H. Chase: *Tales out of School* (Harvard University Press, Cambridge, Mass., 1947), p. 28; J. L. Lowes, J. S. P. Tatlock, and K. Young: "George Lyman Kittredge," *Speculum* 17 (1942) 458–60.

219 *Wilamowitz*. T. Zielinski: "Wilamowitz," *Revue de l'Université de Bruxelles* 2 (December 1931–January 1932).

219 *Verrall*. F. M. Cornford, in the Memoir preceding Verrall's *Collected Literary Essays* (Cambridge University Press, 1913), pp. xxxvii f.

220 *Burckhardt*. G. Pauli: "Jakob Burckhardt," in *Zeitschrift für bildende Kunst*, 9 (1897–8) 97–101; H. Trog in *Biographisches Jahrbuch* 2 (1898) 70–1; H. Wölfflin: "Jakob Burckhardt," *Gedanken zur Kunstgeschichte* (Schwabe, Basle, 1941²) 135–63.

220 *Phelps*. Sinclair Lewis, in *Saturday Review of Literature*, 1 April 1939; G. H. Nettleton: "William Lyon Phelps 1865–1943," *Scientific Monthly* 57 (1943) 565–6; J. J. Reilly: *Of Books and Men* (Messner, New York, 1942), pp. 51–9.

220 *Bergson*. A. Cresson: *Bergson, sa vie, son œuvre* (Presses universitaires de France, Paris, 1941), p. 5.

221 *Wilson*. An unsympathetic picture by A. P. Dennis in *Gods and Little Fishes* (Bobbs-Merrill Co., New

York, 1931), quoted in H. Peterson's *Great Teachers*
(Rutgers University Press, New Brunswick, 1946).
Enthusiastic descriptions in R. S. Baker: *Woodrow
Wilson, Life and Letters* (Doubleday, Page & Co.,
Garden City, 1927), v. 2, c. 12, para. 3; and W. S.
Myers: "Wilson in my diary," in *Woodrow Wilson,
Some Princeton Memories* (ed. W. S. Myers, Prince-
ton University Press, 1946), pp. 36–9. In the same
volume, R. K. Root points out that Wilson estab-
lished the "preceptorial" or tutorial system at Prince-
ton.

226 *Bach.* "*Ich habe fleissig sein müssen: wer es gleichfalls ist,
wird eben so weit kommen*"—Spitta, 1.660.

230 *Browning. Development* is the poem. It also has an
oblique application to the contemporary habit of
breaking up the Bible by "higher criticism."

231 *Byron. Childe Harold's Pilgrimage,* 4.77.

231 *Pitt.* J. E. Sandys: *A History of Classical Scholarship*
(Cambridge University Press, 1908), 2.433 f.

CHAPTER V: TEACHING IN EVERYDAY LIFE

241–2 *The statesman as teacher.* See W. Jaeger: *Paideia* (tr. G.
Highet, Oxford and New York, 1939), vol. 1, pp.
106 f.

247 *the* "*gratuitous action.*" André Gide: *L'Immoraliste.*

Index

GILBERT HIGHET, Anthon Professor of the Latin Language and Literature at Columbia University, was born in Scotland in 1906. He was graduated from Glasgow University and then from Oxford University, where he taught classics until 1938. He is now an American citizen. Besides The Art of Teaching (1950), Mr. Highet's books include The Classical Tradition (1949), Man's Unconquerable Mind (1954), and Juvenal the Satirist (1954). He is also well known for his radio book-talks, some of which have been published as People, Places, and Books (1953).